FOUL PLA

MIKE ROWBOTTOM has written about sport for *The Times*, th
the *Observer* and the *Independent* for more than two decades and is
features writer for insidethegames.biz. He has covered the last six su
Olympics and four Winter Olympics, as well as football and many other
sports. He co-wrote Olympic athlete Roger Black's autobiography *How
Long's The Course?* and is the author of *Usain Bolt: Fast as Lightning*.

FOUL PLAY

THE DARK ARTS
OF CHEATING IN SPORT

Mike Rowbottom

B L O O M S B U R Y
LONDON · NEW DELHI · NEW YORK · SYDNEY

First published in Great Britain 2013

Bloomsbury Publishing Plc
50 Bedford Square
London
WC1B 3DP

www.bloomsbury.com

Bloomsbury Publishing, London, New Delhi, New York and Sydney

A CIP catalogue record for this book is available from the British Library

ISBN 978 1 4081 5579 0

10 9 8 7 6 5 4 3 2 1

Typeset by Saxon Graphics Ltd, Derby
Printed and bound in Great Britain by CPI Group (UK) Ltd, Croydon CR0 4YY

Contents

to cheat: act dishonestly or unfairly in order to gain an advantage

foul play: unfair play in a game or sport

Oxford Dictionary of English

Introduction

'Say it ain't so, Joe!'
– An unknown boy

If the story is to be believed, these words were shouted by a boy, presumably a fan of the Chicago White Sox baseball team, eight members of which – including star player Shoeless Joe Jackson – had just been found to have thrown the 1919 World Series against the Cincinnati Reds. As Jackson stepped from the building in which the damning grand jury verdict had been announced, the disbelieving youngster called out to him: 'Say it ain't so, Joe!'

The phrase may be apocryphal, but it has echoed down the years – the perennial lament of sports fans unwilling to accept that those who have stirred their imagination and earned their loyalty have done so through unfair or dishonest means. In other words, through foul play.

Whether the boy existed or not, his urgent demand resonates, spoken or unspoken, each time another sporting idol is found to have feet of clay. Jackson apparently made no reply. In this he was unusual, as the default position of the sportsman or woman found to have erred tends to be denial, followed more often than not by grudging acknowledgement in the light of clear proof.

Let's say that boy did exist. What might his next utterance have been? Surely another question: 'Why?' Why do sportsmen and sportswomen cheat? What makes them take the decision to break the rules in an area of life where the rules are particularly clear? The answer to that question is probably the same in sport as it is in life: people cheat for advantage, or perceived advantage.

But such gains rest on the Great Unwritten Rule: don't get found out. There are some, many even, who can disprove the phrase 'cheats never prosper'. Not every fraudster gets separated from his ill-gotten loot. Not every sporting figure who has earned fame and fortune by dishonest means is exposed.

One of the conundrums of cheating is that its discovery causes such dismay, given that it is as old as time, or at least as old as humans. And cheating in sport has its own long history.

No sport is clear – not even conkers…

While the fixing of the 1919 World Series was one of the most shocking and high profile of sporting frauds in the last hundred years, misdeeds and shady behaviour exist – and have long existed – in almost every form of contest you care to name. In the so-called big sports – football, rugby, cricket. And in the so-called minor sports – bowls, real tennis, squash, chess, croquet, conkers. To paraphrase Philip Larkin: all sports in time are visited.

This book, clearly, has as its subject matter those who have failed to observe the Great Unwritten Rule. It is not intended to be an encyclopaedia of cheating in sport. Its focus is on that unspoken question – 'Why?' – and its automatic companion: 'How?'

For most sporting cheats, the intended advantage is either glory or money. Or both. But if these are the two main ends, the means by which they are sought are hugely varied, ranging from minor infringements all the way to criminality.

When former Sheffield Wednesday and England defender Peter Swan reflected forty years later on the ban from the game he received for betting against Wednesday in a match they were playing, he concluded: 'My money was on us to lose, and money is the root of all evil.' There is certainly a case to be made for the argument that money is the root of all sporting evil. At one extreme, money is funding – the National Lottery – although such assistance could possibly be seen as a form of cheating, in that it offers a greater level of assistance than is generally available.

For money to act more darkly, however, the dynamic force is gambling, offering gain for those who bet and those who collude. As we will see, this is viewed as the most actively malignant force in international sport – as recent examples in cricket and football attest – thanks in large part to the unwelcome stimulation afforded by internet betting and illegal gambling cartels profiting from the worldwide boom in televised sport. A year before the London 2012 Olympics, the potential threat to competition as a result of the demands of illegal gambling prompted Jacques Rogge, president of the International Olympic Committee (IOC), to declare: 'Sport is in danger.'

Perhaps Rogge is correct. But there have always been malign forces working to distort and undermine sport. A decade earlier a similar warning was sounded in IOC circles, but at that time the perceived threat was that of doping. The battle to eradicate this particular form of cheating from sport has been waged actively for almost half a century now, and the battleground is constantly shifting as those who seek advantage attempt to stay ahead of those charged with finding them out.

A huge range of sports has been affected by doping issues, particularly those that rely upon pure physical capability, such as athletics, weightlifting, swimming and cycling. More worryingly, a huge number of sporting competitors have effectively abused themselves through these means, undermining their health to the point where many have died prematurely. Why would they do that to themselves? What could make them think it worthwhile?

There is a growing body of circumstantial evidence pointing to the inherent dangers of doping – where the bargain made with a healthy body is harsh indeed. And ten years after the fall of the Berlin Wall, hard evidence of this practice emerged as those who had been effectively forced into the doping regime that accompanied East Germany's sporting efforts for a quarter of a century attempted to sue those responsible for a series of ghastly ailments and physical and mental distortions.

Money and doping: both Bad Things

Money and doping, then, are the two most influential elements of cheating in sport, the prime movers in foul play. Both were potent forces in the ancient Olympics, although in fairness the doping which steeped much of the activity could not be described at the time as cheating.

Eupolos of Thessaly. You could call him the Olympic gold medallist of cheating, as he was the first recorded wrongdoer in the history of the ancient Games. According to Pausanias, who wrote a second century AD version of *All You Need To Know About Greece*, Eupolos was guilty of bribing boxers in the 98th Olympiad.

Fourteen Olympiads later, Callippus of Athens was up to no good, apparently buying off his competitors in the pentathlon. Silver medallist. It was a few years on, admittedly, but at the 226th Olympics further misdeeds were recorded from two Egyptian boxers, Didas and Sarapammons, who were fined for fixing the outcome of their match. Joint bronze medallists.

Pausanias was able to gather this information from the bronze statues of Zeus which had been erected over the years on the road leading into the stadium at Olympia, where the Games had taken place since 776 BC. These statues had been financed through fines extracted from Olympic competitors found to have cheated, and were inscribed with the names of the guilty parties along with the details of their misdeeds. This information was accompanied by messages warning others not to cheat and insisting that victory was to be earned through skill and effort rather than by money or other underhand means. Here, then, was early graphic evidence of cheating in sport.

But while filthy lucre was behind so much that was unseemly at the ancient Games, performances were also bolstered in some cases by what we would now regard as doping. Athletes in ancient Greece were accustomed to boosting their performance by all manner of methods, with sheeps' testicles – heavy on the testosterone – the supplement of choice for those wishing to improve their strength and endurance.

Galen, a physician who described the customs of the day in the third century AD, wrote about Olympians drinking large quantities of herbal teas which both hydrated and stimulated with their high content of caffeine – a drug only admissible within restricted limits for today's Olympians. The good physician also reported that certain Olympic competitors had sought to enhance their performance by drinking 'the rear hooves of an Abyssinian ass, ground up, boiled in oil and flavoured with rosehips and petals'.

Whether this concoction would find its way into the World Anti-Doping Agency (WADA) code nowadays is a moot point. But the anti-doping code would surely have little to say about another of the reputed performance-enhancers of ancient sporting times – the practice of drinking a combination of sweat, oil and dust scraped from the skin of Olympic champions immediately after their moment of glory.

Money and doping may have been behind most of the questionable activity of the ancient Games, but the Olympics also embraced other elements that have become key factors in controversial sporting incidents. Let's look, for example, at what happened in the Games of 420 BC.

The Spartans were banned from competing that year, having violated the Olympic Truce imposed during the time of the Games to allow peaceful passage to all competitors. The Greek historian Thucydides describes how Lichas, a prominent Spartan, passed off his winning chariot under the name of a neighbouring state, only for his subterfuge to be detected. Lichas earned himself a good flogging for what is one of the first recorded instances of sporting manipulation. Here, the why is a given; it is all about the how.

In the nigh-on two and a half millennia since Lichas's actions came to light, manipulation has been at the rotten heart of cheating in sport, and down the years it has fallen into two broad categories. Money may set things up, and doping may pump competitors up. Manipulation, on the other hand, is all about making something happen. That is, making the right result happen.

The art of manipulation – basic and applied

Manipulation in its most basic form has involved direct physical actions which are performed illegally with the hope of remaining undiscovered. And there is a second broad form of manipulation within sport which goes beyond direct physical actions, involving more intricate activity. You might describe the two forms as 'basic' and 'applied' manipulation.

Basic, physical manipulation is involved when Lichas enters a falsely credited chariot into the Olympic lists. When Fred Lorz completes the 1904 Olympic marathon and briefly appears to claim victory until it becomes clear he has hitched a lift in a car for eleven miles of the course. When Diego Maradona scores a goal for Argentina en route to their 2–1 win over England in the 1986 World Cup quarter-final with his fist rather than his head (literally, manipulation). When rugby player Neil Back sticks his hand out at an opportune moment to divert the ball out of the hands of Munster's scrum half, Peter Stringer, during the put-in and give his team possession, enabling them to complete their victory in the 2002 Heineken Cup final. (And in both the latter cases the manipulation is successful, in that it does not come to light during the match and both results stand.)

In the same spirit, we see squash players blocking each other, long-distance swimmers hauling opponents back by the legs, athletes attempting to crowd each other out, and team officials switching rugby balls to give advantage to kickers.

Basic manipulation can, of course, be even more base. We are talking here about the perennial presence of violence within the sporting arena: South African rugby player Schalk Burger 'gouges' the eye of Lions player Luke Fitzgerald in 2004; Bill Romanowski establishes a fearsome reputation for intimidation within American football following a series of brutal interventions. And footballers such as Wilf Copping, Norman Hunter, Tommy Smith, Ron Harris and Peter Storey earn similar reputations for physical excess. It's basic. It's bad. But it's part of sport.

Another form of basic physical manipulation involves 'pushing the envelope' without breaking the rules. Instead the rules are bent – albeit, often, into shapes in which they are barely recognisable. Here foul play becomes an art rather than a crime.

Thus Olympic sailor Ben Ainslie relentlessly defends his winning position in a final race by negatively targeting his main opponent, driving him off course and stealing his wind in order to frustrate him. After all, his opponent has done the same to him on previous occasions. We accept this as part of the sport and therefore not cheating.

Following this particular branch line, Australian cricketer Trevor Chappell follows the orders of his captain and brother Greg and bowls the final delivery of a match against New Zealand underarm, to prevent the possibility of them scoring the six they need to tie the match. We don't see this as an acceptable part of the game and it is therefore much less well received.

Further still, the England cricket side touring Australia in 1932–3 employ a hugely controversial form of fast bowling in which the ball rears up menacingly into the body of opposing batsmen, which swiftly earns the name 'bodyline' bowling. The rules were subsequently – consequently – altered. But at the time it wasn't illegal. This was seen as utterly against the spirit of the game and the fallout resulted in a huge drama which upset international relations.

When it comes to the second broad form of manipulation – applied manipulation – we witness a greater level of ingenuity and skulduggery. For example, a Harlequins rugby player is encouraged to bite on a fake blood capsule he has been supplied with in order to precipitate a 'blood replacement' substitution, which will bring on a specialist goal-kicker capable of snatching victory in the closing stages of a match.

Another example: Russian modern pentathlete Boris Onischenko takes part in the fencing element at the 1976 Olympics with an épée that has been wired up to register a 'hit' even though his opponent has not been touched. Another example: rivals for the America's Cup sailing competition become involved in espionage, with divers being apprehended taking covert pictures of hull designs ahead of competition.

We are deep in the heart of sporting wrongdoing here – premeditated illegal activity. But you don't always have to cheat to get the better of your opponent. Between the black and white of wrong and right there is a vast grey area in sport which has to do with getting an edge over others through the use of mind games.

Foul play in shades of grey

This is the area of endeavour explored and celebrated in Stephen Potter's glorious book *The Theory and Practice of Gamesmanship*, in which the newly coined term is defined as 'the art of winning games without actually cheating'. Potter exploits the comic possibilities of stratagems which, while they do not constitute cheating as such, can have the feel of cheating. It is a technique which is widely, perhaps increasingly, employed in sport, particularly at elite levels, where gaining a mental edge over one's opponent is often the crucial factor in contests for which both competitors have been physically honed and relentlessly trained.

Positive thinking is one thing. Every elite performer will enter the fray nowadays having 'visualised' their success and done everything possible to convince themselves that they have the power to win. But mind games can be a little more pro-active than this. If an element of doubt can be placed into the mind of your competitor it will undermine his or her performance. It will cause them to falter at the critical moment. It can, effectively, destroy them. Mind games don't have to be harsh to work. You can start to unravel the opposition's concentration simply by doing nothing – by delaying, by making them impatient. Because impatience leads to imprecision…

Mind games disprove the adage, 'Sticks and stones may break my bones, but words can never harm me.' Words, applied offensively, are devastating. Muhammad Ali's comic-but-cruel – or at times simply cruel – verbal goading before a fight would soften up his opponents before they entered the ring just as surely as if he had been jabbing his left glove into their face for five rounds.

When the Hungarian water polo team met the Soviet Union at the 1956 Olympics, at a time when the Soviets had just restored Communist rule in Hungary by invading it, the match became ritualised warfare. The Hungarians' means of attack was verbal. Having been obliged to learn the language of their occupying force over the years, they were able to torment the Soviet players at every opportunity, insulting them and their families, and generally winding them up. The idea was to get the Soviets so angry that they failed to concentrate on the game and lost. The idea worked.

Sport's moral maze

As a microcosm of life, sport inevitably contains its own moral conundrums. Rules and regulations shift in the effort to frame something which more closely corresponds to what feels right and just, but there are issues and areas where there is no certainty. Thus we can find ourselves in a moral maze.

For instance, when cyclist Floyd Landis – whose 2006 victory in the Tour de France was annulled when he was shown to have doped – went public four years later with other riders whom he alleged had also been involved in illegal performance-enhancing activity, he was effectively shunned by the sport. It was as if speaking about wrongdoing was seen as being worse than doing wrong. When the biggest scandal in the sport broke in 2012, and Lance Armstrong was stripped of the Tour de France titles he had won a record seven consecutive times between 1999 and 2005, the Texan eventually confessed to his doping misdeeds. But that confession contained no other names. Armstrong was rightly execrated throughout the world of cycling for his cynical betrayal of the rules. But could there be an argument that he gained an element of honour for his reluctance to grass anyone else up?

Here's another moral conundrum for you. Erythropoietin (EPO) is a naturally occurring hormone that controls and stimulates the production of oxygen-carrying red blood cells. Why is it that athletes found to have supplemented that process – and hence to have improved their levels of endurance – by taking artificial EPO are penalised, whereas those who can afford to train at altitude, where the body naturally responds to the relative lack of oxygen by creating more red blood cells, are deemed to be acting within the rules?

The power of 'we'

Who decides, ultimately? What role do we, as spectators, as followers, have in the conduct of the sports we follow with such passion and endurance? Is it we who, in the end, are the arbiters of what is deemed fit and proper within the sporting realm?

Certain activities that have become routine in football – tripping an opponent up, say, or feigning injury – are regarded as outrageous by all right-thinking rugby followers. What we have here is a kind of moral relativism – different cultures within different sports, regarding some forms of cheating as being worse than others.

This book will examine the attitude of the sporting spectator to what might be collectively termed foul play, and examine some of the awkward questions that can be asked of the committed fan.

Like the young baseball follower in 1919, we hate to discover that our idols have feet of clay. But such unhappy revelations may prompt us, as followers, to ask if we have been in any way to blame through our expectations, and our partiality.

Does personal bias soften the edges of moral outrage, blur the lines of correct conduct? Which fan has never overlooked behaviour from their own team or representative that would have provoked a howl of protest had it been visited upon them? Where do we draw the lines – for the opposition, or for our man/woman/team – as to what is acceptable? Because those lines seem to shift.

Athletes at the ancient Games had to compete without clothes, in order to prevent any possibility of foul play. If only it had been as simple as that. If only it were as simple as that now.

Doping

'I did it because I felt others in my event were doing it. I thought, "If they can do it and get away with it, then let's have a go."'
– Neal Brunning, shot-putter

Doping in sport is the attempt to make oneself stronger and more capable than one's opponent by illegal chemical means. It goes on a lot.

Faustus and doping: the overreachers

Like Christopher Marlowe's Faustus, any sportsman or woman who dopes is consciously overreaching themselves. While Faustus's pact involved twenty-four years of divine power in exchange for his soul and a one-way ticket to hell, that of the cheating competitor is less extreme. But the dynamic is the same. The possibility of 'magical' power is embraced, with the unspoken concomitant that doping may have a heavy physical and emotional price in future years. In 1988 a survey was conducted among 198 world-class athletes aged between sixteen and thirty-five. They were asked if they would take an imaginary 'wonder drug' that would let them win for five years, even though it would most probably end up killing them. Reportedly 52 per cent said 'yes'.

In 1999, aged twenty-one, Dwain Chambers made his breakthrough to the top ranks by taking the 100m bronze in the 1999 World Championships – with a time of 9.97 seconds, which, once the efforts of his doped years were expunged, remains his personal best. No one who was there in Seville will easily forget his excitement at that achievement; it felt like the start of something big.

But by 2003, when he might have been expected to be near his peak at the World Championships, Chambers had suffered a dramatic fall from grace. A urine sample he had blithely given at his pre-Championship training venue of Saarbrücken turned out to be positive – for the supposedly undetectable 'designer' steroid tetrahydrogestrinone, the acronym for which, THG, began appearing with increasing regularity in the world press.

This substance was developed by a Dr Patrick Arnold for the Californian sports nutrition centre BALCO (Bay Area Laboratory Co-operative). Those who developed and used it called it by a different name: The Clear. In doping terms, it offered exciting possibilities – 'You will be in the clear with this, you'll be ahead of the game and no one will know it, you will be clear away from your rivals' – but it was, in fact, a smooth lie propounded by the hugely persuasive nutritionist Victor Conte, founder of BALCO. Of course, this magic did not come cheap.

At the time of his positive test Chambers was taking not just THG, but also EPO, human growth hormone, and extra testosterone to help him sleep and reduce his cholesterol. He was also regularly injecting himself with insulin to help recovery after heavy weightlifting sessions. As Conte was to write a couple of years later, Chambers was getting 'the full enchilada'. He added: 'Make no mistake, this was an extremely talented athlete before he ever met me. But he came here and got his eyes opened. You can blame him if you want, but he did not seek it out. He just realised there were two sets of rules – the handbook rules and the real rules.'

Chambers was also enduring regular blood testing to ensure that the EPO was not thickening it to the point where it put him in danger of having a stroke. The cost of his first year on the programme was $30,000. 'I wondered what the hell I'd been doing to myself,' he reflected.

Chambers was not the only athlete tempted to overreach himself. BALCO had clients elsewhere in the sport, as well as at the top level in baseball and American football. But without doubt, the athlete who suffered the most spectacular fall from grace in the BALCO affair was the woman who had established herself as one of the sport's great achievers. Marion Jones, winner of three golds and two bronzes at the Sydney 2000 Olympics.

On 14 January 2008 the thirty-one-year-old sprinter and long jumper was sentenced to six months in jail after pleading guilty in a New York court to lying to federal investigators about using performance-enhancing drugs and about her involvement in a cheque fraud scheme. She tearfully announced her retirement from the sport, and thus one of the longest and most dismal tales of doping in sport reached its denouement.

Given that her career followed in the footsteps of her compatriot Florence Griffith-Joyner – whose 100m world record and Olympic victories were widely questioned despite her never having tested positive nor any wrong-doing ever having been proved – Jones was constantly asked about doping, even when she emerged, fresh-faced and ambitious and articulate, as a double world champion in 1997 at the age of twenty.

While laying her plans for the 'Drive for Five' (golds) in Sydney, she spoke of her 'beautiful and lovely sport', adding that she could not understand anyone cheating, because, 'There's something about being first when everything you have done is normal, everything is legitimate.'

In Sydney her first husband, shot-putter C. J. Hunter, tested positive for the banned steroid nandrolone. As Jones comforted her discomposed man-mountain at a press conference she was supported by the figure of a nutritionist who introduced himself as Victor Conte.

It was a hugely unsettling spectacle for the media gathered there. Hunter's normal huge and glowering presence was compromised by contrition. Conte argued that Hunter had been the victim of taking a rogue iron supplement. Meanwhile Jones, on the brink of her greatest athletic enterprise, appeared the calmest and most self-possessed of the trio. Within four years, both men would testify against her.

The operation at BALCO was effectively undone by a single act of human sabotage – although it turned out to be a pyrrhic victory. It was not so much a smoking gun as a dripping syringe. The syringe in question contained traces of THG and it was sent anonymously on 5 June 2003 to the United States Anti-Doping Agency.

An anonymous call from someone describing himself as 'a high profile track and field coach' had alerted the agency to the arrival of this unlooked-for gift, maintaining that it was an as yet undetectable drug that was being used by some sprinters on the west coast of the United States and that the athletes' drug connection was Conte.

Triggering sport's 'Watergate'

The man who set in train what some observers have characterised as a Watergate in sport was revealed a year later to be the sprint coach and former Jamaican Olympic athlete Trevor Graham. 'I was just a coach doing the right thing,' he said. 'No regrets.' Little did Graham realise that an action he clearly intended to have fairly specific results would trigger a crisis in several sports, dragging into the growing scandal a swathe of world-renowned sporting figures. And, eventually, himself.

Accounts differ as to why Graham acted as he did. Conte alleged five years later that the coach had acted out of 'competitive jealousy'. He maintained that the tip-off had been motivated by the fact that one of the sprinters

Graham coached, Tim Montgomery, was starting to be beaten by Chambers, whose doping schedule Conte was overseeing. 'It certainly wasn't done as a noble deed,' Conte added. He characterised it as 'a turf war'.

Another take on the situation suggests that Graham had fallen out with both Conte and Montgomery (who were soon to fall out with each other). Graham was said to have worked with the BALCO owner on an all-encompassing training and doping programme – using THG – to take Montgomery to the peak of the sport. The *San Jose Mercury News* reported in May 2004 that the operation, named 'Project World Record', also received input from the notorious Charlie Francis, Ben Johnson's coach at the 1988 Seoul Olympics where the sprinter was stripped of his Olympic 100m title and world record for testing positive.

According to the newspaper the plan, put in place soon after the 2000 Olympics, was to make Montgomery a world-record holder, and in turn to help promote BALCO's legal supplement, ZMA. Less than two years later, at a meeting in Paris, Montgomery had lowered the world record to 9.78 seconds, and within days he had reportedly split with Graham. Montgomery was soon spotted in Toronto working under the direction of Charlie Francis and alongside Marion Jones, who was by then his partner and would later have a child with him.

By the time the syringe was posted off, an investigation into BALCO by the US Internal Revenue Service (IRS) was already under way. A couple of days after Graham had made his move, IRS agent Jeff Novitzky was sifting through rubbish left by the lab and found an unsent letter from Conte to the US Anti-Doping Agency and the International Association of Athletics Federations accusing Graham of doping his athletes and using a Mexican contact to supply them.

The two men appeared to have pulled the trigger on each other at the same time – and if Conte had apparently misfired, the zealous efforts of Novitzky and his colleagues, who raided the lab on 7 September 2003, would ensure that the bullet eventually hit its mark. The raid uncovered Conte's client list. It contained the names of some of sport's best-known competitors, notably in athletics and baseball.

In the meantime, the provision of a sample had enabled the US anti-doping authorities to find a test, and before long some of the key names on the list were returning positives. For all of them the turn of events was shocking. The product they were taking – 'The Clear' – was suddenly failing to live up to its name.

Would the authorities have uncovered the scandal without Graham's assistance? It will never be known. But Graham's act of sabotage – a judgement it is possible to make with hindsight – had an echo of the doping case that had convulsed the world of sport in 1988.

The rise and fall (and rise and fall) of Ben Johnson

It can be argued that the fall from grace of the Canadian sprinter Ben Johnson, who was stripped of the Olympic 100m title following a positive test for the banned steroid stanozolol, turned on a single moment of human folly. The urine sample which had been tested after the final – won in a world record of 9.79 seconds – had shown up 'a chronic suppression of his adrenal functions'. In other words, Johnson's natural levels of testosterone were depressed. That can happen when long-term ingestion of artificial steroids convinces the body that it doesn't need to bother producing any of its own.

If that fact pointed towards Johnson's guilt, the fact that it was stanozolol which had shown up in his test, in large quantities, was problematic. Not for the IOC, which banned him for two years. But for those in Johnson's camp who, subsequently, would be outright in their admissions that he had been doped for the reason proffered by all those who dope – that is, to keep up with all the others who were doing it.

Neither Francis, who remained an unabashed apologist for doping until his dying day, nor the man who administered Johnson's doping programme, Dr Jamie Astaphan, claimed to understand the finding. At the enquiry set up in Canada in May 1989 under the direction of Government Chief Justice Charles Dubin, Johnson admitted he had lied about taking drugs, and that he had also been taking drugs when he had broken the world record in 1987. As a result, not only was his performance in Seoul annulled, but he was also stripped of his gold and previous world record from Rome.

Yet Astaphan insisted at the enquiry that he had not given the sprinter stanozolol. This steroid's main function is to build muscle, and therefore it is something to use during the months of preparatory training but not in a competition. However, the high level of stanozolol in Johnson's sample suggested it had been taken in the days shortly before he raced. As such it would have been highly detectable, as it requires a period of fourteen days to clear the body's system.

Johnson's camp insisted he had had his last shot of steroids on 28 August, twenty-six days before the final. But they said it was furazabol, not stanozolol, which was the drug at the centre of his programme.

And, puzzlingly, later laboratory tests showed that the stanozolol in Johnson's sample was pure. Stanozolol that has been ingested and urinated would be a broken-down version of the drug. Astaphan later commented that in November 1987 Francis had given Johnson and his training partner Angella Taylor-Issajenko 16 milligrams of steroid in tablet form – four tablets over two days – and both athletes reacted with cramp so bad that they had to take Valium. 'And now, because of the high level Ben tested positive for in Seoul, the suggestion is that he took more than four tablets within forty-eight hours of the race?' he added. 'It just doesn't make sense, even a child can see it.'

At the enquiry, Astaphan speculated that Johnson may have panicked and taken a banned substance during the Games. Morris Chrobotek, a lawyer who represented Johnson, later commented: 'I know that Ben was purchasing stuff from other people. I know that because he told me.' Just to add to the confusion, there were reports of a 'Mystery Man' in the post-race doping control area. Johnson, meanwhile, contended that someone had spiked his drink.

Johnson returned to the sport in 1991, but one year after failing to make the final of the 1992 Olympic 100m event he was banned for life after testing positive for illegal levels of testosterone.

A central conundrum at the heart of doping was voiced by Juan-Antonio Samaranch, president of the International Olympic Committee, in the wake of Johnson's positive test at the Seoul Olympics. Samaranch looked on the bright side. 'This is not a disaster,' he opined, 'for it shows the IOC is very serious, and that we are winning the battle for a clean Games. The gap between our aims and those who are cheating is narrowing.'

So when it comes to doping, a positive is not necessarily negative. Conversely, negatives are not necessarily positive. No news may not be good news.

A short history of enhancement

History makes clear that the urge to enhance performance through chemical means – in sport, in life, in battle – has been strong for generations. This strand of supplementation also runs through many cultures, albeit not always in the form of supplements we recognise as doping substances today. According to Scandinavian mythology, Norse warriors – known as Berserkers – habitually worked themselves into a trance-like rage before battle having drunk a mixture called 'butotens', which may have been prepared from the *Amanita muscaria* mushroom. The 'butotens' also had the effect of massively increasing physical power. It is a phenomenon which has given us the phrase 'to go berserk' – and which makes 'roid rage look like a fit of pique.

In the early nineteenth century, the German missionary and doctor Albert Schweitzer noted how, after consuming certain roots and leaves, the people of Gabon were able to work happily for many hours without being obviously hungry or thirsty. And in the world of endurance walking, which became very popular in Britain in the nineteenth century, experiments with similar methods were being made. One participant, Abraham Wood, wrote in 1807 that he had used laudanum – or opium – to keep himself awake for twenty-four hours while competing against Robert Barclay Allardyce.

The growing popularity of walking races, which could be in excess of five hundred miles, soon gave promoters the idea of branching out into cycling competitions, and by the end of the nineteenth century six-day races were established on either side of the Atlantic. The riders were assisted in their battle against exhaustion by *soigneurs* ('carers') whose range of treatments included nitroglycerine, which was used to stimulate the heart after cardiac arrest and was credited with improving riders' breathing. Riders often suffered hallucinations while participating, which may have been down to a combination of drugs and exhaustion.

The runner who won the 1904 Olympic marathon, Thomas Hicks of the United States, only managed to do so with assistance that would have earned him disqualification had he used it today. The twenty-six-year-old English-born runner struggled badly in the heat, prompting his trainer, Charles Lucas, to come to his aid bearing a hypodermic needle and a bottle of booze: 'I therefore decided to inject him with a milligram of sulphate of strychnine,' Lucas later recalled, 'and to make him drink a large glass brimming with brandy. He set off again as best he could [but] he needed another injection four miles from the end to give him a semblance of speed and to get him to the finish.'

Despite all this, Hicks still had to be helped over the line in a time of 3 hours, 28 minutes and 53 seconds – the slowest winning marathon time in Olympic history. He was reported to have been 'between life and death'. Unlike current Olympic champions, who are able to start cashing in on the marathon circuit, Hicks failed to capitalise on his glorious and costly victory. Sporting agents please look away now: he retired the very next day.

There was no suggestion at the time that he had cheated in terms of what he had ingested. Far from being a banned substance, as it is now, strychnine was regarded as a necessary stimulant for marathon runners, and the official report on the 1904 Olympic marathon acknowledges that it demonstrated how drugs could be of great use to athletes in endurance events.

While cyclists have turned to stimulants and blood boosting to improve endurance, other sports requiring explosive power – such as weightlifting, sprinting, baseball and American football – have shown growing evidence of steroid abuse after the Second World War.

Anabolic steroids were first synthesised in the 1930s, when they began to be used in medicine to stimulate bone growth and treat chronic wasting conditions, such as cancer. But because anabolic steroids increase muscle mass and physical strength, they began to be used in sport and bodybuilding. Known side effects included harmful changes in cholesterol levels, acne, high blood pressure and liver damage. To counteract this, many users took supplementary drugs.

By the mid-1950s steroids were being heavily used in weightlifting, and their use spread to other sports which required explosive muscle power. Paul Lowe, a former running back with the San Diego Chargers American football team, told a California legislative committee on drug abuse in 1970: 'We had to take them [steroids] at lunchtime. He [an official] would put them on a little saucer and prescribed them for us to take and if not he would suggest there might be a fine.'

Central to the attitude Lowe describes is the fact that there are huge financial incentives now existing within the increasingly professionalised world of sport. When relegation from the Premier League to the Championship or qualification for the UEFA Champions League can make a difference of so many millions of pounds to a football club's earnings, the pressure on individuals to do anything and everything to ensure that success must be extreme.

In some cases, the drive to dope may be ramped up, wittingly or unwittingly, by the requirements of particular sponsors. Chambers, for instance, has reflected subsequently upon the pressure he felt to deliver results for his sponsor. If he fell out of the world's top three in the 100m, he related, his salary would effectively be halved. That is serious pressure – even though there is of course no suggestion that the sponsor encouraged Chambers' decisions to act in the way that he did.

The sport of doping – an eternal chase

Doping in sport these days entails its own sport – an eternal chase between those who cheat and those who seek to catch up with them and punish them. The chase could only begin, however, once sporting authorities decided that the age-old phenomenon of taking substances to improve performance was in some cases harmful and/or unfair, and ought to be stopped. Gradually, sports governing bodies began to realise that restrictions needed to be introduced. It took many of them even longer to realise that such rules required an effective method of enforcement, and in some sports that second stride still appears not to have been taken properly.

The International Olympic Committee formed a medical commission in 1967 and produced its first list of banned substances, which included analgesics and stimulants. The IOC began drug testing at the 1968 Winter Olympics in Grenoble and the 1968 Olympic Games in Mexico City. Anabolic steroids, despite suspicions about their misuse, were not added to the IOC list until 1975, by which time a reliable test for them had been established.

The International Amateur Athletic Federation – now the International Association of Athletics Federations (IAAF) – was the first international sports governing body to ban participants from doping, which it did in 1928, but the relative lack of efficient testing militated against effective action. In cycling, it was only when the death of British cyclist Tommy Simpson on the 1965 Tour de France was photographed and filmed, and the use of amphetamines was subsequently shown to have been a contributing factor, that cycling's world governing body, the UCI (Union Cycliste Internationale), was prompted to start banning performance-enhancing substances. Football's international governing body, FIFA, did not begin to frame anti-doping strategies until 1966.

Dopers have very often managed to stay at least one step ahead of anti-doping measures, but their ability to do this was seriously compromised in 1999 with the formation of the World Anti-Doping Agency (WADA), an independent body jointly funded by sporting organisations and governments with the aim of standardising and supervising punishments for doping violations.

From January 2009 there was a concerted effort within WADA to harmonise punishments for doping. Failure to comply with three proposed tests continued to constitute the same offence as giving a positive test. But instead of being expected to provide their whereabouts to testers 24/7, which proved to be unworkable in some cases, elite performers were obliged to specify one hour every day, between 6 a.m. and 11 p.m., when they could be located for testing.

Some years after he had served his two-year ban, Chambers described in his autobiography *Race Against Me: My Story* how he had been advised by Conte on ways to get round the testing system. At a time when athletes were obliged to provide the authorities with a mobile phone number on which they could be contacted twenty-four hours a day if a random test was to be carried out, Chambers said Conte had told him about what he called the 'Duck and Dodge' system.

'If an athlete suspects a trace of a banned substance is still in their body, they fill their mobile voicemail to capacity,' Chambers wrote. 'If the authorities can't leave a message, you can't be tested.' Chambers added, however, that he had failed to take Conte's advice on the day the anti-doping authorities rang him ahead of the test which subsequently proved positive. 'Of course the mailbox was empty – I'm a hopeless cheat – and I'd notified UK Athletics of my whereabouts too,' Chambers added.

Athletics and cycling have become increasingly exercised and engaged with anti-doping, although some of their most profound activity in this area has been a reaction to evidence received purely by chance, rather than through systematic procedure. Conversely, there has been widespread criticism that sports such as football and baseball have failed to address the issue of doping as thoroughly as they might.

Operation Puerto was an investigation begun in 2006 into allegations of blood doping and other procedures being employed by approximately two hundred sporting figures. Of these, a quarter were cyclists and the rest were from a range of sports, reportedly including several high-profile tennis and football players. The cyclists were pursued over their involvement and many received bans, including Ivan Basso of Italy and Tyler Hamilton of the United States. But no football or tennis players were named or punished.

The doping hunt has shifted its ground over the years. In the past, competitors seeking to improve their muscle power and endurance took synthetic anabolic steroids, which mimic the action of the male hormone testosterone. But once reliable tests for steroids were established in the 1980s, cheats began to look elsewhere.

The trend shifted towards employing substances which occur naturally in the body – such as testosterone, human growth hormone (hGH) and human chorionic gonadotropin (hCG), which are harder for the testers to detect

– while the hormone erythropoietin (EPO) boosts red blood cell levels synthetically. In recent years there has been a concerted effort to get hold of those seeking to improve performance by illegal means, and much of the progress has involved the devising of new tests. EPO, for so long indistinguishable from normal blood, can now be tested for. Scientists have also devised a means of detecting human growth hormone, although widespread use of this test has been hindered by problems with funding.

The advent of the Schwarzenegger mouse

Another issue which looms large, but which may not yet be more than a theoretical advance, is gene therapy. Work on developing gene therapy with the intention of addressing wasting diseases and inherited disorders has been going on for many years at London's Royal Free Hospital and University College Medical School, under the direction of Professor Geoffrey Goldspink.

Professor Goldspink discovered that injected genetic material could increase production of a protein called mechano growth factor, or MGF, which boosts muscle mass and improves the muscle's ability to repair itself. By cloning the gene and injecting it into mice – or 'Schwarzenegger mice' as he likes to call them – Goldspink recorded an increase in muscle strength of 25 per cent over three weeks. Given that steroids can manage, at best, a 10 per cent increase over ten weeks, the potential challenge to anti-doping authorities in the future is patently obvious.

The synthetic gene is lodged in a virus so as to gain easy access into any muscle of the body. Some genes will bulk up muscle; others will alter the muscle fibre to make it faster, and thus more suitable for explosive events like the sprint, or slower, thereby boosting its endurance. 'In terms of performance enhancement and sport, it's the holy grail,' Professor Goldspink said. Testing for use in humans was clearly the goal of the project, although in the past the introduction of genetic material has had the unhappy effect of stimulating cancerous cells.

Michele Verroken, an international anti-doping consultant who was formerly Director of Ethics and Anti-Doping at UK Sport, is cautious in her assessment of gene therapy. 'If the technology was there it would already be used for curing illness, never mind about what it could do to improve sporting performance,' she said. 'But the science is very complex. Genetic engineering in theory is something that could happen, but I think in a lot of respects it's a long way off. Doping substances and doping methods are still following a traditional pattern. And although we appear to be finding more positive tests, these cases are better reported now than they used to be, so the number of athletes being caught doping is still broadly the same – around 2 per cent. And there is still a big debate about the anti-doping programme in the current economic climate. Anti-doping costs a lot of money, and governments may have other priorities for spending.'

The problem for the anti-dopers is that they will be unable to detect such genetic alteration directly. There may, however, be the possibility of inferring it from the observation of indirect effects, such as abnormal patterns of protein. It is this approach to anti-doping – individual, holistic and ongoing – which is being adapted with success in cycling. And also athletics.

Shortly before the 2011 World Athletics Championships in Daegu, the IAAF announced its intention to take blood samples from every competing athlete as part of an ongoing programme to develop individual Athlete Biological Passports. Before the championships were over, a blood-testing team operating at the athletes' village had amassed a total of 1,848 pre-competition blood samples from participating athletes.

The Athlete Biological Passports will allow anti-doping experts to register and chart physiological markers over the passage of time, allowing comparison and further scrutiny if required. Scientists will be looking for evidence of banned blood boosters such as EPO and illegal blood transfusions for endurance athletes, while for those involved in power sports the focus will be on steroids and growth hormones. In cycling, this process has been used to determine which competitors should be target-tested. An IAAF spokesman added: 'The data collected will therefore constitute a unique database of reference ranges for various biomarkers in elite male and female athletes.'

On 18 September 2011 the World Anti-Doping Agency announced that the volume of blood tests in the run-up to the London 2012 Olympics would be more than doubled. David Owen reported for insidethegames.biz: 'Meeting at the headquarters of the International Olympic Committee (IOC) in Lausanne, the WADA Executive Committee accepted a recommendation that all anti-doping organisations ensure that not less than 10 per cent of samples collected are blood specimens. Only 4 per cent of all doping control samples collected in 2010 were for blood, mostly for passport programmes.

'WADA said this had been a "key concern", since "an anti-doping organisation ought to collect blood as it cannot purport to have an effective programme in place if there is a loophole in its testing programme leaving room for the possible abuse of substances and methods that cannot be detected in urine analysis such as human growth hormone and blood transfusions". It said the new 10 per cent directive would have a "significant deterrence benefit, regardless of the particular risks associated with the anti-doping organisations' sports".'

The case for Just Saying No

In any discussion about the ills of doping, and how they might be addressed, somebody is always likely to come out with what one might characterise as the default doping argument: 'The athletes and their doctors are always going to be one step ahead of the testers. You may pick off the odd careless or unimportant competitor, but you will never catch up with the really smart ones. It's a waste of valuable resources. Let everyone take what they want and let's see how they do then.'

But is this tempting as a proposition? There are strong reasons to say no. Firstly, such a position is effectively a betrayal of all the innocent athletes and competitors who take part in sport. They are the majority. Secondly, it's a false premise. There can never be equality. Good drugs cost money – as Chambers discovered – and not everyone can afford them.

Chambers has also spoken eloquently about the price dopers pay for their supposed advantages. 'I learned that it may very well be that a certain steroid can give you a fraction of an advantage over a clean athlete at a particular time of the year,' he wrote in his autobiography. 'But if you are increasing your risk of blood pressure, heart disease and diabetes – to name but a few – and end up bald with man breasts and a smaller, dysfunctional penis, I ask you: is it worth it?'

Right there is the answer to the blithe question asked earlier. And it is an answer backed up by much anecdotal and circumstantial evidence suggesting that many elite performers in sports such as athletics, cycling and American football have paid for doping abuse by premature death through heart attack or stroke.

Thirdly and most importantly, then, drugs wreak physical and mental mayhem – and on some occasions deliver the ultimate side-effect. In 1960 the Danish rider Knud Jensen collapsed during the 100km team time trial at the Olympic Games in Rome, fracturing his skull in the fall and dying later in hospital. The autopsy showed that he had taken amphetamine and another drug, Ronicol, which dilates the blood vessels, although it was concluded that he had died of heatstroke. It was also reported that he had swallowed eight pills of phenylisopropylamine and fifteen amphetamine pills, as well as drinking coffee. Five years later, Tommy Simpson, full of amphetamines, meandered to a dead halt on the 6,000-foot-high Mont Ventoux, and there have been numerous other sporting deaths surrounded by suspicions of doping.

But if there is one enormous, terrible reason why that laissez-faire argument should not be countenanced, it is the doping regime discovered in East Germany – systematic foul play that not only distorted sport but damaged a generation of sportsmen and women both physically and emotionally.

East Germany's doping imperative: State Plan 14.25

Following the fall of the Berlin Wall in 1989, documents kept by the Stasi – East Germany's secret police – emerged into public view and provided evidence of a state doping programme which had existed for almost a quarter of a century on a scale never previously seen. It was known, baldly, as State Plan 14.25. What it meant, for a generation of young East German athletes, was a simple choice: follow a state-run programme of doping, or forget about pursuing your career.

In 1977 one of East Germany's best sprinters, Renate Neufeld, fled to the West with the Bulgarian man she was to marry. A year later she said that she had been told to take drugs supplied by coaches while training to represent East Germany in the 1980 Olympic Games. She added that her trainer advised her to start taking pills to improve her performance, telling her they were vitamins. 'I then refused to take these pills,' she recalled. 'One morning in October 1977, the secret police took me at 7 a.m. and questioned me about my refusal to take pills prescribed by the trainer. I then decided to flee, with my fiancé.'

It was not until 1998, nearly a decade after the fall of the Berlin Wall, that the full extent of this operation was revealed in the courthouse of Berlin's Moabit district, as four swimming coaches and two doctors were accused of inflicting grievous bodily harm on athletes who had been in their charge.

They were the first of many indicted, thanks to a team of sixty special prosecutors who had spent years examining files taken from the offices of the Stasi. The list of suspects involved in what was described as 'one of the largest pharmacological experiments in history' numbered almost seven hundred.

The charge sheet for the first of these cases included evidence from seventeen athletes who claimed their health had been destroyed by anabolic steroids – or 'vitamins', as the coaches who doled them out to their young charges preferred to call them.

One teenage girl grew a beard as a result. Another developed a deep voice. The other 'side-effects' included hormonal imbalance, loss of libido, damage to the liver and reproductive organs, mood changes and depression. Rica Reinisch, who won three Olympic gold medals in swimming, said in a magazine interview at the time that she had been fourteen when her coach had first handed her 'the blue pills', adding: 'He said, "Come, little girl, swallow these vitamins. You'll recover better."'

Subsequent trials uncovered a catalogue of damage, and by the time the architects of this policy – Manfred Ewald, the former head of the East German Olympic Committee, and Manfred Hoppner, the doctor who masterminded the doping regime – stood in the dock, evidence had been heard from a group of thirty swimmers, gymnasts and athletes who had been waiting long years to confront the men who had warped their lives in the pursuit of sporting success and national prestige.

Among those who testified was Andreas Krieger, who, as female shot-putter Heidi Krieger, had won the European title in 1986 at the age of twenty-one before her body began to seize up in pain as a result of her drug-taking. Krieger – known as 'Hormone Heidi' on the circuit because of her manly appearance – began training aged thirteen and said she was sixteen when her coach first started giving her little blue pills wrapped in silver paper, telling her they were vitamins.

Krieger found she was able to lift heavier and heavier weights, and was also being offered larger and larger numbers of vitamins. But after her European win she found her back was aching continuously and she needed surgery on her hips and knees. In 1987 she was taking five of the blue pills daily, and yet only managed fourth place.

She described how she began to feel uncomfortable wearing women's clothing, how she began to feel more like a man. But it was only after the fall of the Berlin Wall, when the first of the Stasi files came to light, that Krieger realised she had been given huge doses of testosterone, the principal male sex hormone, to boost her strength, endurance and aggression.

These levels were reportedly two and a half times the recommended dosage in the secret manuals kept by East German sports scientists. Krieger subsequently underwent a sex-change operation. Other sportsmen and women suffered depression, and several committed suicide, after prolonged intake of drugs.

According to a figure obtained by German historian Giselher Spitzer, who researched documents taken from the Stasi offices and photocopied shortly before the end of East Germany's Communist regime, around six hundred athletes were still registered on the doping programme in 1989, and previously up to two thousand had been involved every year.

In the end, the Berlin court gave Ewald, then seventy-four, and his doctor friend suspended sentences, which provoked predictable outrage among those athletes who had spoken out in public to accuse them. 'This is a verdict that cannot satisfy the victims,' said a former discus thrower, Brigitte Michel. Ewald clearly felt he was not at severe risk, given that five years after the Berlin Wall had fallen he brought out an autobiography entitled *I Was Sport*.

And yet the system worked, at least in terms of results. At the 1968 Mexico City Olympics, this country of seventeen million collected nine gold medals. Four years later the total was twenty, and in 1976 it doubled again to forty. The methods perfected by those running that regime produced results in sports such as athletics, swimming and rowing which propelled this relatively small nation into a position where, in the 1970s and 1980s, it could claim to be the third most powerful sporting nation on earth, behind the behemoths of the United States and the Soviet Union.

But Neufeld's testimony stands for all of her fellow athletes, swimmers, rowers... there was no alternative. Victory was required by the state for the state. For those who ran, or jumped, or swam, or rowed, sport had become politics, and politics sport.

The honest cheater

If the means of doping has altered radically down the years, the era in which sanctions have begun to be applied has occasionally thrown up instances of what you might term 'honest cheaters'.

Back in 1992, a not particularly well-known British discus-thrower and shot-putter, Neal Brunning, tested positive for testosterone at the National Indoor Championships in Birmingham. 'Don't bother to test the B sample,' the burly Londoner reportedly said. 'I know what's in it.' Speaking to Brunning a couple of years later was instructive. He was candid. 'I did it because I felt others in my event were doing it,' he said. 'I thought, "If they can do it and get away with it, then let's have a go."'

Many sportsmen and women have reached the position so matter-of-factly articulated by Brunning. In at least one respect it is an entirely justified position. The huge likelihood is that many sporting protagonists have got away with doing things they ought not to have done, and many continue to do so. Every time a paving stone gets lifted on doping in sport, it offers a glimpse into a world teeming with pharmacological misdeeds.

Charlie Francis was for most of his career an unabashed apologist for the necessity of taking performance-enhancing substances – a coaching version of Brunning. 'I'm not going to have my runners start a metre behind,' he once said.

Doping is regarded as a defence method by men such as Francis and Brunning. It's not a case of 'take this, it will really get you out there' so much as 'take this, then at least those other bastards won't be putting one over on you'. Defensiveness, indeed, is endemic to doping and its practitioners. Those who endorse doping, and those who embrace it, strive to feel justified, comfortable even, with what they are doing.

Those who promote doping don't talk about how taking performance-enhancing substances means you are cheating your clean competitors, and they don't talk about how these substances may very well have seriously dele-terious effects on your future health. They talk about the others, the bad guys, who are already out there, taking stuff and stealing their rightful glory. All you are doing is making that playing field level – then you can show everybody; then you can shine.

But the 'honesty' of Brunning and Francis on the subject of doping is rare. When the doping balloon goes up, coaches and managers generally make themselves scarce as their performer becomes aware of a chill wind whistling around them. The message from complicit coaches to competitors is clear: 'Dope, and the world dopes with you; get caught, and you are caught alone.'

It is hard to think of any other track and field athlete, or indeed any other athlete, who has immediately admitted guilt following a positive test as Brunning did. Chambers? One can't help liking him, but the British sprinter's full confession of his wrongdoings was partly precipitated by a slip of the tongue he made while giving an interview to Olly Foster of the BBC, from which it transpired that he had been taking drugs prior to the period which led to his ban. For this accidental 'confession' Chambers incurred additional financial sanctions from the international authorities.

'If you are caught you put your hand up,' Brunning concluded. 'There's no point in doing anything else. It just makes you look like a fool.' When you look at the ways in which some of the world's elite sportsmen and sportswomen have dealt with this awkward moment themselves, it is hard not to agree with his analysis. There is no shortage of bizarre explanations offered.

Doping excuses – sex, beer and male enhancement

Asked to explain three positive tests for the banned steroid Dehydroepiandrosterone (DHEA) between October and January 2010, Olympic 400m champion LaShawn Merritt maintained that they were down to him taking an over-the-counter product to enhance his male part. That proved to be something of a stretch. The international authorities banned him for two years. Merritt has since returned to the sport, his punishment served. But the stigma of a statement released on his behalf at the time of the case may never go away: 'To know that I've tested positive as a result of the product that I used for personal reasons is extremely difficult to wrap my hands around.'

Merritt's area of attempted exculpation was in similar territory to the explanation given by US sprinter Dennis Mitchell after he tested positive for testosterone in 1998. Mitchell claimed his manly hormones had been raised to excessive levels the night before his test because he had consumed five beers and made love to his wife four times, it being her birthday... You picture him working out the figures like someone filling in their expenses sheet. Would ten beers and fifteen sex sessions be too much? Yes. Well how about five and four? Say that, then. Mitchell's story was believed by USA Track and Field but, sadly for him, not by the IAAF, which banned him for two years.

Race-walker Daniel Plaza also brought the 's' word into his defence, explaining his positive test for the banned steroid nandrolone by saying he had had prolonged oral sex with his pregnant wife, a defence based on the suggestion that pregnant women can produce nandrolone naturally. Plaza, too, received a two-year ban, although he was later exonerated.

Sex is not the only excuse-rich zone. There's also food. Tennis player Petr Korda, who tested positive for steroids, claimed his levels had been affected by eating steroid-fed veal. His defence was undone when experts testified that, to achieve the levels he had, he would have to have eaten forty calves a day for twenty years. Britain's former sprinter Lenny Paul also used the food line when he tested positive for steroids as a member of the bobsleigh team, claiming that he had eaten contaminated spaghetti bolognaise.

Justin Gatlin, the 2004 Olympic 100m champion who was subsequently banned for testosterone, maintained that his positive test had come as a result of a masseuse with a grudge deliberately using a cream on him that contained banned substances. The outside interference line was also taken by Johnson in the wake of his 1988 positive for the banned steroid stanozolol. That, he maintained, had been a result of someone spiking the sarsaparilla and ginseng energy drink he took before his race. It had to be that. Because it couldn't have been anything else.

Cuba's high jump world record-holder Javier Sotomayor had the most powerful of defenders in 1999 when he tested positive for cocaine. His country's president, Fidel Castro, told a live TV audience that the test was 'a war against us' which may have been committed by 'professionals of counter-revolution and crime'. Sotomayor was banned. Dieter Baumann, Germany's 1992 Olympic 5000m champion, claimed a positive nandrolone finding in 1999 was the result of someone spiking his toothpaste. Baumann was banned.

But don't run away with the idea that athletics is the only sport to provide ingenious, or just plain ludicrous, excuses. Over the years there has been a fairly choice selection from the world of cycling. In 2004, US cyclist Tyler Hamilton, charged with illegal blood doping, countered that he was a chimera – a person with abnormal genetic cells. 'I have a twin that was never born,' he said. 'That's why my blood contains a different blood-type than my own.'

Gilberto Simoni, twice a winner of cycling's Giro d'Italia, was found to have traces of cocaine in his blood. He said it was because he had drunk some tea which his aunt had prepared for him. Jan Ullrich, Germany's winner of the Tour de France in 1997, tested positive for amphetamines in 2002. He said it had been the 'two little pills' he had taken at a disco the night before the test. When Ullrich's fellow German cyclist, Christian Henn, was found with excessively high testosterone levels in 1999 he blamed it on a herbal mixture taken to increase his fertility – which had been given to him by his mother-in-law.

Cyclist Dario Frigo was caught with an illegal substance in a raid by police. He told them he always carried forbidden substances with him, but had never used any. This presumably worked on the same basis as keeping a cigarette behind your ear, even though you have given up smoking. Frigo said it was just one of his 'weaknesses'. He was also found to have a synthetic blood supplement. His response? 'I can't say which substances were in my bag.'

Floyd Landis, winner of the Tour de France in 2006, offered various explanations for the high testosterone reading which eventually cost him his title. They included cortisone injections taken for pain in his degenerating hip, drinking 'two beers and at least four whiskys' the night before the test – apparently standard fare for cyclists involved in the most gruelling cycle race on earth – dehydration, thyroid medication and, finally, his natural metabolism. The findings, however, pointed to synthetic testosterone, which would not have been created within his system and would have to have been ingested in some form.

The wife of cyclist Raimondas Rumsas was caught with a car full of banned substances, which she claimed were for her sick mother. A year later Rumsas tested positive. He accused his team, Lampre, of doping him. Another cyclist, Frank Vandenbroucke, was found with the banned substance clenbuterol, normally used for asthma. He said it was for his dog.

If there is an amusing side to doping, it is the peculiar excuses some athletes come up with. But the more you look at doping, and what it does to people, and what it does to sport, the less amusing it becomes.

By the 1990s instances of false samples were becoming so common that the authorities altered their rules, stipulating that competitors had to be bare from thigh to chest when providing the urine for tests in order that doping control officers could witness the whole operation. Pretty degrading. But exposure as a doping cheat was a far more degrading process.

For the guilty doper, every knock on the door must sound like heavy footsteps on the stairs at 3 a.m. When he knocked at the door of Austria's sprint champion Andreas Berger in 1993, the tester was greeted by a man looking uncommonly like Berger who announced: 'Oh sorry, my brother is not at home,' before promptly shutting the door.

There was a delay before the householder could be contacted again. It subsequently transpired he had been engaged in catheterising clean urine into his bladder. Painful. And even more painful soon afterwards when he was bursting to urinate. His first sample was taken. But then a wily tester asked Berger to provide a second sample, in his own time. The first sample was clear; the second showed traces of doping, which Berger soon admitted.

When the dope testers called at the home of Ireland's multiple Olympic swimming champion Michelle Smith de Bruin there was another untoward delay before she gave a urine sample that smelled strongly of, and was later found to contain, Irish whiskey. Despite this contamination, it was also found to contain the banned bodybuilding drug androstenedione. De Bruin received a four-year ban, but retained her Olympic titles.

More successful means of manipulating doping test results have involved taking diuretics to cleanse the system before providing a sample. Another method used with widespread success has been that of blood doping. Rather than taking a banned synthetic blood booster such as EPO, competitors employing blood doping simply store some of their own extracted blood, prompting their system to fill the gap in oxygen-carrying red blood cells. Then, on the eve of competition, the original extract – stored in some cases in the family fridge – is restored, thus boosting levels of oxygenated blood and improving endurance.

The ultimate high of the legal loophole

The process of standardising a generally recognised list of unacceptable substances – and therefore making it clear to sportsmen and women what they are free to put into their system – is a continual and necessarily imperfect one. Legal loopholes, technicalities and unforeseen circumstances in this area have led to a succession of controversies within recent years.

At the 1994 World Cup, after Argentina's 2–1 win over Nigeria, Diego Maradona – the man widely regarded as the best footballer of his generation, and perhaps any generation – tested positive for the banned stimulant ephedrine. He was sent home by FIFA, and although Argentina managed to qualify in their group, in the third of the four places, they lost to Romania in the first knock-out match. In his autobiography, Maradona claimed the test result was due to his personal trainer giving him the power drink Rip Fuel. He said the US version, unlike the Argentine one, contained the prob- lematic chemical and that, having run out of his Argentine dosage, his trainer unwittingly bought the US formula.

As an argument, it was plausible. Eight years later, at the Salt Lake City Winter Games, Alain Baxter became the first Briton to win a medal in Olympic alpine skiing as he took bronze in the slalom, later toasting his win in traditional Scottish manner at the Dead Goat Saloon, one of the few drinking establishments in the Mormon stronghold.

But within a few days there was bad news for the man who raced under the name 'The Highlander': he was stripped of his medal after a test showed traces of lev-methamphetamine in his urine sample. Baxter appealed to the Court of Arbitration for Sport (CAS) in Lausanne, where he was effectively cleared, but failed to regain his medal on a technicality.

He maintained that there were two forms of methamphetamine, and that his sample had shown up the form which was not performance-enhancing. He added that it had been contained in the US version of a Vicks nasal inhaler which he had used as a decongestant. The British version he habitually used did not contain the substance.

The CAS panel accepted his plea, and described him as 'a sincere and honest man who did not gain a competitive advantage'. But Dr Don Catlin argued that, as the IOC's banned list did not discriminate between the two forms of methamphetamine, Baxter had failed to follow the principle of strict liability, whereby all competitors are responsible for any substances they ingest, and that by the letter of the law he was at fault. The CAS committee suggested that the IOC rules be modified.

Baxter also passed the ultimate test: his sponsors, including Drambuie, the Scottish whisky liqueur company, stuck with him. Cheers for that.

Four years before Baxter ran into his difficulties with inhalers, a Canadian, Ross Rebagliati, became embroiled in a similarly complicated doping case which highlighted the complexities involved in trying to get all relevant agencies working to the same rules. At the 1998 Winter Olympics in Nagano, Rebagliati – having become the first gold medallist in the newly introduced Olympic sport of snowboarding – stood in danger of having the medal taken away from him when his urine sample showed traces of marijuana, which was on the list of substances banned by the International Olympic Committee.

Rebagliati's defence was an inverted model of the one President Bill Clinton had once used in explaining his youthful contact with the drug – yes, he inhaled; but he did not smoke. The Canadian explained how he had attended a send-off party in Whistler with his friends, all of whom had been smoking marijuana, and claimed he had taken the substance passively.

Other choice new evidence was also revealed. 'It is Ross's belief,' a team spokeswoman said, 'that because of the nature of the substance where he lives in Whistler – in that area it is four times more potent than in any other area – the only explanation he can give is that it was second-hand.'

Rebagliati's defence was intriguing, but irrelevant. The IOC's executive board agreed, albeit by a 3–2 margin with two abstentions, that Rebagliati had taken the central tenet of the Olympic motto – faster, higher, stronger – too literally. The Canadian, however, then profited from a manoeuvre more involved than any he had ever attempted on a snowboard: the legal loophole, involving deft footwork and a 180-degree turn. The IOC's Court of Arbitration for Sports concluded that an ambiguity in the rules on marijuana operating at the Winter Games meant the snowboarder had no legal case to answer. It transpired that the International Ski Federation (FIS) regulations which had been applied by the IOC, offering the option of punishment for anyone whose sample registered more than 15 nanograms per millilitre of marijuana, were drafted with other sports in mind.

FIS officials explained that it was meant to deter sportsmen and women tempted to take the drug to calm their fears before more perilous events, giving the example of ski jumping. The team spokeswoman added that the snowboard slalom in which Rebagliati won his title was regarded by the FIS as a technical sport. 'They believe taking marijuana would have a detrimental effect in that event,' she explained.

Had Rebagliati not been successful in his appeal, then, he would have had the memorable if unfortunate distinction of becoming the first athlete ever busted for a performance-inhibiting drug. Sadly for the twenty-two-year-old champion, life was still far from totally cool. Wearing his medal, he spent more than eleven hours at a local police station convincing officers there was no basis for charging him with drug abuse. It was, Canadian officials maintained, a mere matter of formalities.

But never mind whether what he took was legal or not; was it of any use to him? There was speculation as to whether this would have been performance-enhancing in any way on a testing slalom course. The answer, emphatically, was no – although it may have helped him to come to terms with any spill.

Similar speculation was set in motion when Danny Harris, the US 400m hurdler who won silver at the 1987 World Championships behind fellow countryman Ed Moses, was banned for four years in 1992 after testing positive for cocaine. Harris, a hugely talented young athlete who had ended Moses' unbeaten run of 122 races, was allowed to return to the sport after two years having undergone a rehabilitation course, but was banned for life when he reoffended.

Before Harris's first test there were strong rumours of his drug habit, and two of his training companions in California, British runners Roger Black and Kriss Akabusi, later recalled how he had often turned up late to sessions bleary-eyed and unable to concentrate, usually unable to complete all the required warm-up and schedules. 'The irony of the whole thing was,' Black reflected, 'cocaine was not making him a better athlete, it was making him worse.' The rules abide, however. Even if the drugs don't work, and they just make you worse…

'Nandrolone?' 'Yeah – nandrolone…'

Towards the end of 1998 world sport had become seriously troubled by a strange phenomenon: the nandrolone phenomenon. Discussion of positive doping tests by sporting figures at this time went along the lines of the old Peter Cook and Dudley Moore sketch, in their guise as Derek and Clive: 'Heard about X?' 'X?' 'Yeah, X. Only tested positive, hasn't he…' 'Nandrolone?' 'Yeah, nandrolone… and old Y's just gone down too.' 'Yeah?' 'Yeah.' 'Nandrolone?' 'Yeah. Nandrolone.'

Every time you looked, it seemed, another high-profile athlete had shown up positive for what was an old-fashioned, easily detectable, very much non-designer steroid. There was Doug Walker, the 1998 European 200m champion. Then Mark Richardson, the European 400m silver medallist. Then, inexplicably, Linford Christie, the thirty-nine-year-old former world and Olympic 100m champion, who by 1999, when he tested positive for nandrolone at a minor meeting in Dortmund, was effectively retired. Soon another of the world's most famous sprinters, Jamaica's Merlene Ottey, was charged with the same offence.

Nandrolone had first taken the headlines in 1990 when the then world 400m record-holder, Butch Reynolds, tested positive for it and received a two-year ban despite pleading innocence. But that was an isolated incident; ten years later, the picture was different.

Footballers, too, were falling foul of this substance. In Italy's Serie A and B there were fourteen positive tests for nandrolone in 2000 and 2001, with another forty or so players showing up as borderline with suspiciously raised levels. Among the best known were Juventus's Dutch midfielder Edgar Davids, and Lazio's defensive partnership of Jaap Stam, the former Manchester United player, and Fernando Couto. Frank de Boer also tested positive while on international duty with the Netherlands. Meanwhile Czech tennis player Petr Korda had also tested positive for nandrolone at Wimbledon in 1998 and received a ban, although he was later acquitted.

Nandrolone was far from being a mystery, but the reason why so many sporting figures were testing positive for it was. It emerged that there was one obvious reason: a scientifically proven incidence of the substance turning up in nutritional supplements which should not have contained it. In 1999 the IOC laboratory in Cologne run by Professor Wilhelm Schaencer began a two-year study of nutritional supplements and discovered that a significant proportion – sixteen from the first hundred investigated – had been contaminated during production with pro-hormones which the body metabolises to produce nandrolone.

The defence, once established, began to be employed to good effect. In 2003 seven tennis players were cleared by the Association of Tennis Professionals, which admitted it may have given players contaminated supplements. Also in 2003, Greg Rusedski was cleared of a positive test for nandrolone using the same argument. Of course, a cynic could argue that some sportsmen or women might have been cheating and then employing the contaminated supplements argument. But if that were the case, taking nandrolone appeared to be a curiously clumsy and old-fashioned method of cheating, destined for failure.

Michele Verroken is well placed to offer an overview. She sees the increasing production of sports supplements and drinks to enhance performance as 'a sort of grey area', adding: 'There is an inconsistency about the fact that we are marketing sports foods and drink to athletes – there is a level of hypocrisy going on. They are taken to improve performance, and yet other substances are ruled out.

'Some of the supplements that were causing a problem ten to fifteen years ago have cleaned up their acts. There are more rigorous testing programmes now which offer quality assurance on the products. But you only have to look at the recent case involving the South African rugby players on tour in Britain to see that the system is not foolproof.'

Two Springbok players, Chiliboy Ralepelle and Bjorn Basson, tested positive for the banned stimulant methylhexaneamine (MHA) after their Test match against Ireland on 6 November 2010. A subsequent hearing was told that the substance was present in supplements supplied to the team during the warm-up for their game in Dublin, and both players were exonerated. The South African Rugby Union, however, was criticised for not testing its supplements more comprehensively.

The fear generated by doping, perversely, can equally affect those who are innocent. Many athletes have spoken of the nervousness they feel after performances as they sit and drink and wait to provide a urine sample for the testers. The fear was, and is, that their samples might not be efficiently dealt with, and many memories are still vivid with the case which embroiled former Commonwealth 800m champion Diane Modahl in years of anguish and court action after she was found to have tested positive in 1994. Modahl was made bankrupt and at one point contemplated suicide before winning her appeal – subsequently appearing in the 2000 Sydney Olympics – on the grounds that her sample had been mishandled and neglected.

Money

'I've loved baseball ever since Arnold Rothstein fixed the 1919 World Series.'
– *Hyman Roth*, The Godfather, Part II

No harm in a bet...

What harm can it do to have a little bet? Millions of people get entirely legitimate pleasure – and on occasion, profit – from gambling on all manner of sporting contests. While conventional betting relates to results – West Ham to beat Manchester United, Ruby Rocket to win the 16.20 at Kempton Park – spot betting, a method that has long been employed in the Far East, and which is now ubiquitous thanks to the compound miracle that is broadband and the world wide web, offers gamblers an opportunity to bet on the minutiae of sporting contests, often while contests are still in progress.

Thus you can put money on the number of double faults in a tennis match, or free kicks, corners or throw-ins in a football match, or wides or no-balls in a cricket match. You can also bet on when these will occur within a sporting contest. One mechanism within spot betting which allows certain bets to be placed is spread betting, where a specialist trader will assess the likelihood of something occurring and create a margin of probability over or under which punters are invited to place their bets. This margin then becomes something of a moveable feast as time or money move on.

Whatever the form of betting, it is a truism that the bookie generally does better than the punter. One of the exceptions that proved that rule took place during the 1995 Rugby Union World Cup, when New Zealand's massively powerful Jonah Lomu was casting tacklers around like Gulliver in Lilliput. When Lomu was rested – along with several other first teamers – for the All Blacks' match against the inexperienced Japanese side, bookies predicted that the All Blacks would win what was always going to be a walkover of a match by a large but unspectacular amount, setting the margin between forty and forty-five points.

What the bookies hadn't factored in, however, was the intense ambition of any reserve who gets a chance in the group stages of a World Cup. This match was the chance for the All Blacks second choices to shine, and shine they did as they won 145–17. Those smart observers of the game who had predicted a win well in excess of the offered spread cleaned up, with some winning eighty-three times their stake. Perhaps the sweetest victory of the 1995 World Cup.

Generally speaking, however, making accurate spot betting predictions is a lot more difficult than simply saying you think West Ham are going to beat Manchester United, even though the odds strongly favour the latter team. Such a wager might stem from blind faith. But if you wanted to start making predictions about, say, the number of free kicks that will be given during a match, you are in different, more complex territory. You might operate on the basis of expecting more free kicks than usual, as that would be the only way West Ham could stop Manchester United. The thing is, it's harder, which in turn offers a higher profit potential. Which in turn offers a higher level of temptation.

The devil is in the detail here. Say you were a sportsman involved in one of these contests. Given your ability to influence events, you might decide to make yourself, and perhaps a few of your friends, a bit of extra cash by making a little bet come true – one that would do no harm and have no obvious influence on the result of the match. What harm could there be in that?

In his 2010 autobiography *Taking Le Tiss* the former Southampton and England footballer Matthew Le Tissier admitted to trying to profit from a spot of spread betting in a televised 1995 match against Wimbledon.

Le Tissier described how one of his teammates had friends with spread-betting accounts – then starting to become popular in Britain – who were able to lay some bets for them on the timing of the first throw-in. With bookmakers predicting it would occur after a minute, Le Tissier and his fellow player 'bought' under one minute, with a view to getting the ball out of play as soon as possible after the kick-off.

Thus, if the ball went out after four seconds, there would be fifty-six seconds remaining before the bookies' prediction, and Le Tissier and his friend would stand to win fifty-six times their original stake. As he described it, 'easy money'. But the plan went wrong. Le Tissier 'didn't give enough welly' to the ball and it was kept in, at a stretch, by his teammate Neil Shipperley – clearly not the other player in on the scheme. Le Tissier recalled how he then had to dash around like a mad thing to get hold of the ball and put it out. Had it stayed in play much beyond seventy-five seconds, he added, it would no longer have been a case of winning money, but losing.

'Eventually we got the ball out on seventy seconds,' Le Tissier wrote. 'The neutral time meant we had neither won nor lost. I have never tried spread betting since.' Southampton won the game 2–0, with Le Tissier scoring. After his book came out, the FA said no action would be taken because he was no longer involved in the game.

Le Tissier was a footballer of impeccable technique, but that facility had clearly not carried over to the business of a betting scam. It's interesting, however, to examine the way in which he described the temptation to make the attempt. 'We were safe from the threat of relegation when we went to Wimbledon on 17 April and, as it was a televised match, there was a wide range of bets available,' he wrote. 'Obviously I'd never have done anything that might have affected the outcome of the match, but I couldn't see a problem with making a few quid on the time of the first throw-in.'

There is anecdotal evidence to support the fact that Le Tissier was not the only top-class footballer to attempt such an apparently harmless money-making plan. I once covered a Premier League match in which the apparently pointless early concession of a throw-in was greeted by jubilant celebrations from a number of the home players. Baffling at the time. Now perhaps less so.

Let's repeat. Spot betting is a legitimate pastime. But its specific and limited nature makes it more capable of generating large amounts of winnings. And what gives the manipulation of spot betting a profound and insidious power is the fact that in the minds of sporting protagonists considering such manipulation it can be separated from the suggestion that they are doing something seriously wrong. 'There's cheating, and there's cheating. And this isn't really cheating. Just working the system.' To use an analogy from the world of doping, the abuse of spot betting takes on the status of a social drug – as distinct from one of those serious, performance-enhancing drugs.

The establishment of a tier system within betting abuse may be seen as a dangerous precedent. The limited nature of the venture creates an enclave within sport with a notice over it saying 'harmless cheating'. But that enclave is sited on a slippery slope. If the Southampton exercise was an example of a bit of potentially dodgy dealing, other sporting projects have relocated themselves firmly from the category of spot betting to that of spot fixing, where the sportsman or woman is bribed – or perhaps coerced – into acting in a way that ensures money, and usually that means big money, is won on spot bets.

Cricket oversteps the mark

If we take Le Tissier's bungled scam as being at one end of a continuum, what do we observe if we move along a bit? When three Pakistan cricketers – Salman Butt, Mohammad Asif and Mohammad Amir – were given prison sentences and five-year playing bans in November 2011 after being found guilty of involvement in the spot fixing of no-balls during the fourth Test between England and Pakistan at Lord's in August 2010, it stimulated widespread debate about the moral fibre of a sport which has been synonymous with fair play (although, as it happens, cricket's whites have not been whiter than white since the days when W. G. Grace was in his pomp).

What had the Pakistan bowlers actually done? From the point of view of the spectators at the time, virtually nothing. Three stray deliveries where the bowler's foot slipped over the line. One in particular which seemed like a rather extravagant miscalculation. A momentary oddity. The two New Zealand umpires officiating, Tony Hill and Billy Bowden, said they had felt at the time that Amir's no-ball had been delivered deliberately to England batsman Jonathan Trott, as he had clearly overstepped the mark but bowled the ball short.

'We never suspected a thing,' Hill told the *Dominion Post* in New Zealand. 'There had been a big overstep in particular, and in our minds that was more a deliberate overstep to have a go at Trott, who had been batting so well… it all seemed to be one of those things that fast bowlers have been known to do to get an advantage.'

Writing on insidethegames.biz, David Owen maintained that the sentences handed down to the trio, subject to appeals – Butt, the captain, got thirty months, Asif one year, and the eighteen-year-old Amir six months – were 'preposterous'. His argument was that their actions, 'though corrupt', were 'highly unlikely' to have a significant impact on the game. 'Yes,' he added, 'if England had won by 10 runs or fewer, then the no-balls would certainly have been material; but the chances of that being the case were very low.'

If players are to be given sentences of this magnitude for such an offence, Owen went on to ask, what punishments would be commensurate for those found guilty of actually trying to fix the result of a match? 'Would we lock them up for ten, fifteen, twenty years (the sort of sentences one normally associates with violent crime)?' he wrote. 'Or are we saying there is no moral distinction between acting corruptly in a manner calculated not to affect the result of the match (even if there is a small chance that it will) and doing so in a manner where determining the result is the whole point of the exercise?

'To me, the two examples, though both distressing and wrong, seem fundamentally different. I happened to be at Lord's on the day in question and witnessed a supremely exhilarating day of Test cricket. I simply don't believe the atmosphere of any sporting contest in which one side had been bribed to throw the match would be remotely comparable.'

Many others, however, including a significant number of players and administrators, felt the sentences had not been heavy enough. One former Pakistan captain, Rashid Latif, commented: 'They deserved this punishment. They had it coming.' Darren Gough, the former England fast bowler, said: 'I'm pleased. I would have liked to see the sentences longer, to be honest.' That was also the position of another former Pakistan captain, Mushtaq Mohammad, who wrote that it 'would not have been too much' if Butt, the captain, had received a maximum sentence of seven years.

Supporters, too, appeared to react more harshly to the offences. A year before the court case, when allegations of the spot fixing at Lord's first broke, there were television pictures of angry Pakistan fans burning pictures of their team. It was a shocking image. The faces consumed by flame were not those of deposed dictators, but sportsmen.

Such is the depth of feeling sport engenders, and such is the commensurate anger when the essential bond of trust between the spectator and the protagonist who represents them, and indeed their country, on the field of sporting endeavour is broken. It's guesswork, but you sense that a vox pop of those irate fans a year later would not have produced anything close to a majority believing that the sentences handed down to the cricketers involved were overly harsh.

What lies behind this second position is a reluctance to agree to any kind of sliding scale of wrongdoing within sport. It is the same mindset which holds that those found guilty of serious doping offences should be banned for life, rather than for four or two years. For many within the game the Pakistan trio, in accepting the temptation to fix the timing of no-balls, were literally and metaphorically crossing the line.

Judge Jeremy Cook, who presided over the no-ball conspiracy trial at Southwark Crown Court, made it clear in his summing-up that he felt the case threatened that validating trust between any spectator and the sport they watch. 'Whenever in the future there are surprising events or results, followers of the game... will be left to wonder whether there has been fixing and whether what they have been watching is a genuine contest between bat and ball,' he said. 'What ought to be honest sporting competition may not be such at all.' '"It's not cricket" was an adage,' Cooke added. 'It is the insidious effect of your actions on professional cricket and the followers of it which make the offences so serious.'

In January 2012 Essex cricketer Mervyn Westfield admitted accepting or obtaining a corrupt payment to aid spot betting during a one-day 40-overs match against Durham. The Old Bailey heard how Westfield had agreed to bowl his first over in a way that would let the opponents score 12 runs – for which he received £6,000. In the event, Durham only scored 10 off the over. The twenty-three-year-old bowler was found guilty and served half of a four-month prison sentence.

A subsequent enquiry by the English Cricket Board resulted in Westfield's teammate, the Pakistan leg-spin bowler Danish Kaneria, being banned for life in June 2012 for his part in encouraging Westfield to become involved in the spot betting incident.

An ECB statement described spot fixing as 'a cancer that eats at the health and very existence of the game', adding: 'For the general public, supporting the game and their team within it, there is no merit or motivation to expend time, money or effort to watch a match whose integrity may be in doubt. The consequences of the public's disengagement from cricket would be catastrophic.'

Kaneria refuted the charges, and announced his intention to appeal against the punishment.

The corrosive effect of the 'harmless' bet

By offering sportsmen and women the option of making illicit money at a level where they are still able to tell themselves they are not affecting the overall result, the companies that facilitate spread and spot betting have created a new and potentially damaging phenomenon. Such 'harmless' arrangements are corrosive to trust. And perhaps, in the broader scheme of things, they are not as harmless as they appear.

You could argue that it doesn't matter whether there is a throw-in four seconds into a league game between Southampton and Wimbledon, or four minutes into it. But however innocuous it appears, who can really know what might have happened if that ball had been booted over the line virtually from the kick-off? It might otherwise have been involved in a move which led to a goal. It might have set in motion a passage of play that tempted a player into a tackle which curtailed the career of an opponent. It might have been booted out of play by someone other than Le Tissier four seconds later. And if the elegant midfielder who was never known for his work rate had not sweated to get the ball out of play after seventy seconds, all manner of other things might have transpired.

Equally, one of those no-balls deliberately bowled at Lord's might, if delivered from behind the crease, have been smashed for six, or might have smashed a wicket. 'The moving finger writes, and having writ, moves on.' We can never know how things might otherwise have been.

The trio of Pakistan cricketers had already received hefty punishment from the International Cricket Council's (ICC) anti-corruption tribunal before they appeared in court. Butt was banned for ten years, five of which were suspended; Amir was banned for five years and Asif was given a seven-year ban, with two suspended. But there was a clear sense that these three had paid a heavy price for taking part in something which was more widespread, and which was manipulated by others who had not been called to account.

'It appears that the corruption may have been more widespread than the defendants here before me,' Cooke told the court. 'Whether or not what this court has had to consider is just the tip of an iceberg… lies beyond the scope of the evidence I have heard.' The chairman of the ICC's Anti-Corruption and Security Unit, former Royal Ulster Constabulary Chief Constable Sir Ronnie Flanagan, commented: 'I would have to say it is probably not absolutely isolated. It shows that we can never be complacent, we can never drop our guard, we must be ever vigilant and we will be ever vigilant.'

Fine sentiments indeed. But the awkward truth for the ICC was that this case had not come to light through their efforts, but through a sting operation set up by the now defunct *News of the World* newspaper. In just the same way, two of the biggest drug busts in sport – involving Ben Johnson in 1988 and the BALCO project in 2003 – were precipitated not by the efforts of the drug testers, but by human errors of judgement.

What the case involving the Pakistan cricketers did was to identify players who were susceptible to persuasion on the subject of wrongdoing. But it asked more questions than it answered in terms of how serious the problem of spot fixing is in cricket, or indeed in other sports. The trail from the players led back to an agent, Mazhar Majeed, who was sentenced to two years and eight months. But there was no question of it leading back any further, as it had been the *News of the World* which had set up the request. If money is indeed the root of all evil, it could be argued that this case did no more than pluck a few leaves from its branches.

Peter Swan, Tony Kay, David 'Bronco' Layne

The case involving Butt, Asif and Amir was the first criminal prosecution in Britain for on-field sports corruption since the 1960s, when three footballers were jailed. Had spot fixing been an option for the footballers involved, you fancy they would have preferred it to the course they took. But no such subtleties were available to English footballers back in 1962, when Peter Swan, Tony Kay and David 'Bronco' Layne decided to make themselves a bit of extra cash from Sheffield Wednesday's First Division match at Ipswich Town on 1 December.

For a while, it must have seemed to them as if they had got away with it. No harm done. But on 12 April 1964 the *Sunday People* broke a story that hit English football like an asteroid. Characterising it with customary modesty as 'The Biggest Sports Scandal of the Century', the newspaper accused the trio, two of whom were England internationals, of betting on themselves to lose.

It transpired that in the week of the Ipswich match, Layne told his two teammates how he had bumped into an old friend, the former Everton player Jimmy Gauld, who had spoken to him about money to be made in betting. Gauld said he needed a new match to target, and added that if Wednesday were to lose at Ipswich in their upcoming match some of their players could make a profit. The odds were 2–1. All three bet £50 on the home side to win, and collected a £100 profit after Wednesday lost 2–0. Gauld, subsequently accused of other match fixes in lower divisions, sold his story about the Wednesday match to the *People* for a fee reputed to be around £7,000.

When the case finally came to Nottingham Crown Court in January 1965, Gauld was named by the judge as the 'central figure' in a series of fixed matches. He was fined £5,000 and sentenced to four years' imprisonment for conspiracy to defraud. Swan, Kay and Layne received four-month jail sentences and were all banned for life by the Football Association, although the ban was rescinded after four years and both Layne and Swan rejoined Sheffield Wednesday.

So much for the mechanics. The morality was a little more complex. The three players did not lay their bet on any old match. They laid it before playing at a ground where, they all agreed, Wednesday never seemed to do well. There was an echo here of the kind of calculation made by sporting performers in more recent years regarding the relatively harmless nature of their bending the rules. The thinking here was, presumably, 'Well, we never win at Portman Road no matter how hard we try, so we might as well make a bob or two out of it.'

There was an echo, too, of the 'honest cheat' – a character occasionally encountered in doping cases – when Swan reflected upon his decision more than forty years later. He insisted he had tried in the match, and also pointed out that Kay had been named man of the match in the *Sunday People* of all places. But asked how he might have reacted had the game been scoreless moving into the final few minutes, he admitted he didn't know what he would have done.

'My money was on us to lose and money is the root of all evil,' he replied. 'It's easily done. I could have mis-kicked a ball into my own goal. I could have given away a penalty.' He added: 'David [Layne] and I have asked ourselves many times why we did it. What fools we were.'

What Swan and his colleagues did was regarded as match fixing. But it was never clear exactly what they did or did not do to ensure the desired result. So how do you fix a match or a sporting contest? It's not always a simple process. At times it takes considerable ingenuity. Those seeking to distort sporting encounters will often go for key figures within a team, most obviously the captain. The fact that it was the captain, Butt, who received the longest of the three sentences handed down at Southwark Crown Court in October and November 2011, told its own clear tale of relative responsibility.

Hansie Cronje – 'money for doing nothing'

Unlike a captain in football, who may do a fair bit of shouting or may, like the late lamented Bobby Moore, lead by quiet example, the cricket captain fulfils a far more active and profound role for his team as he orchestrates the fielding, the bowling changes, the batting tactics. He is the nerve centre of the team, and thus the ideal point at which to introduce any virus of foul play. In considering the case of Hansie Cronje, captain of the South African cricket team in the 1990s, we move yet further along the continuum of sporting misdeeds. Money was a motivating force for Cronje, who fell from being a paragon of a cricketer to becoming an emblem for corruption with dizzying swiftness. Sadly, there was less ambiguity here about wrongdoing. Cronje was in a position to make certain things happen, and he used that position.

When South Africa were defeated by England in the fifth Test of their 1999–2000 home series it was not just their fourteen-match unbeaten run in Test cricket which came to an end, but also the reputation of their captain. By the final day of the Test at Centurion, rain had prevented all but 45 overs of play, during which time South Africa had reached 155–6. But on the final morning it emerged that the two captains were going to 'make a game of it'. At the time, Cronje was widely applauded for his sportsmanship in opening up that possibility. A target of 250 from 70 overs was agreed, and when South Africa reached 248–8, Cronje declared. With both teams forfeiting an innings, England thus needed to score 249 to win the Test – which they did with two wickets and only five balls remaining.

And here's the rub. It later transpired that Cronje had accepted money and a gift from a bookmaker in return for making his early declaration. On 7 April 2000, Delhi police announced they had a recording of a conversation between Cronje and a representative of an Indian betting syndicate on the subject of match fixing. Three other players – Herschelle Gibbs, Nicky Boje and Pieter Strydom, were also implicated.

On 8 April 2000 the United Cricket Board of South Africa (UCBSA) denied their players were involved in match fixing. Cronje said the allegations were 'completely without substance'. However, on 11 April Cronje was sacked as captain after confessing that he had not been 'entirely honest'. He admitted accepting between $10,000 and $15,000 from a London-based bookmaker for 'forecasting' results, although not for match fixing, during a recently completed one-day series in India.

Something was clearly amiss, and an investigation – the King Commission – was established to determine the extent of the problem within South African cricket. Soon Gibbs stated that Cronje had offered him $15,000 to score fewer than 20 runs in the fifth one-day international (ODI) at Nagpur. There was also an offer of $15,000 to bowler Henry Williams to concede more than 50 runs in that same match. As things turned out, Gibbs scored 74 off 53 balls and Williams injured his shoulder and couldn't complete his second over, so neither received the $15,000.

On 15 June Cronje released a statement that revealed all his contact with bookmakers. In 1996, during the third Test in Kanpur, he said he had been introduced to Mukesh Gupta, who gave him $30,000 to persuade the South Africans to lose wickets on the last day to lose the match. South Africa were 127/5 chasing 460; Cronje was already out and maintained he spoke to no other players. 'I had received money for doing nothing,' he said. During the return tour, Cronje received $50,000 from Gupta for team information.

In the 2000 Centurion Test, another betting contact was reported to have offered him R500,000 for the charity of his choice together with a gift if he declared and made a game of it. After the match the contact was said to have visited Cronje, giving him two amounts of money (R30,000 and R20,000) together with a leather jacket. The promised R500,000 was not paid.

Cronje said that before the one-day series he had received repeated calls from someone called 'Sanjay' asking him to fix a match. Cronje added that he was offered $140,000 for the fifth ODI if Gibbs scored under 20, Williams went for more than 50, and South Africa scored around 270. On 28 August Gibbs and Williams were fined and suspended from international cricket for six months. Strydom received no punishment. On 11 October Cronje was banned from playing or coaching cricket for life. He challenged his life ban in September 2001, but on 17 October 2001 his application was dismissed. Within less than a year he was dead, killed in a plane crash at the age of thirty-two.

As more and more of the details of these manipulations emerged, cricket was forced to confront an unhappy truth about what had been happening in at least one of its enclaves. It was a traumatic discovery.

But for all the anguish Cronje's revelations caused within international cricket, and most specifically in his home country, an indication of how public perceptions of sporting transgressions can alter came when, less than two years after his death, Cronje was voted the eleventh greatest South African. Whatever guilt he carried, much of it appeared to have been expiated after his death, at least among those who knew him best.

The match fixing scandal of 2000 cost three Test captains their careers: Cronje, Mohammad Azharuddin of India and Salim Malik of Pakistan were banned for life for alleged links with illegal Indian bookmakers. Azharuddin's ban was rescinded after eight years. But the scandal did not mark an end to illegal betting in cricket. Regulating authorities maintain that much of the worldwide network of illegal gambling is based in India, even though it is illegal to bet there except on horse racing. The presence in India of the lucrative IPL (Indian Premier League) Twenty20 tournament offers a clear temptation to err.

Illegal betting on cricket, as we have seen, can be operating on almost every delivery in a match, given that the bet can be about the outcome of each delivery. Professional gamblers typically place numerous spot bets during a match, during which their winnings can wax and wane. Which is where Butt, Asif and Amir come in.

Targeting the ref – Totonero I, Totonero II…

Another classic tactic for those wishing to fix matches is to target the main official, be it an umpire, judge or referee. This moves the moral argument into a different area, given that the referee should be the ultimate arbiter, the man beyond corruption. Players – we expect them to cut corners, don't we? To work a few angles. Referees? Well of course they are always wrong, we know that, but only out of incompetence, not out of badness. It would take all the satisfaction from a good rant at the referee if we thought he had failed to give that obvious penalty because he was corrupt, rather than someone incapable of taking charge of a Sunday league match. Sadly, history tells us this is an inaccurate point of view.

In the space of the last twenty-five years, match-fixing scandals in Italy have erupted like volcanoes. And as with natural eruptions, some episodes have been more serious than others. In 1980 there was the Totonero scandal – named after the Italian description of illegal betting schemes – which involved a systematic attempt to influence results in Serie A and B matches. In 1986 there was more ominous rumbling until, like some hideous franchise, the world witnessed Totonero II. Just when you thought it was safe to lay a bet.

Totonero II involved match fixing from Serie A all the way down to Serie C2 which had taken place over the previous two years, and saw sanctions imposed on nine clubs, seventeen managers and coaches, and thirty-four players. Quite an eruption. Disappointingly for Italian fans, this manifestation was not accompanied by a World Cup win, as the original Totonero had been. But that strange link was to be forged again in 2006, when the Azzurri lifted the biggest prize in football amid the most serious match-fixing scandal ever to have blighted the Italian game.

The scandal that emerged in 2006 has come to be known as Calciogate, or Moggiopoli, a reference to the man found to be at the centre of it: Juventus's general manager, Luciano Moggi. In May 2006 Moggi was accused of fixing matches and bribing referees on a systematic basis. He was also named as being in charge of a network set up to interfere with the Italian FA's referee selection process.

When Juventus had an imminent European match, Moggi would phone Pierluigi Pairetto, the head of the committee which assigned referees to matches in UEFA competitions, who had himself refereed the 1996 European Championship final at Wembley between Germany and the Czech Republic.

How do we know this? Because investigators were already tapping his phone. Transcripts of their conversations were printed in the Italian press. At one point Moggi is very angry after hearing about a switch of officials for a forthcoming game. 'Did you see that they've changed our referee?' Moggi shouts. 'We got Paul Green [Graham Poll], the Englishman.' 'Fuck them,' Pairetto responds. 'The English are all assholes. I'll find out a little bit and inform you.'

A network of corruption and bribery was uncovered, and the punishments that followed were unprecedentedly harsh. Juventus, originally relegated to Serie C1, moved up one division to Serie B on appeal, and had their points reduction lowered from thirty to nine. They were also stripped of their 2005 and 2006 league title wins. Fiorentina, Lazio and Milan, all originally relegated to Serie B, maintained their Serie A status on appeal, but the first two clubs were prevented from taking up their places in the following season's UEFA Champions League, and Milan began season 2006/07 with an eight-point penalty, eventually finishing fourth. But after parleying themselves back into that season's Champions League competition they went on to win it, defeating Liverpool in the final.

A total of nineteen individuals were punished, with Moggi receiving the harshest sentence: a life ban from football. Juventus's 2006 title was inherited by Inter Milan. And referees were a central part of this operation. Where do you go from there?

Another fixing scandal, this time based in Germany, made Robert Hoyzer infamous as a corrupt referee. His career, which began in 2001, saw him officiate in the lower leagues, although he was among officials listed to control German Cup matches. But that career came to an abrupt end in January 2005 after he was suspected of betting on a first-round Cup tie between the regional league side Paderborn and the Bundesliga first division club SV Hamburg on 21 August 2004.

In that match Hamburg took a 2–0 lead, but Hoyzer sent off their striker Emile Mpenza in the first half and also awarded Paderborn two questionable penalties. Paderborn went on to win 4–2. Hoyzer initially denied the allegations but later admitted to them, and it transpired he had ties to Croat organised crime syndicates who had bet large sums on the matches at which he had officiated. He resigned as a referee and resigned his membership with Hertha BSC Berlin. The German football federation, DFB (Deutscher Fussball-Bund), banned Hoyzer from refereeing matches in Germany for life, and soon announced that it was investigating whether or not he had fixed other matches in the regional leagues and second division.

On 28 January 2005 four arrests linked to the Hoyzer case were made in Berlin, one of the key sites being the café where Hoyzer allegedly met with his contacts. On 2 February prosecutors in Berlin announced that police had raided the premises of nineteen suspects in the spreading scandal, and discovered evidence that might have implicated as many as twenty-five people – including fourteen players and three other referees – in fixing ten matches in 2004. Hoyzer had been cooperating with the German authorities and provided much of the information that led to the raids.

But on 12 February Hoyzer was arrested by police after new evidence emerged to suggest that he had fixed more matches than he had already admitted to. On 24 March the German news magazine *Der Spiegel* broke a story that indicated the scandal went far beyond Germany, and possibly to UEFA headquarters. According to the report, Hoyzer told investigators that the gambling ring had the lists of referees and assistants who would work competitive international matches and fixtures in the UEFA Champions League and UEFA Cup about a week in advance of the matches. UEFA does not publicise the officials list until two days before matches.

The criminal charges Hoyzer admitted to carried a maximum prison sentence of ten years, although there was no mandatory jail term. On 17 November 2005 Hoyzer was jailed for two years five months. Following the Hoyzer case the German football federation has imposed a blanket ban on betting on football matches by anyone associated with the sport – players, coaches, referees and officials. Additionally, the federation wanted to reduce the notice on assigning officials to matches to two days, but expanded that to four days when it proved to be unworkable.

In June 2006, just before the FIFA World Cup finals were held in Germany, the left-wing art-technology-philosophy group, monochrom, created an art installation entitled *Café King Soccer* at the NGBK Gallery in Berlin addressing the corruption case that had involved Hoyzer. It seemed that monochrom wanted to reflect on the way that football has always had a kind of creative tension between a working-class culture of subjectivity and a middle-class culture of objectivity whose personification is the referee – a rational, independent figure separate from the maelstrom of passionate mass commitment.

Hoyzer's actions effectively betrayed that position. But the installation also hinted at the idea that he was in some way a tragic character, because he 'acted out his inner self-contradiction as an exemplary civil subject in a publicly effective way'. Hoyzer as Macbeth, then, driven to act in a way he knew to be wrong, to the point where he couldn't go back and therefore might as well go on.

An aesthetic judgement was also made upon Hoyzer's 'exemplary immolation as a scapegoat, which seems to correspond exactly to his role on the field – and *conditio sine qua non* of its perpetuation'. Doubtless voicing the thoughts of spectators throughout Deutschland.

While some parts of the monochrom creation clearly belong in a kind of footballing pseud's corner, there is nevertheless a valid resonance there. Despite all the lessons history teaches us, we still subliminally expect our referees, whether they objectify the middle classes or not, to be figures of basic trust. And when they are not, to borrow from another Shakespearean tragedy, chaos is come again.

Sumo too?

There is, unquestionably, a varying level of expectation from the general viewing public with regard to levels of bribery and corruption in different sports. One of the most extreme examples is that of sumo wrestling. Sumo is suffused with ancient spirituality and has its beginnings in rituals within the Shinto religion. Before any match, the protagonists perform rituals derived from Shinto practice, including a leg-stomping *shiko* exercise to drive evil spirits from the ring, rinsing out their mouths with sacred water and then scattering salt in the ring to purify it.

Before they come to grips – something which happens by instinct rather than command – the two protagonists in the ring practise a kind of breathing known as 'Ah-Unh', which symbolises the first and last letters of the Sanskrit alphabet: the alpha and the omega, the yin and the yang. 'In Christianity you have the Trinity, and in sumo we have something like it too,' one former sumo wrestler explained. 'It's the harmony of three people

– the wrestler on the east, the wrestler on the west, and the referee. It is impossible to express in words.'

Sumo has a profoundly important position in the collective Japanese psyche. But in a survey conducted in 2010 by the Japan Sumo Association (JSA), sixty-five of its seven hundred members admitted involvement in illegal gambling on baseball, cards, mah-jong and other games. Many members of the sumo establishment appeared to have been caught up in what was clearly an endemic problem in a sport where competitors have traditionally been expected to display high standards of behaviour.

When it was announced in July 2010 that top wrestler Kotomitsuki was being banned from the sport after he and his coach had admitted to being involved in illegal betting on baseball – an alleged source of funding for Japan's yakuza gangsters – it had a profoundly disturbing effect, especially as more than ten other wrestlers were also implicated in the betting scandal.

This appeared to be the last straw for the Japanese public TV company NHK. Having televised each of the six annual sumo tournaments since 1953, NHK insisted it would not be screening the next scheduled tournament, in Nagoya, live, following a mass of complaints from viewers. Instead it planned to show brief highlights.

Hardly the standards required in this most ancient of sports. It is little wonder that it has been experiencing problems recently in the area of recruitment. But you have to say, if sumo can become prey to the temptations of illegal betting, where is safe?

In March 2011 Jacques Rogge, president of the IOC, addressed just this question, describing reports of illegal betting within sumo wrestling as 'another frightening example', and adding: 'There have been documented cases of cheating and match fixing in sumo wrestling in Japan. There has been recently a very visible case in cricket. There is no safe haven in the world where nothing happens.'

Rogge was speaking to the press after a meeting that had drawn a group of highly influential figures to the IOC's headquarters on the shore of Lake Geneva in Lausanne. Those present had included ministers from the British, Australian, French and Swiss governments, and representatives from international organisations including the United Nations and Interpol.

All had a common aim: to highlight, and address, a problem within sport which, in Rogge's estimation, had become of even greater concern than doping: irregular betting. The ministers were reportedly 'shocked' to hear that the previous year's figure for illegal betting was an estimated $140 billion

(£86 billion). In confirming this figure at the subsequent press conference, Rogge, with a grim smile, described it as 'a budget much higher than that of many developing nations', adding: 'This is a big problem in the entire world. There is illegal betting where there is broadband internet.'

The meeting also heard that illegal online betting had grown by 70 per cent since 2006, and that betting in Europe was reported to be 'six times higher' than it had been eight years ago. Ron Noble, Secretary General of Interpol, gave delegates details of three recent operations undertaken which had thwarted betting set-ups involving billions of dollars.

In 2007 an operation in China, Malaysia, Singapore and Vietnam involved 260 raids and 400 arrests, and saw $700 million (£430 million) of illegal betting stopped. The following year similar action in Indonesia resulted in 1,000 raids, 1,300 arrests, $17 million (£10 million) of recovered money and $1.4 million (£860,000) of illegal bets stopped. And in 2010 an initiative in China, Malaysia, Singapore and Thailand involving 850 raids netted 5,000 arrests, $10 million (£6 million), and $155 million (£95 million) in illegal bets stopped.

Rogge said betting patterns were clearly established to avoid detection as much as possible. 'We know there are people betting in other continents on European second league divisions,' he said. 'There are bets being taken on fourth division matches in certain leagues, so that shows you the problem. It's for the most popular sports – definitely, yes. But in the popular sports it's not necessarily in the first league or the top teams, it's mostly as we see second division, third division, because of the small exposure to cameras, to supervision, fewer spectators. So if something strange happens it's not going to be seen in highlights for the whole week as would happen with the top match in some professional team sports.'

Jacques Rogge: 'I think that sport is in danger'

Eleven years earlier there had been a similar meeting of minds in Lausanne as governments and assorted agencies had come together to consider how best to co-ordinate efforts to eradicate doping from sport, a meeting which was a precursor to the establishment of the World Anti-Doping Agency. Now there was a new topic on the agenda: betting. 'I think that sport is in danger,' Rogge concluded. 'It's not about the Olympic Games; it's about sport in general.'

Rogge called on governments around the world to clamp down on illegal betting and illegal bookmakers. 'We need their support, they alone have the judicial powers, they can tap telephone calls, they can issue warrants, they can search baggage – we cannot do that,' he said. 'There is a far bigger danger to the total credibility of sport because these are mafia people and they bet at the same time as manipulating the result of a match,' he explained.

Two months later, Rogge's warning was echoed by Sepp Blatter, president of the world football authority, FIFA, at a summit meeting with Interpol with a view to cracking down on illegal betting. An investigation being conducted at a court in Bochum, Germany into what the European football body, UEFA, had described as 'the biggest match-fixing scandal that European football has ever seen' formed the background to the meeting.

Reporting on the summit from Zurich for the insideworldfootball.biz site, Andrew Warshaw said it was made clear that scores of players, officials and referees across both Eastern and Western Europe had been taking bribes to throw up to three hundred matches – not just international friendlies but also Champions League and Europa League fixtures.

The meeting partners had added that, under a new ten-year agreement, Interpol would receive €4 million (£3.5 million/$6 million) from FIFA in the first two years followed by €1.5 million (£1.3 million/$2.2 million) in each of the following eight to try and wipe out the illegal betting rings – many of which were centred in Asia – that Blatter warned could further damage his organisation's credibility.

Blatter said fans had a right to know that matches were being played fairly. 'They will no longer go to football matches if they know they are fixed and if that happens everything that has been created in 107 years in FIFA will count for nothing,' he maintained. 'FIFA would lose all credibility if fans no longer believe in what is known in Great Britain as the beautiful game. It's not enough to go against corruption and bad behaviour on the field of play. We also have to look at those who try to destroy our game.'

Blatter was flanked by a number of high-ranking crime prevention officers from across Europe, notably Commissioner Friedhelm Althans, who was heading the Bochum investigation. Althans said his inquiry was merely 'the tip of the iceberg', adding: 'There is a worldwide network of people active in this field. It is not a matter simply of pursuing individual players and clubs but to attack the evil by the roots.'

Noble, who had sounded a warning for Interpol in Lausanne, added his view of the worldwide malaise. 'Asia is a hotbed of match fixing. During the

2010 World Cup we ran an operation out of Malaysia, China, Singapore and Thailand, and during a one-month operation 5,000 arrests were made, in excess of twenty-six million dollars in cash were seized and illegal gambling dens which handled over two billion dollars' worth of bets were closed.'

We are a world away here from Peter Swan and his mates chancing £50 on a routine defeat at Ipswich. These kinds of figures, reeled out so matter-of-factly by Noble at Lausanne and then Zurich, are truly frightening. And yet sport continually fails to speak in unison on the broad subject of betting. Sports such as racing and football, for instance, integrate legitimate betting organisations into their fabric, either by calling competitions after them or, in the case of football, emblazoning their names across the front of team shirts following sponsorship deals. Betting is an integral element to racing, and has become increasingly so as far as football is concerned.

But the IOC, which first noticed internet bets being offered on Olympic competitions (mainly athletics) at the 2004 Athens Games, looks upon betting in a different light. It responded to the 2004 findings by forming a group to study the issue and in 2006 formalised rules banning all those with accreditation from betting on Olympic competitions. Rogge spoke out about the dangers of betting in the Games and ruled that he would never allow a bookmaker to sign up as a sponsor.

In 2009 the IOC appointed International Sports Monitoring GmbH (ISM), an independent company based in Switzerland, to protect the integrity of Olympic sports by monitoring betting activities on the upcoming Games – the 2010 Winter Olympics in Vancouver and the 2012 Olympic Games in London.

Although nothing suspicious was found during the Beijing or Vancouver Olympics, there is no sense of relaxation over the issue within Olympic circles. 'We should not be naïve; sooner or later this might occur at the Olympic Games and we want to prevent that,' Rogge said. 'Cases of match fixing and other forms of illegal betting are nothing new. They are as old as organised sport itself.

'But with the advent of betting on the internet and the anonymity, liquidity and sheer volume it encompasses, the potential for corruption is at an all-time high. It can be argued that there are temptations and more pressure on athletes, coaches, officials and others to cheat for betting gains than at any other time in the past.

'What's worse, this cancer continues to go largely unregulated in many parts of the world. Illegal or irregular betting – which should not be confused with the legal and regular betting offered by national lotteries and private entities that is a major source of financing to sport – is potentially crippling.

'Each instance that comes to light undermines confidence in sport, which can lead to spectator apathy and drops in attendance, TV viewership and sponsorship. At its worst it can deter people from participating in sports in the first place.'

Running with a fish on your head

More than two hundred years earlier, similar sentiments to Rogge's were being expressed by many jaundiced followers about the sport that had come to be known as pedestrianism. This activity had its roots in wagers between seventeenth- and eighteenth-century aristocrats as to which of their carriage footmen – whose task it was to walk alongside the moving vehicle – would fare better in a walking or running race. There were, however, all manner of variations on this theme, with novelty being considered a prime virtue.

Contests took place between runners and men on stilts. In 1763 it was recorded that a fishmonger ran from Hyde Park Corner to the seven-mile stone in Brentford carrying 56lb of fish on his head. To win the bet involved, he needed to complete the run within an hour, and did so with quarter of an hour to spare. In 1788 another bizarre sporting tourney took place between an elderly, fat man named Bullock and a young man carrying a spurred and booted jockey on his back. History does not record the winner.

By the end of the eighteenth century, however, the public appetite for such contests – which would typically take place at fairs and other such gatherings – had waned because of a lack of outstanding performers and rivalries and also, reportedly, a weariness with the race fixing that had become such a feature of the professional running scene.

In the early nineteenth century pedestrianism's fortunes revived with the arrival of a new champion in the form of Robert Barclay Allardyce, the 6th Laird of Ury. Just as Edson Arantes do Nascimento became famous as Pele, his predecessor as a sporting superstar also operated under a competitive monicker. He was known as Captain Barclay. Even so, Barclay's challenge in 1807 against renowned runner Abraham Wood – which entailed him walking for twenty-four hours with a twenty-mile start over his opponent, who was allowed to run – ended in dubious circumstances in front of a huge crowd at Newmarket.

After Wood had retired at just forty miles, it was discovered that his handlers had given him liquid laudanum – a derivative of opium – after twenty-two miles, and doctors who examined him after he had stopped found him feverish and weak. One correspondent opined that his handlers had given him the drug having secretly laid money on him to lose.

But then match fixing, as Eupolos of Thessaly, Callippus of Athens and Didas and Sarapammons of Egypt have unhappily and officially demonstrated, is as old as sport. If only the ancient Greeks had had broadband. Then the process of turning a dishonest drachma could have been made so much simpler.

Eupolos could have had a quiet word with one of the boxers he bribed simply to take a dive as close to one minute into the third round as he could manage. If Callippus had been after money rather than gold – although Olympic victories led inevitably to money and gifts from your grateful and adoring home polis – he could have had a little chat with one of his rivals and then bet on the wheel of their chariot falling off during the second circuit.

Similarly, Didas and Sarapammons could have laid money against the possibility that each would knock the other down before resuming battle proper to determine who was the better boxer. In short, they could all have done a bit of spot fixing.

Illegal betting, or match fixing, can potentially erode any sporting spectacle. Often this is a process which occurs retrospectively, as the general viewing public realises that such-and-such happened at the behest of so-and-so, rather than spontaneously. That in turn gives rise to erosion in an anticipatory sense. Once the trust has gone, future events are regarded with suspicion and even antipathy.

Floodlight sabotage – The Valley's low point

But of course most people who attempt to subvert sport don't care about sport. And if it proves necessary to curtail the event upon which they are betting, they will do so. The Valley is the ground where Charlton Athletic Football Club have played – bar one season and seven years of wandering between 1985 and 1992 – since 1919. It was in this most traditional of football arenas that a sophisticated scam involving the sabotage of floodlights would have taken place during a visit from Liverpool one winter's evening in 1998 – had police not been tipped off and taken evasive action three days before the game.

They were on hand at the ground on the evening of 10 February to provide an unwelcome welcoming party for a group of four men who had arrived with a car full of highly suspicious-looking equipment. The quartet comprised Wai Yuen Liu, from Hong Kong, and two Malaysian co-saboteurs, Eng Hwa Lim and Chee Kew Ong, whose hotel room was subsequently discovered to contain equipment that would have been useful if you had been wanting, say, to disable a set of floodlights. They also found contacts for a West Ham employee and another person who worked for Wimbledon.

The fourth member of the party was Charlton security supervisor Roger Firth, who was later found to have received £20,000 for his part in a scam thought to have been worth £30 million had it come off. Firth had been paid to let the saboteurs into the ground. But he became responsible for the unravelling of the scam when he attempted to bribe a fellow security guard with £5,000 to let the sabotage occur.

Once it became clear that the intention had been to rig the lights so they could be blown by tripping a switch remotely, investigators saw a pattern emerging which tied this effort in with two previously unsuspected instances in 1997 when matches had had to be abandoned due to floodlight failure in the second half.

The first had been a match between West Ham and Crystal Palace at Upton Park, during which the lights had gone out shortly after West Ham had equalised. The second occurred during Wimbledon's game at their temporary home of Selhurst Park against Arsenal. This time the floodlights went dark soon after resumption of play in the second half, with both sides goalless.

The West Ham and Wimbledon employees whose names were found in the saboteurs' possession were both arrested, but escaped charges due to lack of evidence. The scam was based on a discrepancy between betting rules in Britain and Asia. In Britain, if a match has to be abandoned, even if it is shortly before the final whistle, all bets are off. In Asia, however, there is a pay-off on a match result as it stands if the game is abandoned during the second half.

The betting system worked principally around encounters between larger and smaller clubs in the Premier League. The larger clubs – West Ham, Arsenal, Liverpool – would be likely to attract most of the money, even though, under the Asian betting system, the underdogs would have been given a one- or two-goal 'lead' to start off with.

There would have been a calculated risk for the match in question that Charlton, bolstered by their 'lead', would still be ahead by the start of the second half, at which point the lights would go off and the result would be deemed a Charlton win. This would allow the syndicate which had initiated the scam to make huge amounts of money on wagers. Because of this, it was not a scam which needed to be worked often to work profitably.

Had it not been for the tip-off, it is quite possible that the latest floodlight failure would have been regarded as just another coincidence – although obviously there would have come a point when people began to question the increased incidence of such an event. The suggestion was that another eight similar incidents were in the pipeline. Despite the most careful execution, this would surely have triggered suspicion eventually.

Chris Eaton, a former Interpol official who took up the job as head of security for FIFA, has estimated that 'probably 90 per cent' of both legal and illegal gambling on football around the world stems from South-east Asia, with many of the bets involving European matches.

Eaton added that while match fixers would sometimes target a player who owed money through gambling, another method would involve helping players from poor countries to further their careers with professional clubs, at which point they would feel obliged to comply with any requests.

The World Lottery Association, representing state-authorised lotteries, has estimated that €90 billion is legitimately wagered each year on football games, with the same amount being spent on illegal betting. Eaton says that Interpol estimates the latter figure to be higher.

That the people responsible for the floodlights scam chose to activate it in English Premier League games was actually a huge compliment to the general honesty of the game in this country. It was the high general level of honesty which made it such a tempting target.

English football is enormously popular in Asia, where clubs such as Manchester United, Arsenal and Liverpool have cultivated huge levels of support and where Premier League matches are broadcast live. Blatant match rigging – especially in Malaysia, where more than one hundred players and officials were arrested for corruption in the mid-1990s – had driven disillusioned fans to place their loyalty in English clubs.

But while the targeting was a backhanded compliment in one way, it was also – in simply curtailing a sporting event at the point where a profit was assured – a huge expression of contempt for the sport, and the people who follow it.

Money for art's sake?

If you were, say, Ross Rebagliati, you might be tempted to say of the flood-lights scam that it was 'not cool'. But there is still a school of thought which holds that it can sometimes be 'cool' to fix things like sporting encounters. Many of us will have enjoyed watching Paul Newman and Robert Redford rip off that nasty Robert Shaw in the 1973 film *The Sting*, or perhaps, more basically, watching George Clooney, Brad Pitt et al executing successive intricate casino heists in *Ocean's Eleven, Twelve* and *Thirteen*.

It's undeniable. There is a large element of admiration for well-executed crookedness. What may make this easier to countenance is the fact that in *The Sting* Shaw is a nasty crook, and that in *Ocean's Eleven*, for instance, the money is taken from a casino, which is widely viewed as a mechanism for relieving people of their money in exchange for a sleepless night. But what does this say about us, that we condone someone or something getting comeuppance through means that are equally crooked? One way of looking at this uncomfortable state of affairs is the aesthetic one. Art for art's sake, money for God's sake. But if the money is obtained artfully then the operation has its own validity. From an artistic point of view, that is.

In the 1974 film *The Godfather, Part II*, when Michael Corleone (played by Al Pacino) visits the house of the mildly spoken rival mobster Hyman Roth – whom he will later have killed – the two men sit for a while watching baseball on the television. 'I've loved baseball,' says Roth, 'ever since Arnold Rothstein fixed the 1919 World Series.' Corleone smiles in acknow-ledgement. And there it is: the admiration.

There is another high-profile cultural reference to Rothstein, albeit under the name of Meyer Wolfsheim, in F. Scott Fitzgerald's 1925 novel *The Great Gatsby*. There, Wolfsheim is characterised as a crooked business associate of the mysterious and vastly wealthy Gatsby, who himself is shown to be engaged in ambiguous telephone conversations: '... well, he's no use to us if Detroit is his idea of a small town...' At one point, Gatsby tells the narrator, Nick Carraway, that Wolfsheim is 'the man who fixed the 1919 World Series'. Again, such monumental fiscal wrongdoing seems to carry an aura of wonder about it.

And of course, in the case of Rothstein, the World Series scam was never proven. Rothstein, a legendary New York gambler, once boasted that he could fix anything, and popular history records the subverting of the World Series, a contest at the very apex of sport, as his greatest dark triumph. With their star man, 'Shoeless' Joe Jackson, on apparently invincible form, the Chicago White Sox were clear favourites to defeat the Cincinnati Reds in 1919. Legend now has it that Rothstein bribed eight of the White Sox players, using as leverage their strong dissatisfaction with the level of payment they were receiving from their unpopular owner Charlie Comiskey, to throw the series, having bet $300,000 on the Reds to win.

Chicago, later unofficially renamed the Black Sox by disillusioned fans, slumped to a series defeat, prompting a fever of speculation. The Chicago grand jury that sat on the case the following year heard confessions from several of the players, including Jackson. They had been told no action would be taken against them, but were immediately suspended. As the players made their way out, according to popular legend, a young boy ran up to Jackson and demanded: 'Say it ain't so, Joe!' Jackson, however, later insisted the incident had never happened.

Rothstein, too, insisted that nothing had happened. He told the grand jury he was an innocent businessman intent on clearing his name and his reputation. Prosecutors could find no evidence linking Rothstein to the affair and he was never indicted. 'I was not in on it, would not have gone into it under any circumstances and did not bet a cent on the Series after I found out what was under way,' he said in testimony.

In June 1921, just before the jury trial was due to begin, the players' testimonies mysteriously disappeared and they were acquitted due to lack of evidence. But Kenesaw Mountain Landis, a former federal court judge who was installed as baseball commissioner, upheld the suspensions, declaring: 'Regardless of the verdict of juries... no player that sits in conference with a bunch of crooked players and gamblers... will ever play professional baseball.'

And Rothstein? No proof, no sanction. Two years after the ill-fated World Series, Rothstein was accused of bringing off another betting coup. After his horse, Sporting Blood, had been entered in the 1921 Travers Stakes, he allegedly conspired with a leading trainer, Sam Hildreth, to drive up the odds on his horse. Hildreth entered an outstanding three-year-old racer, Grey Lag, causing Sporting Blood's odds to rise to 3-1.

Rothstein then bet $150,000 on his horse before – guess what? – Grey Lag had to withdraw at short notice claiming a subsequent engagement. The New York gambler cleaned up again, taking over $500,000 in winnings. A conspiracy? It was never proved.

But change the lens on all this, and look at the collateral damage. The 1919 World Series ended the careers of eight leading baseball players, including one of the most talented ever to swing a bat, Joe Jackson. It tarnished for ever the name of the Black Sox – sorry, White Sox. It also compromised any joy the Cincinnati Reds might have had in reaching the apex of their sport. It wasn't glamorous. It wasn't glitzy. It was shoddy and depressing.

Raging bet

That said, for all the simmering resentment the White Sox had about their owner, they did not have to subvert the Series. It could have been worse. They could have been in the position in which a talented boxer found himself almost thirty years later. On this occasion, the Mob managed to do what no boxer had yet managed: floor Jake LaMotta. He had to take a dive against a no-hoper and let the mobsters win their big money before they would allow him his title shot.

LaMotta – who has since been played by Robert De Niro in the 1980 Martin Scorsese film *Raging Bull* – finished his career with a record of eighty-three wins, nineteen losses and four draws with thirty KOs, and was the first man to beat Sugar Ray Robinson. But on 14 November 1947, two years before he became world champion, LaMotta lost in suspicious circumstances at Madison Square Garden, knocked out in four rounds by a relatively unregarded fighter named Billy Fox.

The New York State Athletic Commission, smelling a rat, withheld the purses for the fight and suspended LaMotta, who spent seven months out of the sport. In 1960, after his retirement, he was called to testify before a US Senate subcommittee investigating the influence of the Mafia on boxing. LaMotta admitted at the hearing, and later in his book, *Raging Bull: My Story*, to throwing the fight.

Offering the Mob a chance to cash in with bets on his long-odds defeat – plus giving them a further payment of $20,000 – eventually earned the man from the Bronx his chance, which he took in 1949 when he defeated the French reigning champion Marcel Cerdan.

LaMotta's description of a fix that was reckoned at the time to be far from convincing makes interesting reading: 'The first round, a couple of belts to his head, and I see a glassy look coming over his eyes. Jesus Christ, a couple of jabs and he's going to fall down? I began to panic a little. I was supposed to be throwing a fight to this guy, and it looked like I was going to end up holding him on his feet... By [the fourth round], if there was anybody in the Garden who didn't know what was happening, he must have been dead drunk.'

Here was a clear example of how money can shape and distort sport. There was nothing cool or admirable about it. The realpolitik of illegal gambling was as plain here as it was when the lights went off at Upton Park. Competitors and fans are equally immaterial to the crooked punter, merely means to the end of profit. The sport, and the love of its followers, is polluted in the same way that oceans are polluted with oil. And like oil, illegal gambling is insidious and hard to get rid of.

While glory of the kind for which LaMotta made his calculated decision may be a massive reason for sporting figures to seek illegal assistance through pharmaceutical means, the testimony of Dwain Chambers, the British sprinter who served his two-year ban for taking the designer steroid THG, makes it clear that money is often an equally massive reason.

'My motivation was the fear of what might happen,' commented Chambers, who reckoned that in his first year of working with Victor Conte at the BALCO lab in the United States he spent more than $30,000 on a doping programme that involved THG, the blood booster EPO, human growth hormone, testosterone and insulin, as well as regular testing on the safety levels of his blood. 'I had a £200,000 contract with Adidas that had a clause in it which reduced my salary by half if I was no longer in the top three, so I convinced myself the drugs were working.' It was a lot of money to pay for a European gold medal and a world relay silver, of which he was subsequently stripped.

When you get down to it, money can make a lot of odd things happen in sport. It can make cricketers step over a line. It can make referees blow their whistles. It can turn the lights out. It can also, on occasions, turn brother against brother.

What price brotherly love?

At the 2003 World Athletics Championships in Paris, two brothers born and bred in Kenya reached the final of the 3000m steeplechase. They ignored each other before the race. And after. Why? Money was why. It had caused bad feeling. And it had raised a familiar question: what price loyalty?

The elder brother, Abraham Cherono, was competing for their native country. The younger, Stephen, was competing for the Arab state of Qatar under a new name, Saif Saaeed Shaheen, which he had adopted only a few weeks earlier. Indeed, so unfamiliar had he been with his new identity upon arrival in Paris that he had had to refer to his new Qatari passport to remind himself.

There had already been rumours that Shaheen and his Kenyan compatriot Albert Chepkurui, who was also running for Qatar under the name of Ahmed Hassan Abdullah, had been offered $1 million to switch nationality. After running in the Zurich Weltklasse meeting less than a week after becoming a Qatari citizen, Shaheen denied this figure, but admitted to reporters: 'Qatar will pay $1,000 a month, even after my retirement. In Kenya there is nothing like this. Qatar is a country with a lot of opportunities.'

For 'opportunities', read 'money': this was the attitude of many African nations, who began to fear that all their best talent would simply be bought up and taken away. What balanced that argument, however, was the fact that nations such as Kenya and Ethiopia had such a depth of talent that even the finest departed athlete was likely to be adequately replaced.

At the time, Shaheen compared his switch to that made by Wilson Kipketer, then the world 800m record holder, from Kenya to Denmark. But Kipketer had moved to Copenhagen to study engineering, and had chosen to live there because he loved the place. He also married a Dane in 2000.

When Shaheen wrapped the Qatari flag around himself before setting off on his victory lap in Paris, one nation may have rejoiced, but another cringed. The following year, Kenya managed to block Shaheen from running at the Athens Olympics. IOC rules required competitors changing allegiances to wait for three years after being granted citizenship before they could compete in the Games for their new country, although this could be reduced to one year if both countries involved agreed. Not surprisingly, Kenya was unwilling to come to such an arrangement with Qatar. A month after the 2004 Olympics, however, the new 3000m steeplechase champion Ezekiel Kemboi (of Kenya) was beaten in Brussels by Shaheen, who set a world record in doing so.

In 2005, shortly before the World Championships in Helsinki, the athletics world governing body, the IAAF, tightened its rules on switching nationality to bring them in line with those of the IOC. Shaheen meanwhile continued to compete successfully for Qatar. Shaheen's switch was followed by the 'defection' of almost forty other Kenyan athletes to oil-rich nations such as Qatar and Bahrain. On the eve of the 2005 World Championships, the Kenyan president, Mwai Kibaki, met some of his country's leading athletes and announced: 'Let us resist the temptation to change our citizenship for financial gains.' The IOC president, Jacques Rogge, also spoke out on the subject: 'What is bad is countries or organisations wanting to buy athletes just for the money.'

But what exactly was bad about it? Money for life – it's a no-brainer, isn't it? And while the Kenyans weren't chuffed about an athletics version of the brain drain, there were nevertheless Kenyan voices speaking up for the right of athletes to cash in on their talent. Moses Kiptanui, Kenya's triple world steeplechase champion and former world record-holder, told *Nairobi World News* in 2005: 'I have won more than five medals, but I have got zero from the government.' He said that many past athletes were now living in 'a very, very sparse state… They are very poor despite the fact they have done great things for this country.'

Buying success in football

But what are the legitimate claims of countries and organisations, then? Isn't 'buying athletes' exactly what many other sports have done, quite brazenly, for many years? It happens in football all over the world. And while Italy used to be the place which flashed the biggest money of all – when John Charles moved from Leeds to Juventus in 1957 for £65,000 it almost doubled the British transfer fee record – it is England's Premier League which now attracts the game's richest players – and, of course, payers.

The trend in recent years for the top Premier League teams such as Liverpool, Chelsea, Manchester United and Manchester City to be bought up by fabulously wealthy foreign owners has provoked vigorous debate. While most supporters do not care overmuch who supplies the money if their team is successful, there will nevertheless always be an uneasy fit within any football club between an owner who may see the team as a financial investment and those thousands of supporters who have made an emotional investment.

What can occasion grimly ironic chuckles is the stance occasionally adopted by clubs such as Manchester United, not noticeably underfunded, as they have questioned the validity of the sudden vast investment at first Chelsea and then Manchester City, taken over respectively by business billionaire Roman Abramovich and Sheikh Mansour bin Zayed Al Nahyan, who is said to have an individual net worth of at least £17 billion but – don't panic, City fans – whose family wealth is said to be worth at least $1 trillion.

'You can't buy success' is a comment often heard in football. But is it a statement of fact, or a warning-off? Chelsea patently bought a measure of success, if you count winning the Premier League and FA Cup as a success. Had John Terry not slipped as he took his penalty in the shoot-out at the end of the 2008 Champions League final against Manchester United, that statement of fact could have been made without even a measure of circumspection. And in 2012, lo, it came to pass as the Champions League was finally obtained.

But the players who become part of these massive instruments of wealth also take on an ambiguous position. They can be bought and sold. And yet when they arrive at a club they are expected to demonstrate loyalty and to connect with supporters who were there years before they arrived and will be there years after they depart. The annoying fashion among scorers for kissing the club badge on their chest in celebration is, in many cases, no more than an empty gesture.

On occasion, however, a genuine connection between a player and their supporters can be fashioned despite the millions of pounds sloshing around in the background. The arrangement whereby top Argentina internationals Carlos Tevez and Javier Mascherano signed for not-very-top-at-the-time Premier Leaguers West Ham in 2006 had a vexed financial back-story, which would result in West Ham being fined £5.5 million the following year for breaching Premier League rules relating to players who had third party financial agreements. Reports at the time suggested more prestigious Premier League teams had been put off such a signing because of stipulations put in place by Media Sports Investments, which owned both players' rights.

But aside from all the financial wrangling, Tevez – despite a poor start – earned himself a place of genuine affection among the Upton Park fans, a bunch of people not easily fooled, with his inspirational displays towards the end of a season in which the team managed to escape from what had at one point seemed certain relegation. That Tevez should secure the club's Premier League status in the last match of the season by scoring the only goal in their game against Manchester United was, in its way, a perfect ending. Tevez moved on to West Ham's last-day opponents for £20 million the next season after being voted the club's player of the year. But when he returned to Upton Park in different colours, he was warmly applauded by supporters who had not forgotten his vital, if unlikely, contribution in 2006–07.

In sport, loyalty used to be a virtue. Today it is a commodity. Rare indeed is the Premier League player who fulfils the old definition of loyalty – that is, someone who remains devoted to a particular cause. Jamie Carragher at Liverpool. Ryan Giggs at Manchester United. And... erm...

The changing commercial nature of the game appears to be distorting our understanding of loyalty, which, rather than being a measure of longevity, is now becoming a qualitative assessment. Thus Tevez could be said to have been loyal to the West Ham cause, albeit for only one season. As supporters, we understand the new position. Players are not necessarily execrated for moving clubs – unless they transgress one of the ancient rules of geography by switching to a team deemed to be bitter rivals. Thus Sol Campbell became 'Judas' for moving from Spurs to Arsenal, and Wayne Rooney encountered massive antipathy at Everton after leaving them for Manchester United – what might he have endured had it been Liverpool, you wonder. Tevez was no longer flavour of the month at Old Trafford after moving across the city to City. But then he soon became something short of flavour of the month there as well…

Buying success in cricket

The same volatile, monetised system is now established in cricket, where the creation of the hugely lucrative Indian Premier League (IPL) in 2008 with franchised teams playing a Twenty20 format has created an instant micro-climate to match that of football's English Premier League. The initial auction for the eight team franchises to be established in different Indian cities attracted ninety bids from immensely wealthy corporate figures such as Vijay Mallya, Anil Ambani, Sunil Mittal, Kishore Biyani and Lord Swraj Paul. There were bids too from film stars such as Shahrukh Khan and Hollywood actor Russell Crowe. And bids also came in from at least two Premier League teams, members of the National Basketball Association, and two foreign banks with operations in India. This was always going to be a going concern.

The first auction, concluded on 24 January 2008, attracted a total in excess of $723 million. When two more teams were added to the League in 2010 – based in Karachi and Pune – the former was bought up for $333 million, and the latter for $370 million. Based as it is in a country where cricket has a massive and fanatical following, the IPL is estimated to have a brand value of more than $4.5 billion.

According to the Annual Review of Global Sports Salaries by sportingin-telligence.com, the IPL is the second highest-paid league in the world based on pro rata first-team salaries behind the National Basketball Association. It is estimated that the average annual salary of an IPL player is $3.84 million. In a kind of hyper-version of the National Football League's annual draft, players become lots for auction themselves each year – with a maximum price of $2 million – as the franchises gather to build their squads for the forthcoming season.

And loyalty? Well, that's on the market too, of course. In 2009, for example, England's naturalised South African Kevin Pietersen was eagerly sought by two of the leading IPL teams. Vijay Mallya, the Indian liquor baron who owned the Bangalore Royal Challengers – and the Force India Formula One team, for that matter – made it plain that he was prepared to pay the maximum for Pietersen's flamboyant hitting power. But there was another challenger in the form of the reigning IPL champions, the Rajasthan Royals, whose coffers had been recently supplemented by some $14 million or so from Bollywood actress Shilpa Shetty. All eight of the existing franchises wanted Pietersen, but less than half of them were thought to be able to afford his salary if they secured him. In the end, Pietersen was secured by the Mallya spending power, for whom he played two seasons before his services were bought up for a third season by the Deccan Chargers.

The National Football League, the National Basketball Association, the English Premier League, the Indian Premier League: all revel in the publicity of ever-escalating fees and salaries as they bolster their brands with the world's top talents. Spending big money is a part of the glitz and glamour of the sport, as intrinsic as the extravagant dresses on Oscars night or the flamboyant hats at Ascot on Ladies' Day.

But what price loyalty? Occasionally, amid the seething seas of lucre, it is possible to discern a small, principled action. Such was the case when Lionel Messi, arguably the best footballer in the world, took his club Barcelona to court to force them to allow him to play for Argentina at the Olympics. It seems that Mammon cannot get its rapacious claws into every aspect of our sporting life.

Manipulation I – basic level

'Are there any diving schools in London?'
– Jürgen Klinsmann

While money and/or the pursuit of personal or political glory may be the driving forces of foul play, aided and abetted by doping, the question of how you actually get ahead of your opponent, or opponents, is one which needs to be answered in most sporting arenas by physical actions. Without these actions – whether they are clearly foul play, or whether they merely push the rules to their furthest acceptable limits – the victory is not achieved. If you want to get ahead, you need to DO something. You need to manipulate your circumstances.

'The Hand of God'

Manipulation in its most basic form has involved direct physical actions which are performed illegally with the hope of remaining undiscovered. And there could be no more literal example of manipulation than that employed by Diego Maradona at the 1986 World Cup, when he diverted a high and inadvertent back pass from England's midfielder Steve Hodge over the oncoming England goalkeeper Peter Shilton with an upraised fist clenched just above his straining head, giving Argentina the lead in a quarter-final they eventually won 2–1 en route to securing the Cup itself.

Unfortunately – from an English point of view, that is – the referee, Ali bin Nasser of Tunisia, was unable to distinguish what millions of others saw clearly and immediately: a player of five feet five inches, albeit a very athletic player of five feet five inches, finding an illegal way to get the ball over an advancing six-feet-one-inch goalkeeper with his own arms raised. Also unfortunately, the referee did not think to consult with his Bulgarian linesman, Bogdan Dotschev.

The fact that Maradona provided Argentina's second goal through one of the most electric bursts of dribbling the game has ever witnessed may have mitigated his offence in many eyes, but there was no hiding the action which provided sport with one of its highest profile cases of foul play.

At the press conference after the match had finished, Maradona described his first goal as having been scored '*un poco con la cabeza de Maradona, y otro poco con la mano de Dios*' ('a little with the head of Maradona, and a little with the hand of God'). He later added: 'I was waiting for my teammates to embrace me, and no one came... I told them, "Come hug me, or the referee isn't going to allow it."'

Bobby Robson, England's manager at the time, was mild in his comments, describing Maradona's action as the 'hand of a rascal'. Almost a quarter of a century later, a similar phrase became public currency in the wake of a controversy involving another celebrated footballer, Thierry Henry, who briefly showed the dexterity of a basketball player before setting up the French goal which earned France a 2–1 aggregate victory over Ireland in their play-off for a World Cup place in 2010.

More than one newspaper nodded to Maradona's mighty misdeed by running the headline: 'Hand of Gaul'. You could see what the sub-editors were getting at, but it never really caught on. Henry, who had almost scooped the ball in his efforts to prevent it from going out of play, admitted immediately what he had done. That is, almost immediately. That is, after the match was over. He blamed the referee, Sweden's Martin Hansson, for not spotting the offence. 'I will be honest, it was a handball,' Henry said. 'But I'm not the ref. I played it. The referee allowed it.' You have to ask, if Henry had been truly honest, would he not have admitted what he had done immediately? Then again, if he had, could the referee have disallowed the goal on those grounds? Probably not.

The 2010 World Cup in South Africa produced another famous – or infamous – example of basic, indeed literal, manipulation when Uruguay's forward Luis Suarez handled on the line in the final minute of their quarter-final against Ghana to block a header from Dominic Adiyiah that would otherwise have given the African team a 2–1 lead. Suarez was sent off, but the penalty was missed and Uruguay ended up winning the penalty shoot-out after extra time.

The discussions and justifications that followed these notable handballs on the football field will be discussed later. But they are egregious examples of the most basic form of manipulation in a sporting arena.

'The Hand of Back'

Rugby Union has endured similar moments of manipulation – classically in the case that has since become known as the Hand of Back. The closing moments of the 2002 Heineken Cup final in which Leicester became the first team to retain the trophy generated a controversy that will not be forgotten, or forgiven, by their opponents, Munster. The Irish team were 9–15 down, but had forced play deep into the Leicester half and had the put-in to a scrum under the English side's posts. But their scrum half Peter Stringer found the ball being clawed out of his hands, straight back to the Leicester side of the scrum, thanks to the blatant sleight of hand of the Leicester flanker, Neil Back. Whereupon the cup-holders swiftly recycled the ball and ended the game by clearing to touch. Back's infringement was not spotted by the referee, to the clear anger of several Munster players. Back's teammate, the England captain Martin Johnson, wrote later of the incident that 'in an ideal world, no one would cheat', adding 'but that is unrealistic'. He went on to say that in rugby 'part of the skill, part of the fun, almost', lay in 'getting away with things'.

More recently rugby union has provided two more high-profile cases of manipulation. The 2011 World Cup in New Zealand swiftly proved particularly testing for kickers of all nations as they struggled to master the flight of the official balls supplied. When a perfectionist such as England's fly-half Jonny Wilkinson misses five kicks, including four in succession – as he did in the opening group match against Argentina – suspicions about the ball are natural.

But the action of England officials during the subsequent group match against Romania, where Wilkinson was aided and abetted in changing the ball before he attempted two conversions, earned instant punishment from the Rugby Football Union, which suspended kicking coach Dave Alred and conditioning coach Paul Stridgeon from attending the next group match, against Scotland.

The regulations state clearly that conversions need to take place with the same ball that was grounded for the try. The England kickers believed that one of the eight numbered balls provided for the match in Dunedin was better suited for kicking, and this was the one handed over by Alred and Stridgeon. 'In the heat of a World Cup match these guys have made a mistake, and they have paid for it,' said the England manager Martin Johnson. Others in the RFU clearly felt there was a little more deliberate intent involved.

Earlier in 2011, switching of the ball in a different context had caused another controversy. This incident happened during Wales's home Six Nations match against Ireland. As the Irish forwards gathered to form a line-out, a ball boy threw a different ball from the one that had gone off to Wales's hooker Matthew Rees, who swiftly threw it to his unmarked colleague Mike Phillips. With the Irish team in confusion and disarray, the scrum half made great headway down the left-hand edge of the park and eventually touched down for a try that was converted. Wales ended up winning by six points. The converted try had made all the difference.

Rule 19.2d of the International Rugby Board regulations is explicit: 'For a quick throw-in, the player must use the ball that went into touch. A quick throw-in is not permitted if another person has touched the ball apart from the player throwing it in and an opponent who carried it into touch.' Jonathan Kaplan, the referee, very clearly consulted with the Scottish touch judge, Peter Allan, who evidently felt that the same ball which had gone out had been the one quickly thrown-in. This was clearly an attempt by the Welsh to pull a fast one, and they got away with it.

Unpleasantness in Barcelona

Hands, of course, do not have to be involved in such manipulation. Another infamous example of a competitor attempting to ensure victory – albeit in this case for a teammate – by clear physical means occurred during the 1992 Olympic 10,000m final. By the closing stages of the race the leader, Kenya's Richard Chelimo, was being tracked by Khalid Skah of Morocco. It is usually crowd noises which draw attention to perceived wrongdoing in sport, and such was the case here as spectators in Barcelona's Montjuic Stadium began to vent their displeasure at what they were witnessing with boos and whistling.

The cause of the growing displeasure was a feeling that Skah was beginning to receive illicit assistance from his fellow countryman Hammou Boutayeb, who, when the two leaders lapped him, accelerated to regain the 'lead' ahead of the Kenyan, effectively checking Chelimo's progress.

As the ferment grew, so did feelings of uneasiness about what was happening. Was this a coincidence we were seeing? Or a piece of opportunistic gamesmanship? Such judgements are not always simple, either at the time or in retrospect. In the press box, two members of the same national newspaper exchanged harshly diverging opinions.

After staying up with the action for almost three laps, Boutayeb eventually relinquished his 'lead' and the two gold-medal contenders then made a final run for the line, which ended with Skah bursting past his Kenyan opponent in the final few metres to win by one second. When the delayed result emerged, Skah had been disqualified. But fourteen hours later he was reinstated on appeal.

At the previous year's IAAF World Championships in Tokyo – Skah's first big international championship – the Moroccan felt he had been ganged up on by Chelimo and another Kenyan who went on to win the 10,000m title, Moses Tanui. A deflated Skah then lost the 5000m final to his main rival, Kenya's Yobes Ondieki.

The day after the Olympic final Skah received his medal to a summer storm of boos and whistles as the bulk of 65,000 spectators did all they could to let him know he was not forgiven. The Moroccan clapped and offered his wolfish grin in response to the general disapproval. Chelimo, predictably, received huge acclaim; Skah shuffled over on the podium to take, rather than shake, his hand and earn some esteem by association. 'If somebody shouts, the rest follow them,' Skah said afterwards. 'Almost all the people are not very close to the athletics world. I deserve this medal.' He paused for a moment before adding: 'My name will always be engraved in the history of the Olympic Games.' Which was true.

The following year Skah finished behind five Kenyans at the World Cross Country Championships, with Ismail Kirui, one of Chelimo's brothers, taking the bronze. But it was another Kenyan runner, Dominic Chirui, who voiced their sense of satisfaction. 'We are just avenging what Skah did in Barcelona,' he said.

Making sure the right man wins

But how had they done this? By adopting the same kind of 'team' tactics they had objected to a year earlier, it seemed. Running as a team was of course more acceptable in cross country, where a team event ran in tandem with the individual race. But such was the Kenyan domination of the event that they were able to openly manipulate the individual honours at the same time as securing their national victory well before the end of the race. In 1993, after William Sigei had taken the gold, it transpired he had been effectively waved through by his fellow Kenyans on the instruction of their coach, who explained afterwards that Sigei had proved himself the best runner in training.

Sigei's victory in the men's senior event, which was led for all but the finishing straight by his teammates Dominic and Ismail Kirui, was worked out to the last detail. 'In the last five hundred metres I slowed my speed so that Sigei could come through,' Dominic Kirui said. 'In our training before the race, when we were doing speed work, we saw that Sigei was just better. It was decided that Ismail and I would make good pacemakers for him.' The man who laid the plans, Kenya's national coach, Mike Kosgei, beamed with pride afterwards. 'Sigei was our darling in the race,' he said. 'When he was running on his own in third place, I told him to stay there. We didn't want anybody to jostle or spike him.'

Man-ipulation on the rugby field

Jostling and spiking, of course, along with kicking, gouging and shirt-pulling, also have their place in the unfair field of physical manipulation – or, if you like, man-ipulation.

And here we return to the rugby field. Prop forward Jason Leonard, who earned 114 caps for England and played in their winning World Cup final of 2003, was known as a master of the dark arts of the scrum, although his reputation did not extend to foul play. Leonard first represented England in 1990 in a lively affair against Argentina in Buenos Aires – the first sporting fixture in that country involving British opposition since the Falklands hostilities of 1982.

He recalls his fellow forward Wade Dooley raking a white-shorted figure on the English side of the ruck, and then realising that England as well as Argentina were wearing white shorts. England's No. 8 Dean Ryan emerged, with lacerated shorts, soon afterwards. After beating their hosts, England lost against them a week later when Leonard recalled Dooley was 'taken out from the kick-off' and had to leave the field with damaged ribs.

A match against the same opposition at Twickenham produced more unpleasantness. Leonard recalls one of the Argentinians, Federico Mendez, falling to the floor in a scrum and trying 'to grab Jeff Probyn's meat and two veg'. Mendez reportedly got 'a stamp in return', and soon afterwards felled England's towering forward Paul Ackford with what Leonard described as 'a big hit from his blind side'. Leonard added: 'I didn't see the punch as I was scrapping with one of their guys.'

England's victory over France in 1991 secured the Grand Slam, and brought Leonard up against a man he described as one of his heroes, Pascal Ondarts. Leonard recalls fondly how he got 'a big uppercut' from his hero in the first scrum, and 'smacked him back' in the second, adding: 'We didn't have any problems after that.' Can you imagine such a sequence of events in football? Yet none of these incidents left Leonard harbouring any strong feelings. All just good, plain violence?

When the British Lions toured South Africa in 1974 under the captaincy of Willie John McBride, they went twenty-two games unbeaten and won 3–0 in a Test series marked by even higher levels of violence than usual. With officiating at the matches being undertaken by referees from the home nation, the Lions decided to take some preventative defensive measures, and came up with the gloriously expressed notion of 'getting their retaliation in first'.

The arrangement was that if the call '99' went up, every member of the Lions side needed to misbehave violently with his nearest opponent, a policy that depended on a natural reluctance on the part of any South African official to send every member of the touring side from the field. Lions followers particularly cherish video evidence of what has come to be known as the 'Battle of Boet Erasmus Stadium', which shows the British and Irish full back J.P.R. Williams – a doctor in his other life – running more than half the length of the pitch during one such call to arms in order to launch himself at Moaner van Heerden.

Thirty-five years later, when the two teams met again at Test level, a similar level of violence was involved, although the nature of one of the incidents caused extreme offence on the Lions side. The Lions' Welsh scrum half, Mike Phillips, described the behaviour of South Africa's captain Schalk Burger in the first minute as 'disgusting' – unusually harsh words for a sport where what is tolerated would be enough to provoke riots in football.

Burger's offence, in what was his fiftieth appearance for the Springboks, was to gouge the Lions' Luke Fitzgerald in the right eye. Gouging is seen as one of the most heinous and dangerous of practices in rugby, and although Burger was sent to the sin bin, the Lions were angry that he did not receive a red card. Burger was eventually banned for eight weeks after being cited by the match commissioner, Steve Hinds. But by then the battle had been won and lost, as South Africa had taken an unbeatable 2–0 lead in the series.

While the Lions were unhappy with the protection they received from the match officials, their management team were angry at the reaction to the gouging incident from South Africa's coach Peter de Villiers, who claimed the Burger incident was 'all part of the sport'. Fitzgerald said after the game that he had tried to remove Burger's fingers from his right eye and believed it to be a 'strange' decision that the flanker had been given only a yellow card. 'I was surprised not only by the actions of one professional player against another, but that a player of Burger's quality and experience would do something like that.' Phillips expressed himself less diplomatically. 'It was a clear red card. You can't do things like that, it's disgusting,' he said. 'Guys were swinging punches off the ball. We can play hard, we can play tough, but we try to play within the rules.'

Gouging has always been a no-no as far as rugby players are concerned. But there has been a profound shift of perception concerning certain other violent features within the game. Phillips's complaint about punches being thrown off the ball would have provoked a quizzical reaction from some of his Lions predecessors who were operating at a time when such activity was almost viewed as part and parcel of the action.

Players who are seen punching their opponents on a rugby pitch nowadays are generally sent off, even though there is still some feeling in the sport, perhaps among its older followers and former players, that there should be more leeway given. As spectators we might feel, viscerally, that a punch given and a punch given back, in the context of what is one of sport's more monumentally physically challenging games, represents honours even. All part of the sport.

Violence – a way of sport

The context is what helps to justify such an argument. Were two chess players to exchange blows, we might feel very differently. Were two American footballers to exchange blows, we might feel the same way about it. The latter sport had its own ruthless practitioner of intimidation in Bill Romanowski, who, by the time he ended his career with a final season for Oakland Raiders in 2002–3, had won four Super Bowl Championships and established himself as one of the game's most brutally effective operators as a linebacker.

Romanowski has been involved in numerous altercations with both teammates and opponents. In 1995, when he was with the Philadelphia Eagles, he was ejected from a game – and subsequently fined $4,500 – for kicking the Arizona Cardinals fullback Larry Centers in the head. Two similar incidents occurred during the 1997 season while he played for the Denver Broncos. In the first, he was fined $20,000 after a helmet-to-helmet hit on the Carolina Panthers quarterback Kerry Collins in a pre-season game resulting in Collins sustaining a broken jaw. In the second, Romanowski spat in the face of 49ers wide receiver J. J. Stokes during a regular-season game in response to being taunted.

Two years later, while still with the Broncos, Romanowski was fined a total of $42,500 for three illegal hits plus a punch thrown at the Kansas City Chiefs tight end Tony Gonzalez, and was also fined an undisclosed amount for throwing a football and hitting Bryan Cox of the New York Jets in the crotch. They called it ball abuse.

Explicit examples of violence can have the effect of changing the culture within a sport. This happened within rugby union after an incident during the Lions tour to New Zealand in 2005 provoked more bitter debate and subsequently reshaped opinions – and, crucially, interpretation of the rules – within the game. During the first Test against the All Blacks, the Lions in general, and their captain Brian O'Driscoll in particular, appeared to have been targeted inside two minutes. O'Driscoll was lifted by two New Zealand players and deposited on the ground in such a manner that he broke his shoulder and could play no further part in the tour.

At the time, no action was taken against the home players, who maintained they had not meant to seriously harm their opponent. O'Driscoll and the Lions management, however, characterised the action as a deliberate spear tackle. The incident generated considerable ill-feeling and controversy, and the international rugby authorities revisited their rules over the matter of tackles in which players are upended. By the time of the 2011 World Cup, referees were operating under an instruction to go for a red card first in the event of any player suffering from what had come to be known as a 'spear tackle'.

The Wales captain Sam Warburton felt the effects of this readjustment just eighteen minutes into his side's semi-final against France, when he was sent off for a tackle which deposited the French player Vincent Clerc wincingly upside down on the turf. There were many within the game who argued that Warburton's tackle was not a spear tackle, as, having tipped the French winger in his initial contact, he made no attempt to drive him down but rather dropped him, like a dog realising it had picked up something it shouldn't. The general consensus was that Warburton's tackle had been rash, but that a yellow card, particularly at such an early stage of the match, would have been more appropriate. The letter of the law, however, supported the referee, and it was an expression of the concern felt within the game for a form of manipulation which had the potential to be seriously damaging to players.

When things get bumpy

Physical manipulation – one on one – has a part in many sports. Even supposedly non-contact sports such as squash – as James Willstrop, England's 2010 Commonwealth silver medallist, recounts: 'There was one occasion when a player headbutted another on court, but generally there is nothing as violent as that going on. That said, things can get bumpy on court. I was playing an opponent recently and there were a couple of occasions where he was leaning on me and giving me a bit of verbal. He had a little go at me, so I made it my business to have a little go back at him. But that's all part of the game. I would never call it cheating.

'Squash is a ferocious, physical sport. Of course there are some instances of bad sportsmanship – you have that in any sport – but there are relatively few examples in our sport in my experience. It is generally a down-to-earth game. As squash players, we are not rich. We are not famous. The bottom line is that we tend to travel around the world together. We might occasionally share rooms. We will see each other every week, so there is not really room for any kind of bad feeling.'

Squash has been trying hard to get into the Olympic movement. Badminton is already there, although it is not without blemish. At the 2006 Commonwealth Games in Melbourne, home player Ashley Brehaut employed a contentious method of serving with the racket marginally (but still illegally) above the waist. When Brehaut pulled his little stunt at 19–19 in the deciding game, his New Zealand opponent took exception, shouting out, unambiguously, 'You're a fucking cheat, Brehaut.' The Australian was docked a point, but did prosper as he went on to win the game 22–19.

Swimming is even less of a contact sport than squash – or at least, it should be. But in long distance swimming the rules get a bit soggy round the edges. At the women's 10km swimming race at the Beijing Olympics, for example, Britain's Cassie Patten won the silver medal as she finished just one and a half seconds behind Russia's Larisa Ilchenko. But rather than celebrating, Patten angrily sought out one of her opponents – Angela Maurer, who had finished fourth – and had a very public row with the German, accusing her of hauling her back by her legs in order to gain an advantage.

The twenty-one-year-old Patten was up in the lead on the Lake Shinyi course for more than two hours, despite her legs often being clipped by the closely packed swimmers behind her, before the Russian came through to win in the final hundred metres. The alleged tug on Patten's legs, which might have earned the German a yellow card, was missed by the judges attending the race in a boat alongside the swimmers.

Patten, who was seen pointing angrily at Maurer and then holding on to her arm by way of demonstration, commented: 'I had my legs pulled. I'm just annoyed because I didn't get to savour looking up and coming home because of that negative. It's unsportsmanship. I would never pull on some-one's legs, so I would never assume someone would do it to me. But at the end of the day, I've got one of these,' she added, pointing to the medal around her neck. 'And she hasn't, so that's enough.'

Maurer did not admit to the misdeed, but her comments were faintly reminiscent of those made by Neil Back in another context: 'It was really crowded going around the corners. There was a lot of grabbing and pulling. I have to say I was no angel either.'

The loneliness of the 400m runner

While there are many examples where manipulation has allowed sportsmen and women to get ahead, there are also examples where such attempts have backfired. Take the rather clumsy turn of events that took place in the Olympic 400m final at the 1908 London Games. If Great Britain and the United States enjoyed a 'special relationship' back then, it was left severely strained by the circumstances of this race.

The favourite to win was the British runner Lieutenant Wyndham Halswelle, a twenty-six-year-old Scot who had served in the Boer War and had won the silver medal at the Athens Games two years earlier. Having set an Olympic record of 48.4 seconds in the semi-final, Halswelle was joined in the final by three Americans: John Baxter Taylor, William Robbins and John Carpenter. Already ill feeling had been generated between the US team and their hosts, stemming initially from the refusal of the athlete carrying the Stars and Stripes, Ralph Rose, to dip the flag to the Royal Box containing King Edward VII. This was in the days before the introduction of separate, staggered lanes for individual 400m runners and, given the make-up of the final, British officials, fearful of an American team effort, had stationed themselves every twenty yards around the track.

Robbins took a twelve-yard lead by the halfway point, but was passed by Carpenter and Halswelle as the field approached the home straight. Halswelle then attempted to pass the American on the outside, only to be pushed wider and wider as Carpenter altered his course. This was a tactic legally employed in US racing, but British officials called foul and broke the tape before Carpenter could cross the line. Taylor was also pulled off the track by men in blazers.

Predictably, there was a big old row that went on for half an hour before the track was cleared. Carpenter was disqualified for obstruction and a rerun was scheduled two days later, but this time with string dividing the lanes. Both remaining Americans refused to participate, however, which meant Halswelle, with no strings attached, had to run around in splendid isolation to claim his gold in fifty seconds. He did not find it at all splendid, however, and subsequently quit the sport.

Football's hard men – and how to handle them

While you might classify some of the capers which have occurred on rugby pitches over the years as manipulation, or perhaps extreme manipulation, the word which probably applies in many cases is intimidation. In this, rugby has been conspicuously matched by football, albeit that the level of accepted violence in the latter sport is dramatically lower.

The 1960s and 1970s saw a core of footballers celebrated for their bone-crunching capabilities, players such as Norman Hunter and Billy Bremner of Leeds United, Tommy Smith of Liverpool, Ron Harris of Chelsea, Nobby Stiles of Manchester United, Peter Storey of Arsenal. These are men who made their name by manipulating – physically manipulating, that is – their opponents. With this kind of player, what you saw was what you got. Even if it hurt a lot.

What do you do if your opponent kicks you? Well, you can of course kick him back. Or, being a little cleverer, you can attempt to get him into trouble – and yourself out of it – by exaggerating the violence meted out to you. Or even, on occasion, anticipate it and dive to the ground in apparent agony. This is an approach to physical manipulation – physical manipulation of oneself, one might call it – for which Germany's Jürgen Klinsmann was renowned by the time he joined Tottenham Hotspur in 1994. Thus when he arrived in north London he carried two big handicaps as far as British spectators were concerned. One, he was German, and Germany, since 1966, had always beaten England, whether it required full time, extra time or a penalty shoot-out. England's only hope appeared to be if it went to alphabetical order. And two, Klinsmann had a reputation as being a world-class diver.

Perhaps the most outrageous example of the flaxen-haired German's talent for toppling occurred during the 1990 World Cup final, where a spectacular effort in the sixty-fifth minute resulted in Argentina's Carlos Monzon becoming the first player to be sent off in the game's ultimate showpiece. Monzon's was a reckless challenge, with studs flying, and you could argue that he deserved to go for that. But as TV replays showed, the Argentinian did not make any serious contact with Klinsmann, who turned his defensive spring into a fresh and ambitious enterprise. When he returned to earth, Klinsmann clutched his head. Perhaps, after all, it was a mental problem.

The trait of making the most of any foul, or any intent to foul, or in fact any action whatsoever, in order to earn a free kick or a penalty was undoubtedly rife in the continental game before it took root in the English game. Like the clogging it is designed to counteract, such activity is a matter of physical manipulation, even if the manipulation is of oneself and involves a higher degree of imaginative enterprise.

But the idea that it had 'come over with the continentals' was patently false. A quarter of a century before the flamboyant German arrived at White Hart Lane, Manchester City's buoyant little forward Francis Lee had made an art of earning penalties in a manner which Klinsmann would have recognised. It was not always a question of cheating, more a case of exaggerating or, in some cases, anticipating a defensive challenge and, how shall we say, embellishing it. And so Lee would pick himself up out of the Maine Road mud and, after offering a cheeky grin to his teammates, would thump the resultant spot kick high and unerringly into the net. Lee was thus the perfect player for any team: goal-maker, and goal-taker.

Although Lee was one of the best exponents of this questionable practice, he was far from being the only one operating in the Football League at the time. But the arrival of Klinsmann refocused the gaze of the domestic game upon this particularly questionable aspect of play. It soon became evident, however, that Klinsmann was a smart cookie. At his introductory press conference, on a day when the tabloids were raging over the arrival of the 'Stuka dive-bomber', Klinsmann amiably enquired of the media present: 'Are there any diving schools in London?' And when he scored on his debut against Sheffield Wednesday at Hillsborough, the German had already prepared a masterpiece of an ironic statement – he celebrated with an exuberant, full-length dive along the turf, and was swiftly joined by teammates doing likewise. It was like watching a bomb disposal expert disabling a piece of ordnance with one deft snip of his pliers.

Klinsmann went on to become a hugely popular player, not just with Spurs fans, but with English football fans. It was, essentially, a double manipulation on the German's part. Firstly he manipulated the rules, and then the audience. It was brilliant.

Going down easy

There was always a kind of charm and grace, sometimes even a balletic comedy, about Klinsmann's falling to earth. Sadly the same could not be said of others who practised this dubious art. The 1998 World Cup, for instance, produced an infamous piece of simulation from Croatian defender Slaven Bilić during his side's semi-final defeat by France. Bilic, charged with marking the big French defender Laurent Blanc as a free kick came in, attempted to hold the veteran, who shrugged him off. After a moment of hesitation Bilic collapsed, clasping his forehead. He later admitted he had been acting, and had done so at the prompting of a teammate. Blanc, despite protesting his innocence, got the red card, which meant he missed a World Cup final on home soil at the end of his long career. One can only guess at his feelings as he saw France beat Brazil 3–0.

In 2011 Joey Barton offered an interesting variation on the Klinsmann double manipulation as he played one of his last games for Newcastle United, against Arsenal at St James' Park, before being transferred to Queens Park Rangers. The combustible Scouser was outraged when Arsenal's debutant, Gervinho, made the most of a challenge in the penalty area by a Newcastle defender. Barton angrily pulled the Ivory Coast forward to his feet and remonstrated with him.

As the two grappled, Gervinho appeared to slap Barton on the face. After a delay of perhaps a second, Barton, who is far from being a stranger to serious fisticuffs, fell as if poleaxed, and although he subsequently got a yellow card for manhandling the Arsenal player, Gervinho saw red and walked. Soon after the match, through the miracle that is Twitter, Barton admitted to the wide world that he had 'gone down easy'. When interviewed by BBC Five Live he added that he was not proud of the way he had behaved. Thankfully, no Arsenal player had seen fit to haul him furiously back to his feet before dropping like a stone under his minimal contact and setting in train a reaction which involved a Newcastle colleague pulling him angrily back up, whereupon…

In September 2009 the European football body, UEFA, had attempted to put down a marker on this contentious practice by banning Arsenal's Croatian striker Eduardo for two matches for diving in a challenge with Celtic's keeper Artur Boruc to win a penalty in a UEFA Champions League match on 26 August. It was a punishment in line with the two-match ban levied on Lithuania's Saulius Mikoliūnas following a penalty he won against Scotland during a Euro 2008 qualifier. But the ban was overturned on appeal. 'We were able to show there was contact between the keeper and Eduardo and that the decision should be annulled,' an Arsenal statement said.

Arsenal's manager Arsène Wenger had described UEFA's initial action as a 'witch hunt', adding that any action against the Croatian would set a dangerous precedent, with tens of similar incidents taking place every week in European football. The UEFA statement said: 'Following examination of all the evidence, notably the declarations of both the referee and the referees' assessor, as well as the various video footage, it was not established to our satisfaction that the referee had been deceived in taking his decision on the penalty.' Matters of simulation, patently, are tricky ground when it comes to sanctions.

In the wake of the decision Eduardo's teammate, Robin van Persie – who has been accused more than once of exaggerating defensive challenges made upon him – offered an insight into the thinking behind what some regard as questionable practice. Van Persie was happy to admit that he had overreacted to contact on occasion. The Dutch international argued that, if fouled, 'You are in the right to show in a way to the referee that you are pushed. That's not really diving. It's just saying, "Come on, he just pushed me, so I can't score now."

'You sometimes make a little movement with your arms or with your body,' he added. 'But I don't think that's really cheating. I never have the intention to dive. Just to play honest football. I am against divers. It is just not honest, but it is difficult. Sometimes you are knocked off balance a bit and it looks funny.'

W. G. Grace – the bad bits

But let's not be thinking that football is the only breeding ground of attempts to physically manipulate the fortunes of sport by just-about-fair means or foul. Let's look at cricket. Going way back. W. G. Grace, famously, was a man of many talents. A medical practitioner, he played football for the

Wanderers – the Manchester United of their day – and won the 440 yards hurdles in the National Olympian Games at Crystal Palace in August 1866. He later became the first president of the English Bowling Association, and took up golf in a serious fashion.

However it is as a cricketer, indeed The Cricketer, that he is best remembered. The man who played the first-class game as a Gloucestershire and England all-rounder for a record-equalling forty-four seasons, heavily bearded for most of that time, and portly towards the end of it, made a mark on his sport and his society as much by the force of his personality as by the mastery of his batsmanship. W. G.: the initials alone were enough to announce him for the largest part of his life, but this son of Bristol was also known as The Champion and, in his later years, The Old Man. Nobody ever called him The Manipulator – although on occasions they would have been justified.

W. G. Grace might have been invented to vex Australians. A report in an Australian paper that appeared in 1874, soon after the great figure had taken part in an England tour, had this to say about him: 'We in Australia did not take kindly to WG. For so big a man, he is surprisingly tenacious on small points.'

Despite the fact that he was nominally an amateur – given his professional status as a surgeon – Grace wanted to win at all costs. Sometimes this tendency worked against him, as in the 1882 Test when Australia beat England on an English ground for the first time, leading to the satirical obituary in the *Sporting Times* newspaper which set in train the Ashes series – being the ashes of English cricket – which is still biennially contested today.

Australia's match-winner on this momentous occasion, Frederick Spofforth, took 14 wickets, reportedly 'fired up' by a characteristic piece of gamesmanship from W. G. in which Australia's batsman Sammy Jones was unsportingly, but strictly legally, run out. There were other examples of W. G.'s lordly disregard of the rules, or his propensity to bend them. In a match against Surrey at Clifton in 1878 the ball reportedly lodged in his shirt and he simply began making runs, stopping only at the eventual intervention of several fielders. He claimed afterwards that he would have been out – for handling the ball – had he tried to remove it. Following a discussion, the fielding side managed to beat him down to three scoring runs. Given W. G.'s athletic pedigree, one wonders how long he might have been prepared to carry on running if the opposing players had not stopped him.

Grace also had an angle when it came to tossing the coin at the start of matches. As the coin flew, he would call out 'The Lady'. Sovereigns at the time had Queen Victoria on one side and Britannia on the other. Another celebrated example of Gracemanship occurred when he once refused to leave the crease when he was given out, apparently responding to the official with the raised finger: 'They've come to see me bat, not you umpire.' There was some truth in this, given that signs outside cricket grounds where W. G. was due to appear would often indicate that the price of entry was sixpence – or a shilling 'if W. G. plays'.

The brutal effects of 'fast leg theory bowling'

If Australian cricket disliked W. G., it loathed Douglas Jardine, captain of the England side that arrived to contest the Ashes in the 1932–3 series. And you could understand why. First, though, you have to understand why Jardine did what he did.

Australia had won the previous series in England, with their majestic batsman Don Bradman scoring 974 runs at an average of 139.14, an aggregate record that still stands. As the next series loomed up, Bradman was maintaining his average at around 100 – twice that of any other batsman in the world. In order for England to have a chance of winning, something had to be done about the Don. That was the basis of the thinking behind what has come to be known as 'bodyline' bowling, the tactic Jardine's men employed to devastating effect in a series which they eventually did win, 4–1.

To limit the opportunities for Bradman and his colleagues, the England captain asked his two fast bowlers, Nottinghamshire's Harold Larwood and Bill Voce, to pitch the ball short and in line with the leg stump, so that it reared up into the body of the receiving batsman. It was described as fast leg theory bowling. In order to maximise the effectiveness of the shock tactic, Jardine also studied how to congregate fielders on the batsmen's leg side.

When the Test series got under way, English journalists wrote of fast leg theory bowling, while their Australian counterparts referred to bodyline bowling. Larwood took 10 wickets in the first Test, as the hosts lost by 10 wickets in Sydney, albeit with the unwell Bradman absent. Australia's captain, Bill Woodfull, apparently came under pressure to allow his bowlers to retaliate in kind for the second Test. He refused on principle.

Perhaps unnerved by what had happened in the first Test, Bradman hooked his first delivery – a non-bodyline delivery from Bill Bowes – and was caught out for a golden duck. Jardine, normally staid, capered in delight. But Bradman returned to score a match-winning century.

The third Test in Adelaide witnessed the height of the controversy, as Woodfull was struck under the heart by a delivery from Larwood and was clearly in agony for several minutes. Jardine promptly told his field to close in to bodyline placings on the leg side. The crowd unrest grew. Woodfull was eventually out for 22. When the England manager, Pelham Warner, visited the Australian dressing room to offer his sympathies, the Australian captain was reported to have rebuked him with the following words: 'I don't want to see you, Mr Warner. There are two teams out there. One is playing cricket. The other is making no attempt to do so.'

The following day a delivery from Larwood, albeit a non-bodyline delivery, was mishit off the top edge by wicketkeeper Bert Oldfield and the ball flew up to hit him in the head, fracturing his skull. The Australian Board sent a letter to the MCC accusing the English team of being unsportsmanlike. The MCC objected.

The reaction of the Australian crowd to Jardine's new idea was one of swiftly rising outrage. During the third Test there was jeering after many of the England deliveries, and police had to intervene to prevent a riot taking place at the Adelaide Oval. The reaction on the part of English players and followers of the game was, as one might expect, more ambivalent. Gubby Allen, an amateur fast bowler who was a member of the touring side, refused to bowl the fast leg theory deliveries. Warner later made it clear that he did not care for the tactic but made no comment during the tour. There was no public criticism, either, from former England amateur captains such as Lord Hawke and Sir Stanley Jackson. Some observers pointed out that Australia's fast bowlers McDonald and Gregory had employed similar tactics against England in 1920–21, although the Australians staunchly refuted this.

Too close a call

While the manipulative efforts of W. G. over the years were instinctive reactions emanating from an obdurate state of mind, the formulation of 'fast leg theory bowling', as it is not known, was of a different order. But such actions correspond to the instincts of elite sportsmen and women, who are all engaged in pushing themselves towards their limit and naturally seek anything that is not actually illegal if it will give them even the smallest incremental advantage – which, at their level, is the difference between success and failure.

More than thirty years later another calculated manipulation by an England captain proved to be effective in the short term, but damaging in the long term, as it once again provoked debate within cricket over what did or did not constitute proper behaviour.

In 1967 England were led by Yorkshire's Brian Close – who had taken over from Colin Cowdrey the previous year for the final Test against the West Indies, who were already assured of the series with a 3–0 lead – and engendered a fighting spirit in the home side which saw them salvage a defiant final victory.

A three-match home series against Pakistan was going well; the first match was a rain-affected draw and England won the second. Before the final match, Close captained his county, Yorkshire – who were then in pursuit of a hat-trick of County titles – against Warwickshire at Edgbaston.

The host team had been set a target of 142 to win in one hour and forty minutes. When the match ended they had got perilously close, reaching 133–5. But Yorkshire had earned their draw. What they had also earned, however, was massive disapprobation for the tactics employed by Close, who had slowed play down to the point where only twenty-four overs were bowled in that time, and only two in the final quarter-hour. It was physical manipulation, employed to tactical purpose.

In the wet conditions, Yorkshire had made much of the need to dry the ball, and their tactics had aroused numerous members of the Edgbaston crowd to vent their disapproval.

Yorkshire's chairman Brian Sellers sent an apology to the MCC, the guardians of the game, who were then in charge of touring England sides. A couple of days before he captained his country in the final Pakistan Test – which England were to win by eight wickets – Close was told that the MCC had overruled the selectors and that he would be stripped of the captaincy for the forthcoming tour of West Indies. The replacement would be Colin Cowdrey.

Cricket's 'most disgusting incident'

Crowds have reacted vehemently to other instances of manipulation through physical means. In 1981, Australia's captain Greg Chappell took a decision during a one-day international against New Zealand in Melbourne for which he will always be remembered. It provoked the New Zealand prime minister of the time, Robert Muldoon, to describe it as 'the most disgusting incident I can recall in the history of cricket'.

Even Chappell's fellow Aussie Richie Benaud, commentating for Australian TV, described the act as 'disgraceful', adding: 'It is one of the worst things I have ever seen done on a cricket field.' The Australian prime minister, Malcolm Fraser, was also censorious, describing what had happened as 'contrary to the traditions of the game'.

Perhaps only in cricket could an action within the rules of the game engender such outrage. As Chappell's younger brother, Trevor, prepared to send down the final delivery of the match, New Zealand needed a six to tie the match. Under the orders of his captain, the youngest Chappell proceeded to bowl his last effort underarm, thus precluding any possibility of a Kiwi final flourish. As he ran up to do so the eldest Chappell brother, Ian, commentating on the match, had instinctively shouted out: 'No, Greg, you can't do that!' and the hugely experienced Test player maintained his critical line afterwards. The Australian side, meanwhile, were booed from the field by their supporters – victorious.

Such a reaction would have told the Australian captain all he wanted to know about the moral virtue of his choice, despite it being legal. It remains one of life's ironies that the sport which gave us the phrase 'just not cricket' as a yardstick of anything improper has been beset by so many questionable incidents. It is also interesting to note how an utterly harmless delivery has occasioned such opprobrium whereas so many more perilous ones have passed without comment.

Umpire Denness fans the flames

We are also on the sporting borderline in cricket when we consider the question of appealing to the umpire for a dismissal. It's a legitimate part of the game, and there will have been innumerable occasions when an umpire who has a scintilla of doubt about raising his finger will have found the courage to do so amid the loud expectations of the fielding side. But, like the bouncer, such encouragement can be overdone. The difficulty comes in judging at what point this manipulation oversteps the mark.

In 2001 there was an almighty hoo-hah during India's match against South Africa in Port Elizabeth, when umpire Mike Denness – the Scotsman who played Test cricket for England – sanctioned six of the visiting players for variant manipulations he felt were beyond the rules. Four players were suspended from the following Test for 'excessive appealing', one for inability to control his team's behaviour, and the sixth – Sachin Tendulkar, the icon of the Indian game – for ball tampering.

But rules are all about interpretation, aren't they? And back in India – guess what? – the interpretation was that Denness had acted outrageously. Effigies of the unfortunate umpire were burnt amid allegations of racism. The Indian Cricket Board threatened to call off the Test series unless Denness was replaced for the next match, and although the umpire was supported by the International Cricket Council, the South African board decided to replace him, and also to ban him from attendance at the forthcoming third Test.

The ICC subsequently stripped the second Test of its official status, and charges against all but one of the six named were dropped. The ICC insisted, however, that Virender Sehwag serve his one-match suspension for excessive appealing. That must have been for excessive excessive appealing...

Harsh life on the ocean wave

Murky waters indeed. But then not everything is crystal clear in sport, particular once competition gets under way. Which brings us to the incomparable British sailor Ben Ainslie.

You can tell something about Ainslie simply by observing his Olympic career. In his first Olympic appearance, at the 1996 Atlanta Games, he won silver. At his next four Games he won gold. This is clearly someone with huge talent who has managed to fine-tune his approach to a consistently unmatchable level. It could be argued, however, that his racing experience in Atlanta – which Ainslie, being Ainslie, regarded as a gold lost rather than a silver won – was most significant for him as an Olympic competitor. Because it was there that he learned how to turn silver into gold next time round – and it was done partly through matching and indeed bettering the manipulation employed by his victor in 1996, the Brazilian sailor Robert Scheidt.

Ainslie has described how Scheidt was the dominant figure in the Laser – a single-handed dinghy – when he began racing that class in 1994, and how he modelled himself on the Brazilian and his 'active and aggressive' style in particular. In 1996 the nineteen-year-old Ainslie learned for himself how that aggressive approach worked for Scheidt. The Briton lay in silver medal position before the final race, and after much pre-race manoeuvring the organisers put up the black flag – an indication that any boat jumping the start line at the next attempt would be disqualified.

'Robert was pretty cunning,' Ainslie recalled, 'because he was sitting near the committee boat and must have heard them call out his sail number, that he was over the line, so he just sheeted in and started over the line with ten seconds to go, knowing he was over it. When one goes, others go because they don't want to be given the jump. So about twenty boats went. I was among them and we all got disqualified and the net result was that Robert won the gold and I got the silver. Yes, in its way it was brilliant.'

Four years later in Sydney the positions were reversed, and a couple of abandoned starts meant Scheidt was forewarned about the Briton's tactics. But he still couldn't stop him. Ainslie managed to get into a perfect spoiling position a matter of seconds before the start, and he soon isolated the Brazilian as the rest of the fleet sailed away, blocking his wind and weaving across his path. There was apparently plenty being said between the two boats.

In the end, Scheidt broke clear after ramming the Briton's boat, and then set off to try and catch the distant race ahead. Scheidt almost made it, taking advantage of a huge wind shift, but with Ainslie desperately catching up to see if more action was required, the Brazilian was penalised and the gold was secure with the Briton.

Bryn Vaile, who won gold for Britain with Michael McIntyre in the Star Class at the 1988 Seoul Olympics, has had close hand experience of the nitty gritty of competitive action on the water for thirty years as a sailor and national selector. 'You can effectively stop an opponent by sitting in their wind,' says Vaile. 'It is called covering. It was originally introduced as a defensive measure, but what someone like Ben does is use it as an aggressive tactic. It's aggressive covering, if you like. You use the rules aggressively, rather than defensively.

'It's similar to the kind of manoeuvring you can get in Formula 1. There are times when Ben's objective is to manoeuvre things so that he gets to cross the line ahead of a particular opponent. For instance, at a recent Olympic test event in Weymouth, Ben needed to make sure a Dutch opponent did not get into the top ten in one of the races, so with five minutes left before the race begins he goes for him and stalls him, forces him away from the start line.

'He pushes him so far back that by the time the race begins he has got boats in front of him and a lot of dirty air to get through before he can reach them. He ended up forcing the Dutch opponent so far away from the start in the pre-race manoeuvring period that he only crossed the line himself in around seventeenth place. But he still won the race.

'It is something that happens all the time in fleet racing. If your main rival is in sixth place and you are one place ahead of him you can make him drop back down the field by aggressive covering. As long as he doesn't reach a certain position in the race, your overall position is protected. It's quite legal. It's happened to me, and I've done it to other people. Sometimes you are the rabbit, and sometimes you are the hunter.

'When Ben went to his first Olympics in Atlanta in 1996, the Brazilian, Robert Scheidt, made sure he got gold and Ben got silver by using that tactic. Ben didn't forget that. And when they were at the Sydney Olympics four years later, Ben replied in kind – and did it better.

'If you find someone is covering you, either before or during the race, there are a lot of ways you can try to break free. You can try and use another boat by getting it in between you, or you can try and use the committee boat to block the person covering you. Sometimes you can get free by using a group of boats to disrupt your pursuer.

'Or you can do a tacking battle, where you tack rapidly right and left, right and left, maybe fifteen or twenty times in a row. Then it comes down to which sailor has the better manoeuvring skills and can keep their speed up at the same time. These kinds of tactics come into play, usually, in the last race of a series, or maybe the second from last, when the points position gets tight. And the fact that every competitor has one discard race in a competition can also have an influence on when it happens.

'Ben's friend Iain Percy, who has won Olympic titles himself, describes him as "the most competitive man in the world", and I know what he means. There is something of Ayrton Senna, or Michael Schumacher, in him. Ben is fantastically confident in his own ability. He can multi-task, and still maintain top speed. Robert Scheidt is the same. He is one hell of a sailor.'

Sailing beyond the limits

Such activities on the water are within the rules – just. But there are times when such physical 'hustling' in sailing goes beyond what is deemed acceptable to those involved with the sport. Such an example occurred in the Sail for Gold regatta on the Olympic course at Weymouth a month before the 2012 London Games got under way. In the decisive medal race Britain's

Olympic Laser sailing champion Paul Goodison was pursuing his major London 2012 rival Tom Slingsby. The Australian had arrived at the final race in gold medal position, but Goodison, in fifth place, had a chance of silver as he trailed the leader by a boat's length, well clear of the chasing field. Slingsby, however, then took the decision to 'cover' Goodison, blocking him and slowing him down, and kept it up for the rest of the race, leaving the Briton vulnerable to the pack behind. As the wind pushed the fleet together on the final run, Slingsby's Australian teammate Tom Burton and Philipp Buhl of Germany slid past on the line to take silver and bronze respectively, with Goodison having to settle for fourth place.

The Briton accepted that 'covering' was 'definitely part of the game', but added: 'This incident wasn't really part of the game, though. The guy that was realistically closest to beating Slingsby overall (Burton) was four hundred metres behind. What he did was to make sure that his Australian mate got as close as he could to attack me at the end. It's a bit frustrating. There's two boats who are a long way in front, and if we'd finished in that order he would have won the gold medal and I would have won the silver. So slowing down until the pack catches up is not really going to affect his result, but it could end up affecting mine. And unfortunately I made a mistake on the last bit that allowed the two guys closest to me to go past in the last twenty metres. It was frustrating because it was my mistake.'

Goodison, who admitted the incident had led to a 'stand-up row' between himself and Slingsby in the pub the following night, added: 'If you are doing what you have to do to win, that's acceptable. If you are doing something that is going to influence people, the other guys, without affecting you at all, that's probably out of order. Tom looked at it in a different light, that if one boat gets past him then he might start slipping back, and that's why he's argued he was defending so hard against me. We agreed to disagree on that.'

Making a late run for the line

Athletics history has offered up numerous examples of the most basic of manipulations – attempting to secure victory in races through the expedient of joining them at a later stage than your opponents. It sounds impossible, but it has been done on many occasions, even if not with ultimate success. At least, we trust not. Assuming that Pheidippides really had run all of the twenty-five miles from to Marathon to Athens in 490 BC to herald the Greek victory over the Persians – and if he had only jogged round the agora before making his big announcement he certainly paid a heavy price for his subterfuge when he immediately dropped dead – then the first marathon runner known to have tried to blag a victory over the marathon distance was Fred Lorz. But in order to do that the American required the mechanical assistance of a car, which carried him for eleven miles of the route before it broke down and he 'finished' the course.

What happened at the 1972 Olympics was similar as Frank Shorter, the American who won the marathon gold medal, entered the stadium to a puzzling reception of boos and whistles. What Shorter didn't realise at the time was that this opprobrium was directed at the young West German running ahead of him who had been first to enter the stadium and had briefly convinced his home crowd that he was the winner. Perhaps Shorter still hears those calls as he looks at his gold medal now. Let's hope not.

But if we accept that neither Lorz nor the young German seriously expected to get away with their pretence, such was not the case with Rosie Ruiz as she crossed the line to win the 1980 Boston Marathon in what was then the third fastest time recorded: 2 hours, 31 minutes and 56 seconds. There were soon, however, some puzzled glances among the authorities, who had never heard of her and who, what's more, had not been aware of her during the main part of the race. None of her fellow competitors recalled running with her either.

The answer was simple. Rosie had registered for the race, thus getting her official number, but had jumped out of the crowd and started running at the final half-mile. Despite the grimace on the line, she had hardly had time to break sweat. Before long, the victory garland was awarded to its rightful owner, Jacqueline Gareau. It transpired that Boston had not been the only scene of a Ruiz deception; she had qualified to run there by running the New York Marathon. By running some of it, and by taking the Manhattan subway for much of the way.

In 1993 Herman Matthee was stripped of his gold medal from the fifty-five-mile Comrades ultra-marathon in South Africa after it transpired that he had proposed an even simpler means of advancing his cause – video evidence showed he had ridden in a taxi for almost twenty-five miles of the route. History does not record whether, like Fred Lorz, Matthee claimed it was all a prank.

There was a horsey kind of echo of the marathon spoofs – if such a thing were possible – on a foggy afternoon in January 1990 when Landing Officer, a 23/1 long shot ridden by Sylvester 'Sly' Carmouche, emerged from the mists as victor. A surprising victory, and a bogus one. It transpired after not too much investigation that Carmouche had dropped out of the mile-long race while lost from view and then rejoined the field as they came round again before galloping to glory. In retrospect, Carmouche probably wished he hadn't overegged the pudding by finishing twenty lengths clear.

Twins peak

In 1999 the Comrades race witnessed a more novel attempt at subterfuge. It turned out that Zimbabwean twins Sergio and Arnold Motsoeneng, who were virtually identical, had decided to win the race from Pietermaritzburg to Durban by sharing out the running. They alternated the work by changing over at mobile toilet stops and taking it in turns to keep up with the action in a car. Sergio finished ninth, earning one of the ten gold medals on offer, although runners behind him were puzzled as they did not recall him overtaking them.

The gold medal was swiftly returned when photographic evidence showed fatal flaws in the twins' plan. A picture taken around the halfway point showed a scar on Sergio's right shin which had disappeared by the finish line. Other photographs confirmed that the brothers had worn their wrist watches on different arms. These were details that might have come straight out of one of Agatha Christie's Hercule Poirot mysteries.

Sergio admitted the hoax and agreed to hand back the medal and the nine thousand rand he had won. 'He lives with his parents and ten brothers and sister in a two-bedroom house and the family had run into financial difficulties,' a lawyer said. 'That's why the brothers tried to pull off the trick.'

Ten years later Merseyside twins Nazim and Zabid Mohammed employed their own version of tampering in a league cricket match, when Nazim, a bowler, swapped with his batsman brother at the end of an innings. A life ban was imposed after discovery of the ruse – Zabid, unlike Nazim, was left-handed.

Such unfortunate turns of events helped to inspire many anti-cheating techniques that are now standard in marathons, including extensive video surveillance and RFID (radio-frequency identification) chips worn by all runners that monitor the times at which they arrive at various checkpoints.

The sad transatlantic subterfuge of Donald Crowhurst

Ocean racing, particularly of the long-distance variety, is peculiarly taxing to the body and spirit, and there have been sailors who have proven unequal to the task. One such, sadly, was Donald Crowhurst, who employed an aquatic version of the tactic used by some of the marathon's more notorious competitors.

An amateur sailor, Crowhurst entered the 1968 *Sunday Times* Golden Globe Race with the idea of raising publicity for a handheld radio direction-finder which used marine radio beacons. His chosen boat, a trimaran, was untested and liable to capsizing, but Crowhurst had a plan to allay this tendency: an inflatable buoyancy bag. It was a great idea that failed in only one respect. He didn't get around to adding it. Crowhurst also left having forgotten many of his vital supplies in his haste. He was never seen again.

Swiftly realising that neither he nor the boat were up to the task upon which they had embarked to such fanfare from followers and sponsors alike, Crowhurst simply sailed about in the South Atlantic and suggested, through misleading radio reports, that he was leading the race. This caused competitor Nigel Tetley to push his ship beyond its limits in an effort to catch up with his phantom opponent, and despite being well ahead of the field Tetley was forced to abandon ship as it broke under the strain.

When Crowhurst's boat was eventually found, unmanned and adrift, on 10 July 1969, the logbook he had left, containing rambling philosophy, confession and snatches of poetry, made it clear that he had suffered agonies of conscience upon hearing of Tetley's fate, and had apparently determined upon suicide.

Fosbury's virtuous manipulation

Sporting manipulation doesn't have to be crooked. Before the 1968 Mexico Olympics, high jumping typically involved the 'straddle' technique, namely manoeuvring over the bar face downwards. Back in the day, some had achieved success with a scissors-kick method, but this was generally outmoded.

In preparing for the 1968 Olympics, however, a young US high jumper called Dick Fosbury had developed his own revolutionary technique of leaping over the bar backwards, with back arched. He had worked on this variant over a period of years, despite coaches suggesting he stuck with the straddle technique.

But the Fosbury Flop, as the technique has come to be known, won him the 1968 US Olympic trials, and the 1968 Mexico Olympic gold medal with an Olympic record of 2.24 metres. Four years later, at the Munich Olympics, twenty-eight of the forty high jumpers used the same method. Nowadays, it is universal. It was one of the most beautiful of sporting manipulations – legal, original, successful.

The dark side of Subbuteo

That said, the Beautiful Game will always be football. We have now examined examples of the kind of physical manipulation that erodes, and at times destroys, that beauty. Such physical forces also exist, sadly, in the game which has helped so many while away hours that might otherwise have been spent doing homework. Yes, we're talking here about Subbuteo. It's a table football game – or carpet football game, depending on where you spread out the green baize-like playing surface – and it has at its heart the aesthetic pleasure of bowls, in that the three-quarter-inch footballers, each set on their own weighted hemisphere, will follow a curve to left or right depending on which side they are flicked by the finger of a player.

Just as woods make for the jack, these little totems, which can be bought or painted in one's favourite team strip, pursue their own biased paths towards a waiting ball which, in the old form of the game, is almost as big as they are. The pleasure when they connect, particularly if they have circum-vented a defender en route, is great. Unlike bowls, however, these players can also slide in a straight line across the green cloth of the pitch – again, if set in motion with a flat, central flick.

Flick. Not push. As anyone who has wasted long hours playing this game will tell you, pushing is cheating. Pushing is illegal manipulation, a slur on the game. Essentially, some part of the hand with which you are propelling the player has to remain in stationary contact with the surface. Any kind of shovelling action is not on. Pushing. Shoving. Chivvying (the last being a Scottish term). The errant action has many names, but they all amount to the same thing.

If this has been the most obvious area of dubious manipulation within the game, however, it has probably been run a close second by actions relating to the lightweight goals, with their little coloured nets. Sad to relate, the sudden shifting and OCD 'straightening' of these lightweight goals has taken the impetus out of many an attack.

And unlike outfield players, the goalkeepers – whether they stand with bent knees and arms awaiting developments, or whether they are models already created in the act of flinging themselves towards an imaginary ball with both arms outstretched – have no independence of movement. Instead, they are attached to either a wire or a plastic stick which pokes out behind the goal to be manipulated by their handler. Which has encouraged the practice, when an incoming shot is expected, of simply whizzing the keeper to left and right to maximise the chances of connecting with the ball. Not on.

Peter Adolph, who lodged an outline patent application for the game in August 1946, chose a neo-Latin title for his game meaning 'hobby' after being refused permission to call it Hobby in English. But given the domestic controversy his brainchild would generate for future generations of players, Adolph might have been better off calling it Argument.

Manipulation II – applied level

'The rules say nothing about the foot gear of a high jumper, but the federation has to take a stand on this phenomenon.'
– Paul Mericamp, spokesman for the IAAF

The range of physical manipulations employed in sport aimed at bending or, frankly, breaking the rules is vast. But there is another layer to manipulation which is just as widespread and arguably more pernicious. As opposed to basic manipulation, applied manipulation requires, as its name implies, forethought and ingenuity. Applied manipulation operates beyond, or beneath, the level where you gain unfair, or barely fair, advantage by doing something with either your body or that of your opponent. Applied manipulation has to do with third parties, inanimate objects – and it employs a bewildering array of props.

Bloodgate – no joke

Let's take a recent example. Where do you go if you want a fake blood capsule? A joke shop, of course. There's a good one in Clapham Junction which was popular with Harlequins rugby union club a while back, before one of their jokes backfired.

In retrospect, the image of the Quins' full back Tom Williams walking off the pitch at the Stoop during the Heineken Cup quarter-final against Leinster in April 2009, red poster paint 'blood' brimming over his lips, looks ludicrously artificial – like something out of a lame Dracula film.

Harlequins lost 6–5, but the result might have been different had Nick Evans, the recognised goal-kicker who came on as Williams's 'blood replacement', not missed with his late drop-goal attempt. The blood pellet option had been planned in advance as a means to manipulate the substitution system for tactical reasons. Williams compounded the sense that all was not as it should be at the time by winking at his teammates as he came off. Never a good tactic in a televised match – just ask Cristiano Ronaldo.

A subsequent disciplinary hearing found that the capsules had been bought by club physio Steph Brennan under the instruction of Quins' director of rugby, the former England forward Dean Richards. While the outcome was not funny for Quins, the activity on the day did have a genuine element of farce about it. Williams told the hearing that he had put the pellet in his sock after Brennan had come on to the pitch and handed it to him, before pulling it out after a contact and trying to bite on it. The capsule fell out of his mouth, however, so he had to pick it up and start all over again.

He went on to describe how, with Leinster officials apparently shouting at him that the blood 'wasn't real', he had asked the club doctor to deliberately cut his lip with a scalpel and they had had to find a room to themselves in order to do this. A picture was subsequently taken of his lip; it was a neat cut, requiring no stitches. In August 2009 Richards received a three-year ban from the game. Brennan was banned for two years, and Williams for four months. Harlequins were fined £259,000 for what came to be known, inevitably, as Bloodgate.

No matter how hard Harlequins try to put this unfortunate episode behind them – and they have already tried very hard – it will always be there, like a rogue tramp in a wedding photo. For so many reasons it takes its place in a kind of inverted Sporting Hall of Fame which is already crammed with misdeeds and manipulations great and small – a Hall of Sporting Infamy, if you will. Imagine you could take a tour around this hall. What might you find?

Dodgy pipes, torn gloves, lead weights and baggy trousers

In the late 1980s an illegal system was discovered which had been built inside an Austrian thirty-five-footer racing boat used for international competition. The ingenious and nefarious alterations were designed to enable water to be distributed around the boat to provide extra ballast. It was a bit of a clumsy job, by all accounts, and was discovered when the boat was sold on. You'd have thought those responsible would have got rid of the evidence beforehand, wouldn't you? Similar skulduggery reportedly took place in the 1970s and 1980s, when regular night racing at sea involving quarter-, half- and one-ton boats took place. Under cover of darkness lifeboats were sometimes suspended over the side, which was equivalent to having an extra man on the rail.

Alterations of a different kind were alleged to have assisted Muhammad Ali – then plain Cassius Clay and yet to win his first world heavyweight boxing title – during his 1963 fight against Britain's Henry Cooper at Wembley Stadium. Many believed that the US boxer was prevented from losing by some shady manoeuvring – in other words, applied manipulation – on the part of his trainer, Angelo Dundee.

It was Cooper's misfortune that when he hit Clay with his best punch, a left hook – otherwise known as 'Enery's 'Ammer – there were only a few seconds left until the bell for the end of the fourth round. It was also luck – good or bad, depending on which way you look at it – that Clay was prevented from falling to the canvas when his arm caught in the ropes. Clay managed to get back to his corner at the end of the round, but was clearly still dazed, and Dundee appeared to revive him with smelling salts – which were, strictly speaking, a no-no. What Dundee did next, he later admitted, was to open a small tear that had already appeared in one of Clay's gloves before telling the referee that new gloves were required, a tactic which delayed the start of the fifth round. Clay was able to mount a cagey defence upon resumption and went on to win on a stoppage after Cooper was cut above his eye.

So how much time did Dundee's efforts earn his fighter for the purposes of reorientation? Cooper, who died in May 2011, always said it delayed the fight by between three and five minutes. But Colin Hart, the highly respected veteran boxing and athletics writer for the *Sun* newspaper, insists this was not so. 'I've studied the tape and timed it,' he said. 'Five seconds. That was all the extra time Clay got. Of course five seconds can be a long time for someone who is trying to clear their head. But all those claims about a minute's delay or more are just a myth. It was nowhere near as long a gap as some people have said it was.

'Clay got knocked over at the end of the fourth round and he was still very groggy when the bell went. Dundee wasn't exactly cheating, but what he did try to do was exacerbate the situation by trying to make the split in the glove worse. The gloves weren't changed. There were no other gloves at ringside, and if they had had to go back to the changing rooms it would have taken fifteen minutes. So the fight continued with the split glove.' After this fight the rules were changed so that spare pairs of gloves would always be on hand at ringside.

And the lumps of lead? Cooper, it later transpired, had been guilty of his own, admittedly harmless, manipulation before the fight. Never a big man in the heavyweight division, the Londoner had trained so hard that he was probably around 27lb lighter than Clay, but he said he had disguised this at the weigh-in, for fear Clay might gain encouragement, by inserting lead into his boots.

Six years after that fight alterations to sporting wear of a different kind created a mini-scandal in the sport of ice hockey. The goalkeeping trousers owned by National Hockey League (NHL) keeper Tony Esposito, it was discovered, had a mesh sewn into them to prevent pucks from going through. That web of deceit was swiftly banned, of course.

Bats and balls

In cricket, fielders and bowlers are allowed to polish, clean or dry the ball, but no artificial substances may be applied to it – only spit and sweat. It is also illegal deliberately to roughen one side of the ball or to damage the seam on the ball. If you do that it adds to its asymmetry, meaning air will pass over one half of it faster than the other, resulting in a deviation in flight. Allegations about tampering are almost as old as cricket itself. There have been claims about all kinds of substances being 'innocently' used to exaggerate the effect of the ball's flight, including hair gel or oil, sugar – fielders sucking boiled sweets – and even lip balm.

The thing is, with all the television coverage of the game, more and more examples are being shown up. And what becomes increasingly clear is that this is an offence *sans frontières*. Eyebrows were raised in 1976, for instance, when England's John Lever was able to get large amounts of swing from the ball on the unhelpful pitches of Delhi and Madras during a tour of India. There were suggestions from the Indian side that Lever's habit of occasionally passing the ball over his eyebrows may have been designed to rub a vaseline-like substance on to it, but no charges were ever brought.

In 1990 New Zealand's Chris Pringle – having taken a career best of 11 for 52 in the third Test in Faisalabad – produced a variant of the classic justification-for-doping argument in defending his own tampering with the ball. Pringle said he had done it because he was convinced the Pakistan bowlers were doing the same thing. This mindset is doubtless behind all manner of shady or downright dark sporting deeds. As is the case in so many doping incidents, one of the underlying factors is fear, or at least trepidation about potential rivals and opponents, allied to a lack of trust in those with the authority to prevent such abuses to act effectively. Paranoia plus opportunity equals infringement. It doesn't have quite the same ring as $E = mc^2$, but that doesn't mean it isn't just as true.

Pringle would presumably not have been surprised that, two years later, the Pakistan bowlers Wasim Akram and Waqar Younis were accused of gaining large amounts of reverse swing by altering the finish on the ball. No evidence was ever adduced for this, however. Two years later it was the England captain, Michael Atherton, who was facing awkward allegations for his conduct during a Test match against South Africa at Lord's in 1994 after television cameras caught him reaching into his pocket and then rubbing a substance on the ball. Atherton denied ball tampering, claiming that he had dirt in his pocket which he used to dry his hands. Strictly speaking, not cheating. He was summoned to the match referee and was fined £2,000 for failing to disclose the dirt to the match referee.

Pakistan's Waqar Younis became the first player to receive a suspension for ball tampering in 2000. He was fined half his match fee after it was ruled that he had lifted the seam off the ball during a game against South Africa in Colombo. The following year six Pakistan players were fined for ball tampering in a domestic one-day competition, the Ramadan Cup, and in 2003 Pakistan bowler Shoaib Akhtar was banned for two one-day Tests and fined 75 per cent of his match fee after TV cameras had shown him scratching the surface of the ball during a match against New Zealand.

In January 2004 Rahul Dravid of India was fined after TV pictures showed him applying a half-sucked lolly to one side of the ball in a match against Zimbabwe. The successful reverse swing applied by England bowlers in the following year's Ashes series against Australia was aided and abetted by saliva sweetened by eating mints, according to the autobiography later published by England batsman Marcus Trescothick. In 2006 an alleged ball-tampering issue overshadowed a Test match between Pakistan and England, whereby Pakistan refused to take to the field for the evening session after being penalised five runs for ball tampering in the afternoon. Cameras caught the umpires discussing the condition of the seam. Pakistan were believed to have intended a protest against the decision by delaying their return after tea. However, while they were refusing to play, the umpires awarded the game to England in accordance with the laws.

A deal was then agreed between the English and Pakistani cricket boards to allow the match to continue, and the Pakistani team resumed the field fifty-five minutes after the umpires first took to the field for the resumption of play. Umpires Darrell Hair and Billy Doctrove, however, declined to continue the game, maintaining their decision that Pakistan had forfeited the match by refusing to play. As a result of Pakistan's forfeiting of the game their captain Inzamam-ul-Haq was charged and found guilty of 'bringing the game into disrepute', though he was cleared of the charges relating to 'changing the condition of the ball'.

Similar controversies have occurred in Major League Baseball (MLB), where doctoring the ball with spit is punishable by immediate dismissal from a game and a subsequent ten-game suspension. A row over ball-tampering erupted during the second game of the 2006 World Series when television pictures showed Detroit Tigers pitcher Kenny Rogers with what appeared to be a foreign substance on his pitching hand. Rogers maintained the substance was merely dirt from the mound, and complied with a request from the umpires to wash his hands at the end of his second inning. No further action was taken, but the issue was pursued extensively in the media, who referred to the controversy as either Dirtgate or Smudgegate. What would the sporting world have done without the Watergate scandal?

Almost twenty years earlier veteran pitcher Joe Niekro was playing for the Minnesota Twins when his opponents accused him of doctoring the ball. When umpires made Niekro turn out his pockets, a piece of sandpaper and an emery board fell out. Niekro received a ten-game suspension. Niekro's brother, Phil, who was also a pitcher, reportedly sent him a power sander with a fifty-foot-long extension cable.

It is not just the ball that has been the subject of attempted manipulation in baseball. For many years there have been insinuations about players inserting cork into the interior of a baseball bat, to make it lighter, and thus easier to swing, without reducing its hitting power. In 1994 Albert Belle of the Cleveland Indians was accused of corking. One of his teammates came up with a cunning plan to switch the bat that was under investigation with another standard one. Unfortunately, however, the bat that was submitted for inspection carried another teammate's signature on the handle, which rather spoiled the effect. Belle was suspended.

The most public exposure of 'corking' came in 2003, when the bat belonging to Sammy Sosa of the Chicago Cubs shattered in the middle of a game, spraying the field with bits of cork. Not much arguing with that. However, a 2007 study found that corked bats absorb more kinetic energy than uncorked bats, and so don't technically hit the ball any further.

Megaphone abuse at the Berlin Olympics

Some dark manipulation took place on behalf of the host nation at the 1936 Berlin Olympics, where home oarsmen Willi Kaidel and Joachim Pirsch were strong favourites in the double sculls rowing event. You could tell that because der Führer turned up for their final, and he wasn't one of those Führers given to saying things like, 'Never mind, the main thing is that you have taken part.'

The British pairing of Jack Beresford and Dick Southwood had noted during the qualifying rounds that the Germans were getting away to flying starts, as they had worked out that the megaphone the starter lifted to his lips in order to issue the commands was so large that it effectively blocked his view of the crews. Thus the home pair would get in one or perhaps two strokes before any of their opponents.

In the final, however, Beresford and Southwood came through to win what Beresford, who had already earned two Olympic golds and two silvers, called the sweetest race of his career. The Britons had simply done the same thing as the Germans at the start, proving the truth of the old maxim: If you can't beat them, join them; then beat them.

The British pair raced their final in a new, lightweight wooden shell which had been specially constructed for them and shipped over to Berlin ahead of the Games. Their new boat, however, mysteriously disappeared in transit, before investigations by a fellow British rower who had been working in Berlin as a coach to German crews prompted an investigation – and the boat, which had been transported by rail, was discovered in sidings. Odd, that.

Athletics – ideally equipped for manipulation

Athletics is a hugely varied and often very technical sport, employing a wide range of hardware. An ideal arena, then, for a spot of applied manipulation. During the 1980s there were reports that an official anxious to see new heights achieved in the pole vault at his meeting had arranged for the pole to be filled with sand so that it was less easy to dislodge. Another tactic was said to be used by a leading vaulter of that time. It was alleged that he would visit venues at which he was due to compete and loosen the bolts on the framework holding up the bar, thus allowing contact force to be dissipated through an unusually sympathetic structure which would sway and shake as if it were undergoing a religious conversion.

Technical sports, it seems, offer greater scope for skulduggery. At the 1980 Moscow Olympics the doors at either end of the stadium were seen to be open whenever home javelin throwers were about to perform, thus improving the aerodynamics. Equally mysteriously, by the time competitors from other nations had made their preparations, the doors were shut. It may have been coincidence, but Russia's Saida Gunba took silver in the women's javelin, and home throwers Dainis Kula and Sergey Makarov took gold and silver respectively in the men's event. An idea that flew...

In 1999 a British discus thrower, Perris Wilkins, was investigated by UK Athletics after an official alleged he had tried to switch his regulation 2lb discus for a lighter one while taking part in the CGU World Trials at Birmingham's Alexander Stadium. The investigation took in the circumstantial evidence that all of Wilkins's best performances had taken place at low-key meetings, including his startling British record of 66.64 metres in 1998 at a Midland League meeting. But in his first international outings the previous year he had only managed 53.16 at the European Championships, where he finished second last, and 55.39 in the Commonwealth Games, where he was eighth. No charges were ever brought on those grounds against Wilkins, however, who was sanctioned three years later when he was banned for life following a second doping offence.

During the 1950s the high jump event witnessed some crafty manipulation by Soviet competitors. When Russia's Yuri Stepanov produced a world record in the high jump of 7 feet 1 inch (2.16 metres) early in the summer of 1957 it provoked surprise among observers of the sport who were unfamiliar with this new talent. Stepanov had not even made the Soviet Olympic squad at the previous year's Games in Melbourne. And when, shortly afterwards, Russia's Olympian Igor Kashkarov (who had cleared only 6 feet 10½ inches to finish third at Melbourne) managed a jump of 7 feet ¼ inch, questions began to be asked.

When the French daily *L'Equipe* published a picture of Stepanov in action, interest swiftly focused on his shoes, the soles of which looked unusually thick and bouncy. In Moscow the high jumpers' coach, Nicolai Komenkov, insisted that there was nothing wrong with the soles. But no chance was offered for them to be examined, and so the IAAF got involved. 'The rules say nothing about the foot gear of a high jumper,' said the IAAF spokesman Paul Mericamp, 'but the federation has to take a stand on this phenomenon.'

Before long the rules did say something about suitable footwear for high jumpers and the spring-heeled-Jack soles were banned. But Stepanov's world mark stood.

At the 1987 World Athletic Championships in Rome the home long jumper, Giovanni Evangelisti, won the bronze medal. It was then discovered, however, that home officials – and they know who they are even if the world remains officially unsure – had simply added a bit on to the distance he managed.

So simple, and yet so effective. Or so it would have been, had the Italian media not prompted an investigation by printing the incriminating data. In April 1988 the IAAF officially amended the result, which meant that Evangelisti, a legitimate bronze medallist at the 1984 LA Olympics, did not add a valuable medal to the home tally. Bronze went instead to Larry Myricks of the United States.

Indoor games

It may pain some readers to learn that that very nice man, Michael Palin, has been found to have cheated at conkers. This shameful episode in the life of the former Monty Python comedian turned travel writer and broadcaster took place in 1993 during a competition held on the Isle of Wight – Mecca for conkerers, in case you didn't know.

Palin was found to have committed two of the prime crimes of the conkers competitor: not only had he baked his conker, he had also soaked it in vinegar. Not nice, but these things have to be faced full on if they are to be properly addressed. At least he didn't paint his conker with clear nail varnish, as some have.

Elsewhere, the staid game of bridge got a right old shuffling during the 1965 world championships, when it transpired that teammates Terence Reese and Boris Schapiro were communicating illegally through body language. Vigorous digging actions signified spades, while an ostentatiously turned backside indicated trumps. Actually no, the communication took place through fingers. For instance, two fingers held together indicated two hearts held, and two fingers held apart indicated five.

It sounds almost as complicated as working things out fairly. But when officials noticed something was amiss, the two players were dropped from the British team. And although the British Bridge League cleared them,

Reese and Schapiro got two fingers from the world ruling body, which found them guilty.

Even that quintessentially cerebral pastime, chess, has been disfigured by allegations of cheating. The advent of new technology has enabled and tempted many amateur players in recent years to take lengthy 'toilet breaks', where they have sometimes been found consulting miniature chess computers. In one case this misdeed was discovered when an official stood on the bowl in the neighbouring stall and looked over the dividing wall. In 2006 the world chess champion himself, Vladimir Kramnik, was accused of visiting the toilet 'suspiciously often'. OK, it was fifty times during the game. But then these games can go on a long time. And chess is a nerve-racking business.

Boris Dis-Onischenko and his magic sword

An épée is a kind of sword used in fencing. But the épée wielded by the Soviet Union's modern pentathlete Boris Onischenko at the 1976 Montreal Olympics was not a regulation épée. It was a kind of magic épée in a way, because it meant Onischenko didn't need to hit his target to score points. His misdeed became a front-page story around the world, firstly because it took place at the Olympic Games, and secondly because it was so staggeringly cynical and blatant.

By the time he got to the Montreal Games, Onischenko – an army officer from the Ukraine who had won individual silver and team gold for the Soviet Union at the 1972 Olympics – was one of the most highly respected protagonists in a sport which has its roots in the notion of chivalry, courage and resourcefulness, and encompasses five knightly accomplishments: fencing, riding, swimming, running and shooting. His successes in the fencing discipline, however, derived from a classic case of advanced manipulation: Onischenko's épée was wired up with a hidden circuit-breaker that he was able to activate to record a 'hit' on the electric scoring system even though his blade had not made any contact.

Suspicions began to be raised during the team competition when the Soviets took on Britain. In a fight against Adrian Parker, the automatic light indicated a hit for Onischenko even though he had not appeared to touch his opponent. When the same thing happened in his next fight, against another highly experienced British competitor, Jim Fox, the latter raised an objection and the weapon was taken away to be investigated by the Jury of Appeal.

Onischenko fought on with another épée – and, no doubt, a sick feeling of apprehension. He was soon disqualified, automatically knocking the Soviet team – defending champions – out of the running. The Ukrainian was swiftly removed from the Olympic Village and was soon Back In The USSR. He has not been seen outside it since. Of course, all the British newspapers loved it. Next day the headlines were all about 'Dis-Onischenko'.

Recalling the incident many years later, Fox – who took full advantage of the Soviet absence along with Parker and third colleague Danny Nightingale by winning the team gold – reflected sadly on the fall from grace of a man who had not just been a rival, but a friend. Before the news of his disqualification had come through, Fox said, Onischenko had come up to him and apologised.

Eternal youth

In recent years, track and field statisticians have noted an increasing number of runners who have falsely declared their age in order to win youth or junior titles. In 2006 this prompted the president of the IAAF, Lamine Diack, to proclaim: 'We shall treat the matter with the same seriousness as doping.'

Diack's comments followed cases where birth details were incorrectly supplied on behalf of two Kenyans, Thomas Longosiwa and Emmanuel Chamer, who obtained passports bearing lowered ages with the intention of taking part in the World Junior Championships in Beijing. Longosiwa was arrested and charged, while Chamer was let off after owning up. Both athletes dropped out of the event.

Two other Kenyan-born athletes now representing Bahrain were also arrested in June 2006 and briefly held before being released. They allegedly changed their ages to participate in the previous year's World Youth Championships in Morocco and junior races at the 2005 World Cross Country Championships in France.

At the 2008 Beijing Olympics concerns were raised over the ages of several of the Chinese gymnasts, including three of their team champions, He Kexin, Jiang Yuyuan and Yang Yilin, and the IOC announced an investigation into the matter. The allegation was that these Chinese athletes were ineligible to compete as they were not sixteen – the minimum age limit announced by the International Gymnastics Federation (FIG) in 1997 to prevent an increasing trend of younger gymnasts being entered in senior competitions, with a mind to preventing injury and undue stress and pressure on children involved. The Chinese authorities denied the allegations.

Concerns about He's age had been expressed before the Games began, but following her stunning victory on the uneven bars they intensified. Two official Chinese gymnastic websites had reportedly given He's date of birth as 1994 before they were both 'blocked'. She commented: 'My real age is sixteen. I don't care what other people say. I want other people to know that sixteen is my real age.'

Despite widespread doubts, the IOC accepted the Chinese position. But investigations showed up a further discrepancy at the Beijing Games involving a Chinese gymnast who had won an Olympic medal eight years earlier. The investigation was protracted, but in 2010, almost ten years after she had won a women's team bronze medal at the Sydney Olympics, Chinese gymnast Dong Fangxiao had her medal taken away by the FIG, thus giving the team bronze to the fourth-placed United States. Officials spotted that Dong had registered as a national technical official at the 2008 Beijing Games, giving her date of birth as 23 January 1986, even though her birthday according to the FIG database was 20 January 1983. This meant that when she had competed in Sydney she had been only fourteen.

In 2001, Bronx baseball pitcher Danny Almonte earned renown for throwing the first perfect game in the Little League World Series, the hugely popular US annual event, on behalf of his team, 'The Baby Bombers'. The proud youngster was pictured receiving an award for his prowess from the Mayor of New York, Rudy Giuliani. His powerful performances became a little easier to understand when it transpired he was actually two years older than he should have been to take part in a competition devised for twelve-year-olds – information which only came to light when a suspicious rival team employed a private investigator to look into the case.

Driving over the limit

If Formula One was *Wacky Races* then Michael Schumacher would be Dick Dastardly. Schumacher won his first world title in 1994, but the achievement came against a background of controversial activity on behalf of the German and his Benetton team which you might characterise as applied manipulation.

Although Schumacher got away to a fabulous start by winning six of the first seven races, his momentum was checked when the international governing body, the FIA (Fédération Internationale de l'Automobile), found that Benetton were using gearbox software specifically outlawed by regulations and which was deemed to be a kind of 'launch control', allowing the German to make perfect starts.

At the British Grand Prix, Schumacher was penalised for overtaking on the formation lap, only to apparently ignore the penalty and a subsequent black flag, which means all drivers must return to the pits. He was disqualified and given a two-race ban. Schumacher claimed there had been a communication problem between the race stewards and his team.

Schumacher was also disqualified after winning the Belgian Grand Prix, when his car was found to have illegal wear on its skid block. These checks to the German's progress allowed Britain's Damon Hill to catch up in the drivers' championship, and by the time of the final race of the season, in Adelaide, Schumacher led by just one point.

On lap thirty-six Schumacher hit the guardrail on the outside of the track while leading before returning to the track. He then moved to the left, ahead of Hill in the Williams. The Briton then switched right to try and overtake on the inside of the next bend, but Schumacher moved across as well, colliding with the Williams before flipping out of the race. Hill made it to the pits, but the car's left suspension wishbone was broken and he had to withdraw, leaving the German as champion. Many Formula One insiders blamed Schumacher for the incident, as did, not surprisingly, the British media. It was a highly controversial incident, but the race stewards judged it as a racing incident and no action was taken.

If some people had been prepared to give Schumacher the benefit of the doubt in 1994, they were probably less inclined to do so after the collision in 1997 at the same stage of the championship. Once again Schumacher, by now with Ferrari, led into the final race by one point, this time from Jacques Villeneuve, driving the Williams FW19. Towards the end of the race, in Jerez, Schumacher's car developed a coolant leak and his level of performance went down. It looked as if he might not last to the end of the race.

As Villeneuve approached to pass him, it looked as if Schumacher provoked an accident between the two cars. Whatever the root of the action, the German's car came off worst in the collision and he retired from the race as Villeneuve was able to proceed to the end, winning four points which earned him the title. Afterwards, Schumacher was disqualified for unsportsmanlike conduct.

Too much information

Here's a question. You have been given a mass of documents you should not have which require photocopying. Do you: a) use your home printer to carry out this lengthy job; or b) go down to the local photocopying shop and get to work in full view of the bloke behind the counter?

Strange as it sounds, this question is based on a real case: Dossiergate, as it's now known in motor-racing circles. In 2007 at the High Court in London, Ferrari pursued a compensation suit against Mike Coughlan, senior designer of the McLaren team, which was found to have been in possession of confidential design documents belonging to the Italian company. Coughlan was subsequently sacked and banned, and McLaren were fined £50 million and stripped of all their points in the 2007 constructors' championship.

The High Court heard that Ferrari had been tipped off about the espionage when Coughlan's wife walked into a photocopying shop in Woking with a 780-page dossier from Ferrari and began copying it. A staff member from the shop, who happened to be a Ferrari fan, realised that all was not well and got in touch with the Italian team. 'We would not have found out about it were it not for a tip-off by the photocopying agency,' said the Ferrari QC.

After serving the two-year ban imposed by the FIA, Coughlan was given a second chance as he was appointed chief engineer to the Williams team. 'I sincerely regret my actions and I fully accepted the penalty given to me by the FIA,' Coughlan said. 'I can only hope I can earn back everyone's respect.'

Information for such a tactically dense game as American football is at an absolute premium, so spying is potentially crucial and requires covert surveillance of your opponents through a variety of means. One of them is to stand opposite their officials and video the signals they are giving to their players, although this is high risk, as Bill Belichick, coach of the New England Patriots, discovered. He was disciplined by the NFL (National Football League) for covertly videotaping signals being given by New York Jets' defensive coaches during a match on 9 September 2007. Belichick was fined $500,000, the Patriots were fined $250,000, and they lost an original first-round selection in the following year's NFL Draft.

Information was also at the heart of a strange case involving the Munster rugby union team a year after the club had endured the 'Hand of Back' in losing their Heineken Cup final against Leicester. Perhaps through the workings of divine justice, they appeared to profit from a more intricate piece of manipulation before a Heineken Cup tie against Gloucester.

Needing to beat their English opponents by a margin of at least 27 points, and to score at least four tries in so doing, the Irish club's chances of progressing to the last eight looked slim indeed – until a Limerick taxi driver provided them with a sheet of paper carrying all the English club's tactical plans for the vital Pool B match.

Perhaps coincidentally, Munster progressed, after winning by a margin of 27 points (33–6) and scoring four tries. The driver, Tom McDonnell, said he had found the information in the back of his cab after giving a Gloucester official a lift before passing it on to the Munster hotel via a rugby-playing intermediary. Gloucester's director of rugby, Nigel Melville, was unconvinced, insisting that someone had stolen one of the sheets that had been put under the doors of the players in their own hotel.

Such a prosaic set of circumstances pales in comparison to one of the most concerning of sport's applied manipulations – which has occurred, if reports are to be believed, for a number or years: underwater espionage, related to the hugely prestigious and hugely costly America's Cup sailing challenge.

In 1983 Australian multimillionaire Alan Bond's *Australia II* boat became the first non-American yacht to win the America's Cup racing series in 132 years, greatly aided by a winged keel produced by noted designer Ben Lexcen. When the boat was undergoing its trials in Newport before the racing began, great care was taken to drape canvas over its hull and keel – to keep the revolutionary new keel a secret from an American crew skippered by the brashly competitive Dennis Conner.

'We call it a modesty skirt,' explained the *Australia II* boat manager, John Longley. 'We like to keep our lady's private parts hidden.' With only three weeks of the phoney war left, the US sailors started to ask awkward questions about the mysterious keel. Most pertinently, was it legal? That question was officially settled: it was. Four days later the head of the rival US *Liberty* team was writing to the Dutch laboratory where Lexcen had finalised his design, asking them to build the same design for the US team. Request refused.

Soon Warren Jones, the executive director of the *Australia II* team, was asking direct questions of the US syndicate: 'The NYYC [New York Yacht Club] has stated that it had only recently become aware of the details of the *Australia II* keel. We would like to know where these details were obtained, since it is common knowledge that we keep all the details of our boat secret,' he said. The American syndicate spokesman Robert McCullough responded: 'I don't think it's illegally obtained. I can assure you that we didn't go after it; it was given to us…'

If foul play had been involved, it would not have been for the first time in this competition. In 1934 the defending US boat was found to have copied the revolutionary headsail of the challenger. Before the America's Cup series of 1992 – when, for the first time, the old 12-metre class boats were replaced by larger vessels – technical advances became even more important, and there were a spate of attempts at spying which affected both some of the challengers and indeed Dennis Conner's defending boat, *Stars & Stripes*.

The New Zealand challengers, headed by Sir Peter Blake, were the target more than once, prompting defensive measures to be put in place. 'We put divers in the water to make sure no one's down there with cameras,' he said. 'And if anybody is stupid enough to swim in at night time, we have a surprise for them.' This was thought to be an underwater sonic wall.

On 30 January 1992, after the first round robin of the Louis Vuitton Cup – the competition which establishes which will be the official challenging boat in the America's Cup – had got under way, Blake went public with another incident: 'This morning our divers saw another diver in the middle of a yacht pool with a camera.' Two members of the Kiwi team dived in and were able to apprehend the interloper, who turned out to be a US Navy diver. His camera was seized after it emerged – as it were – that he was intending to sell information to the highest bidder.

Dodging the doping bullet

Applied manipulation also has a role to play in getting away with doping. Which explains the whizzinator. It's a phallic object. In fact, it's a phallus. Not a real one, clearly, but a realistic one – in fact, there are a variety in different colours – which is widely available on the internet. This artificial phallus is designed to be attached to a bag containing clean urine, which is hidden about a competitor's person. It's a waste of time and effort if that competitor can give a clean urine sample all on their own, of course. In some cases, apparently, the bag containing clear urine has been lodged up a competitor's anus.

At the 2004 Athens Olympics, the Hungarian who won the discus gold was disqualified and banned after the urine samples he provided before and after competition showed evidence of belonging to different people, indicating tampering. The thrower also refused a request to be tested shortly after his competition in Athens. It was never proved how he had supplied differing samples, but informed speculation pointed towards possible use of a whizzinator-type device. The name of the thrower involved was Adrian Annus.

There was a historical forerunner of this kind of operation. During the 1978 Tour de France, Belgian cyclist Michel Pollentier was thrown out for a crude attempt to fix a doping test with the help of a rubber tube and a bulb of urine after taking the race leader's yellow jersey following a punishing ride up Alpe d'Huez. According to one report, officials conducting the post-stage test became suspicious when 'Pollentier began pumping his elbow in and out as if playing a set of bagpipes'.

Bowls – and deviation

The world of sport has seen a wide range of cricket balls with pre-picked seams, corked baseball bats, that kind of thing. It has also seen 'roll-straight' bowls – specially calibrated to make a beeline for any jack. Getting a wood to roll correctly is not always a simple matter, of course. Bowls expert David Rhys Jones, whose longstanding commentary work for the BBC earned him the soubriquet 'the voice of bowls', recollects the distressing case of Margaret Letham, a Scottish player who encountered an unexpected challenge when on the verge of winning the women's world outdoor singles title in Moama, New South Wales in 2000.

'The gold medal seemed to be hers when she defeated Ireland's Margaret Johnston (the most successful woman bowler in the game) in a group match,' Rhys Jones recalls. 'Johnston responded by challenging Letham's bowls, which she alleged were "too straight". Bowls is all about bias, of course, and the curved path of each bowl must equal or exceed that of a Master Bowl that represents the minimum bias. Straight-running bowls (i.e. those that swing less than the Master Bowl) make life too easy, and are deemed to be illegal.

'The bowls were tested overnight on a testing table – and failed the test. A distraught Letham was stripped of the points, which were added to Johnston's total – and it was Johnston who went on to head the table, qualify for the final, and win the title. There was no suggestion that Letham had tampered with the bowls, or was deliberately cheating – she had been given the bowls especially for the world championships by a leading manufacturer. Other similar bowls failed the test, too.'

Rhys Jones adds that it is the manufacturer who has the duty of testing and then stamping bowls before putting them on the market. These tests then need to be carried out regularly – 'like an MOT'. He adds: 'It has been known for bowls to be tampered with. Rubbing the bias side with sandpaper or emery cloth changes the template of the bowl, and alters the bias.

'And, although bowls is all about bias, it is generally felt that reducing the bias makes it easier to get near the jack, so there is often a great deal of hostility towards those who have "straight" bowls.'

Letham was so upset about the turn of events which had halted her aspirations in the individual event that she did not bother to turn up for the sixth-place play-off match. But she felt a little happier by the end of the championships, having won the pairs title with fellow Scot Joyce Lindores.

Rhys Jones also recalls another occasion on which applied manipulation within bowls triggered one of the most controversial incidents to have taken place in the sport. It occurred at the 2009 Asia Pacific Championships in Kuala Lumpur, where the New Zealand four skipped by Gary Lawson – a player who had been described as 'the Bad Boy of New Zealand bowls' – were accused of throwing their last group game in order to manipulate a better draw in the knockout stages.

Having already qualified for the quarter-finals, the Kiwis allegedly calculated that by losing to Thailand in their final game they would avoid their arch-rivals Australia in their next match. Four dropped shots on the penultimate end certainly had the effect of losing them that match. The consequent maths within their group meant that Canada missed out on progressing, and the Canadians, suspicious, asked Bowls New Zealand to investigate rumours that all had not been as it should have.

Kerry Clark, the chief executive of Bowls New Zealand, got on about as well as you might have expected with the Bad Boy of New Zealand bowls, and this incident stirred uncomfortable and none-too-distant recollections of a similarly awkward affair in January of the previous year.

On that occasion, at the World Championships held at Christchurch, a Kiwi quartet skippered by Lawson was found to have deliberately dropped shots against Ireland, an action which had the effect of ending whatever slim hopes of success were being maintained by Scotland. 'We are taking it seriously,' said Clark at the time, 'and we're dealing with it in terms of our constitution, which does have a misconduct provision in there where misconduct is defined as including deliberately losing or attempting to lose a game of bowls or playing unfairly.' The New Zealand four were reprimanded by Clark, but then sailed on to win the world title.

Now the Kiwis' conduct in the match against Thailand was duly investigated. Lawson's three teammates, deemed to be mere accessories, were fined NZ$1,000 each, while the skip was fined NZ$5,000 and banned for six months. After further legal action, however, the case was altered. The fines were rescinded, and all three of Lawson's colleagues were deemed eligible for the upcoming Commonwealth Games in Delhi. The ban on Lawson, however, remained.

The New Zealanders' attempt to second guess the process of qualification ended up backfiring, as they still came up against Australia and were put out of the competition by them. 'The decisions and findings of the BNZ judicial committee are accepted,' a chastened Lawson said afterwards. 'We accept that our actions were contrary to the rules.'

Badminton – and calculation – at the London 2012 Games

The London 2012 Olympics, broadly speaking a triumph beyond even the organisers' fondest imaginings, were nevertheless marred by an unprecedented controversy in the badminton competition, from which four of the teams in the women's doubles were disqualified for 'not using one's best efforts to win'. Matches between two South Korean pairings and their Chinese and Indonesian opposition turned into a shuttlecock version of a slow bicycle race as the teams appeared to be outdoing each other in their efforts not to win, methods of which included deliberately missing shots and serving woefully.

Gail Emms, Britain's 2004 silver medallist in the mixed doubles, who was commentating on the matches, made her own personal comments in the aftermath. 'I have had volunteers really, really upset and emotional – they were crying because they couldn't believe this was going on at the Olympic Games,' she reported. 'They have been working so hard to make this sport, this competition, perfect and they have just seen four women's doubles pairs not live up to what they believe in. It has been really, really hard. There have been a lot of strong words. It was so embarrassing. Bear in mind there were six thousand people inside Wembley Arena who had paid good money to watch top-level, elite, world-class badminton. They basically got a show where my two-and-a-half-year-old could have won one of those matches. It was so shocking. The girls were serving so far out it was very embarrassing. What happened was just truly disgraceful. This is the Olympic Games – it is not very much in the Olympic spirit.'

But as Emms pointed out, the roots of this problem lay in the Badminton World Federation's introduction of round-robin matches to the format, which offered competitors the opportunity of engineering more favourable draws for the subsequent knockout section by using a 'tactical' defeat. 'Every badminton tournament that has ever been played is usually knockout, so if you win you are still in the competition, and if you lose you go home,' she said. 'The idea was to have group stages to show more badminton on the TV, to give the non-dominant countries in badminton more of a chance to play in the Olympic environment. It has just really backfired. As soon as I heard it was group stages, I think it was six or seven months ago, I said instantly that means you can fix the way you go through in your draw. I knew this was going to happen. It was put to the BWF many times. They ignored the warning signs, thinking it would be fine.'

The London 2012 chairman, Lord Coe, told a press conference the following morning: 'It's depressing. Who wants to sit through something like that? It's unacceptable.' Coe's discomfort was heightened by the fact that IOC president Jacques Rogge, who had sounded a clear warning on the danger of match fixing in world sport a year before the Games had got under way, had been a spectator at the Wembley Arena on the previous day.

The expelled players include Chinese world champions Wang Xiaoli and Yu Yang, who were accused by other players of attempting to throw their 'dead rubber' in order to avoid playing China's No. 2 ranked pair before the gold-medal match. The Chinese players' actions appeared to trigger a response from pairs from South Korea and Indonesia, who in turn tried to lose to counter the Chinese intentions. The BWF met the following morning after charging Wang and Yu, Greysia Polii and Meiliana Jauhari of Indonesia, and two South Korean pairs, Jung Kyung-eun and Kim Ha-na, and Ha Jung-Eun and Kim Min-Jung, of not using their 'best efforts' to win the matches. There was no suggestion of any betting being associated with the matches, but the circumstances were seen as being profoundly damaging to the Games. South Korea head coach Sung Han-kook admitted his two pairings attempted to throw their matches against the Chinese and Indonesians, but said it was in retaliation against the Chinese team who instigated the situation.

Thomas Lund, chief executive of the BWF, made a careful statement to reporters in the aftermath of the controversy: 'I would like to underline that it is the responsibility of the players, and team members, and the entourage around them to live up to the standards in our regulations – the players' code of conduct – to go after winning every match. That's the bottom line.'

The badminton controversy at the London 2012 Olympics garnered numerous reactions on social media. One observer with a long memory recalled how Britain's double scullers Dickie Burnell and Bert Bushnell had been similarly creative with the options of their draw en route to winning gold at the 1948 London Olympics. Shortly before he died in 2010, Bushnell revealed: 'Dickie decided we should lose the first heat so as not to meet the Danes in the semi-final. I wouldn't have had the nerve to do that. We could have won, but we didn't, and came into the semi-final via the repêchage, avoiding the Danes.' The Danish favourites were eventually vanquished in the final along with the Uruguayan pair. It did not go unobserved either that, on the eve of the London 2012 Games, the BBC had run a drama programme celebrating the pair's unheralded win at the London Games sixty-four years earlier.

The argument broadened. What should be done if a coach rested key players during a preliminary match, or if a swimmer or athlete was seen not to be putting in maximum effort during a heat in order to conserve energy? The answer to the last example was provided in the course of the London Games – but it was hardly a clear one.

Algerian middle-distance runner Taoufik Makhloufi, one of the favourites for the 1500m, was initially thrown out of the Olympics after dropping out of his 800m heat on the day before he was due to run in the 1500m final. Having qualified for that final it was reported that Makhloufi no longer wanted to run in the 800m but that his National Olympic Committee had failed to withdraw his name before the deadline. Thus Makhloufi dropped out of the two-lap race after jogging just 150 metres.

His action drew an immediate response from the International Association of Athletics Federations, which disqualified him from the evening's 1500m final. A statement from the IAAF said the referee 'considered that he had not provided a bona fide effort and decided to exclude him from participation in all further events in the competition under rule 142.2'.

However, an IAAF spokesman said the athlete could be reinstated with a medical certificate from a doctor explaining he had an ailment that troubled him but which could clear up and allow him to compete in coming days. Surprise! Makhloufi was subsequently reinstated in the final after the Algerian federation insisted he had a knee problem and that the organisers knew about it. And despite his knee problem, he produced a sprint finish which earned him Olympic gold. 'It was the will of God,' he said. 'Yesterday I was out. Today I was in.' Commenting on the presence of the Algerian in the field, Kenya's defending champion Asbel Kiprop said, 'He should have been allowed to run. It was not a big offence.'

Slippery customers

Judo is a sport known for its sense of honour, so cases of judoka bending the rules are very limited. Should anyone's sense of fair play falter, there are three referees operating as well as officials constantly reviewing live footage, so the opportunities for wrongdoing are slight.

Some judoka may try to wear a smaller outfit – known as a 'gi' – to make themselves more difficult to grip. And when tired, some will undo their belts momentarily to pause the contest and get a respite. But the case of one slippery character, Yoshihiro Akiyama, has created waves in recent years.

The thirty-five-year-old Japanese judoka won the prestigious 2001 Asian Championships and 2002 Asian Games, which saw him selected for the 2003 World Championships. Once there, he earned three wins in the -81kg category to make the semi-finals, but all his victims claimed his gi was slippery. He was made to wear a reserve gi and lost the semi-final and bronze medal match.

The following year Akiyama moved to mixed martial arts with Japanese organisation HERO's, the new extension of Fighting and Entertainment Group's K-1 promotion. But in a 2006 bout against the legendary Kazushi Sakuraba the former judo player was accused of 'greasing' – that is, applying a body oil to make himself difficult to get hold of.

Akiyama won by stoppage but the result was overturned to a no-contest as K-1 announced he had applied lotion to his body. His prize money was withdrawn and he was indefinitely suspended.

In 2005 one of Zimbabwe's leading youth athletes, Samukeliso Sithole, winner of seven titles in the previous year including his country's only gold at the Southern Region Championships in Botswana, hit trouble. The problem was that while Sithole had competed in a female competition, he was found to be a man named Ngwenya Mduduzi, who was charged with impersonation and causing psychological damage to female athletes and received a four-year jail sentence.

Home-town judges – the theory

Sport has a long and troubled history of sporting manipulation by those who stand in judgement. There are those who say that any sport which requires the deliberation of a judge to decide on merit is not a proper sport. Football, rugby, tennis – these, the argument holds, are the real McCoy, whereas gymnastics, diving, ice skating and ice dance are of lesser sporting merit because the scoring is less clear-cut and more subjective.

Because of that intrinsic subjective element, it is hard to find clear evidence of misdeeds with regard to the judging of sport, although there is a legion of anecdotal evidence, much of it involving tales of partiality to home performers – that is, the existence of 'home-town judges'. Recently, UK Sport – the body responsible for administering the funding of Britain's Olympic and Paralympic programmes – addressed the phenomenon of 'home advantage' by analysing past Olympic results.

There are two clear schools of thought about what it means to perform at a home Olympics. The first says it's inspirational, and certainly the number of aspiring British Olympians who have spoken about the supposed motivational power of competing on home soil in 2012 is evidence for this position. They can't all be blindly following the advice of their media trainers. But the second school of thought, voiced by former US Olympic 200m and 400m champion Michael Johnson, among others, is that performing at home simply increases the pressure on performers to live up to escalating expectation. (Not that he did so badly with his 200m world record of 19.32 seconds at the 1996 Atlanta Games.)

The argument over this topic goes on, and will continue to do so. But what the UK Sport officials found, and acknowledged, was that there was indeed a recorded, quantifiable example of 'home advantage' at different Olympics over the years – and that home advantage could be seen to operate in the area where sports were judged. With the best will in the world, it seems – and certainly without the best will in the world – judges tend to err towards the home competitors at any Games.

Academic studies attempting to document what happens when a home team or athlete appears to thrive have looked at four main factors to do with the crowd, learning or familiarity, travel and rules. It has also been surmised, not too adventurously, that the bigger the crowd, the bigger the effect on the match official.

As is often the case in areas such as these, science merely seems to confirm what everyone thinks they knew already. Thus sport acknowledges these factors with well-worn phrases: the 'home-town decision' and, where referees and judges are concerned, the 'homer'.

Statistical surveys of summer and winter Games have identified a particularly marked advantage for home nations where medals are awarded by judges. And crowd noise is thought to be a telling factor in aligning judges with home individuals or teams.

So in sports such as boxing, gymnastics, and ice dance or figure skating, if you are competing at a home Olympics you can realistically hope to get, how shall we say it, rub of the green, the benefit of the doubt. And if you're not competing at a home Games? Well, then you are at risk of becoming a victim of applied manipulation by your opponents – premeditated and unfair treatment.

Such applied manipulation took place during the 1966 World Cup finals – at least, as far as many of the Latin American nations taking part believed. They alleged that the organisers, and by extension the referees – football's mobile judges – were working in favour of European teams, and specifically the England team. One statistic adduced was that of the thirty-two matches, all but seven had European referees. The additional fact that Uruguay and Argentina made their exits in the quarter-finals to Germany and England respectively, in controversial games controlled by English and German referees respectively, was also seen as unfair.

Plus, of course, there was the officials' collective failure to protect the Brazilian seen by many as the world's greatest player, Pele, who was brutalised by Bulgarian and Portuguese players as his side failed to progress from the group matches. And there was the fact that the host nation, England, got to play every one of their home games at Wembley. England's semi-final against Portugal had been due to be played at Goodison Park, Everton's ground, but there was a late switch by FIFA – whose president at the time was England's Sir Stanley Rous. The official reason for the change of heart was commercial. No one would have argued that Wembley would not be a sell-out for the match. But was that the only reason?

Home-town judges at the boxing ring

While sporting rivalries thread through the history of any big event, there will also be a deeper and darker narrative involving judged events, where all too often the forces of reaction and national prestige exert undue influence on the action. As graphic evidence for this, it is hard to beat the photograph taken at the moment the decision was announced as to who had won the 1988 Olympic light-middleweight title at the Seoul Games.

The referee, with an ambiguous expression on his face, holds up the arm of home boxer Park Si-Hun. But rather than exulting, the South Korean is looking across at his opponent, Roy Jones Jr, with an expression of shock. Jones Jr, meanwhile, stares, hands on hips, taking in the fact that – as he suspected – he has just found himself on the wrong end of one of the most outrageous judging verdicts ever handed down to a practitioner in the noble art of boxing.

The nineteen-year-old from Pensacola, Florida had spent the best part of the three rounds that had just come to an end raining punches on Park. Compubox, a private company that kept a record of all connecting punches for the US television network NBC, offered clear evidence of how the bout had gone: Jones registered eighty-six hits, his opponent thirty-two. It seemed that the only way the American could have won his gold would have been by a knockout, as he had hinted beforehand: 'I know how tough it is to get a decision against a South Korean.'

Three of the five judges ruled that the Korean had earned a victory. The uproar over a result that was so clearly unjust was such that many Koreans rang local radio and TV stations to complain. Park himself apologised to Jones, telling him through an interpreter: 'I am sorry. I lost the fight. I feel very bad.' On the victory stand, Park raised Jones's arm to mark what he felt was the true result.

Inevitably there were accusations that officials within the Korean Amateur Boxing Association had bribed or coerced some of the judges to give the result to their man. One of the judges announced soon after the fight that the decision had been a mistake. Eventually, all three who had voted in favour of Park were suspended – an IOC investigation in 1997 found that they had been inappropriately entertained by Korean officials. But the result was allowed to stand.

Park's progress to gold had been, shall we say, charmed, since the start. Two of his victories, although not as blatantly unearned as the one in the final, had surprised most independent observers and engendered fury among his East German and Italian opponents. When the quarter-final result against Vincenzo Nardiello was announced, the Italian dropped to his knees and beat the canvas in frustration before running out of the ring and screaming at the jury.

In his first round, Park had been extremely fortunate not to be disqualified for two illegal blows to the hip and kidney of Abdullah Ramadan of Sudan, who doubled over in agony. The Australian referee seemed reluctant to disqualify him, however, and deferred to the judges, who ruled that, as Park had not been cautioned, Ramadan had retired.

The referee would certainly have borne vividly in mind the disturbing scenes in the boxing arena two days earlier when home bantamweight Byun Jong-Il lost his bout to Alexander Hristov of Bulgaria after being docked two crucial points by New Zealand referee Keith Walker for illegal use of the head.

The decision sparked fury within the home ranks and Byun's coach, Lee Heung-Soo, ran into the ring and hit Walker on the back. Soon several other Koreans had joined the coach and rained down blows upon the shocked Kiwi, who had to be defended by fellow referees. Even one of the security guards took part in the attack, aiming a kick at Walker's head as he made his shaky way out of the ring. Meanwhile, a US boxing judge, Stan Hamilton, sustained a serious cut on his arm when he threw it up protectively as a Korean coach attempted to smash the Bulgarian president of the Referees' Committee over the head with a plastic box. In the aftermath, a tearful Byun staged a silent protest in the ring, where he was eventually given a chair. He stayed put for more than an hour.

Part of the fury of the attacks on Walker stemmed from the erroneous belief that he had officiated at the previous day's narrow and controversial defeat of the host nation's light flyweight favourite Oh Kwang-Soo, at the hands of Michael Carbajal of the United States. Part of the fury went back four years to the Los Angeles Olympics, where Koreans felt officials had been biased in favour of US boxers, and were particularly incensed by the dubious defeat of their light welterweight Kim Dong-Il at the hands of home fighter Jerry Page. And so on and on it goes, like a Greek tragedy.

And at the ice arena...

Eighteen years after the LA Games, another Olympics on American soil – the winter version at Salt Lake City – reopened old wounds between the US and South Korea. The event which caused the discord was short-track speed skating – a notoriously volatile sport which, at the same Games, produced the farcical finish that left Australia's Stephen Bradbury free to glide slowly over the line with arms raised to take gold in the 1000m after all four of his opponents had crashed ahead of him on the final bend.

One of those fallers was the home nation's Apolo Anton Ohno, whose desperate attempts to make amends in the subsequent 1500m final appeared to have ended in failure as he was narrowly beaten to the line by South Korea's Kim Dong-Sung. However, Ohno had earlier raised his arm to signal that he was being impeded by Kim as he attempted to pass him with three laps remaining. The Korean appeared to drift to the inside, checking the American's progress.

The South Korean was subsequently disqualified for 'cross-checking', which ignited a fire of indignation in his home country that crackled and burned for years afterwards. For many Koreans, this was Los Angeles all over again. The Koreans took their appeal all the way to the IOC and the Court of Arbitration for Sport (CAS), without success. Thousands of protest letters, some of them including death threats, were sent to the IOC and to Ohno. At the FIFA World Cup later the same year in South Korea and Japan, two South Korean players celebrated a goal against the United States by mimicking what they clearly thought had been the exaggerated reaction produced by Ohno when he thought Kim had skated into his line.

The chain of events which saw two couples being given Olympic gold in the figure-skating pairs event at the 2002 Winter Games in Salt Lake City seemed impossible to follow at the time, and is still mysterious.

Jamie Salé and David Pelletier of Canada skated what most knowledgeable observers reckoned to be a flawless free programme, which commanded the majority of the marks. And although the Russian pair of Yelena Berezhnaya and Anton Sikharulidze had won the short programme – the other element of the event – an obvious technical error in their free programme indicated to most neutrals that the Russians' long run of success in this event, which no pair outside the Soviet Union had won since 1960, had come to an end.

But gold went to the Russians, with the judges from China, Poland, the Ukraine, Russia and France placing them first. The judges from the United States, Canada, Germany and Japan gave the event to the Canadians. It was a split along political and geographical lines that was entirely expected – not counting the presence of France in the first group.

Rumours immediately circulated that there had been some kind of agreement between the Russian and French judges whereby the Russians would reciprocate by voting for the French pair in the ice dance. This was never proven, although the French judge, Marie-Reine Le Gougne, and the head of the French skating federation, Didier Gailhaguet, were both suspended from the sport for three years, despite there being no official investigation.

Meanwhile the IOC was putting pressure on the International Skating Union (ISU) to sort things out as the media outcry in the US and Canada grew more strident, and on 15 February Ottavia Cinquanta, president of the ISU, and Jacques Rogge, president of the IOC, announced in a joint press conference that the Canadians would be awarded gold, but that the Russians would be allowed to keep their gold as there was no evidence of wrongdoing on their part and four of the other eight judges on the panel had marked them ahead. As things turned out, the French pair won the ice dance, with the Russians second.

And in the gymnastics hall

Like skating, gymnastics has also endured numerous awkward questions relating to judging decisions – but none more probing than those asked in the wake of the 2004 Athens Olympics, where it seemed the whole judging system was going into meltdown, creating major doubts over a number of medal awards.

The most vexatious of all issues came in the men's all-around competition, where Paul Hamm of the United States, despite dropping to twelfth place after a disastrous fall on the vault, his fourth discipline, came back with excellent performances on the parallel bars and the high bar to win gold by a margin of 0.012 points, the narrowest in Olympic history, over Kim Dae-Eun of South Korea, with Kim's compatriot Yang Tae-Young third.

But there was immediate controversy as the FIG ruled that Yang had been given an incorrect starting value of 9.9 in the parallel bars, rather than 10.00, due to a misunderstanding by the judges of one of the moves he was due to perform. Had the correct starting value been operated, it was claimed, Yang would have won gold. The FIG suspended three judges, but said the result would stand.

Hamm's supporters pointed out that he had performed his routine in the knowledge of what he needed to do to surpass the Korean, and that he could have adjusted the level upwards if he needed a greater margin. Eventually – and ludicrously – Bruno Grandi, president of the FIG, sent a letter to the United States Olympic Committee to be passed on to Hamm, describing Yang Tae-Young as the 'true winner' of the gold medal, and stating: 'If (according to you [*sic*] declarations to the press) you would return your medal to the Korean if the FIG requested it, then such an action would be recognised as the ultimate demonstration of Fair-play by the whole world. The FIG and the IOC would highly appreciate the magnitude of this gesture.' Very swiftly, the IOC made it clear that it would appreciate no such thing. Yang took his appeal to the Court of Arbitration for Sport, unsuccessfully.

Soon after the all-around final there was further embarrassment for the sport as Bulgaria protested against the decision to award their world champion, Jordan Jovtchev, silver in the rings behind the Greek competitor Dimosthenis Tampakos, who enthused the home crowd by taking his country's first gold in the event in the history of the Games, doing so by a margin of just 0.012 of a point. The Bulgarian team insisted that the Greek's score had been given too high a degree of difficulty. 'What Tampakos did was much easier,' said a spokeswoman.

It was a judgement that aroused widespread incredulity. Even the bronze medallist Yuri Chechi of Italy, winner of the event at the 1996 Olympics, recognised an injustice. As soon as the final results appeared on the scoreboard, Chechi pulled Jovtchev in front of the camera and gestured towards him as if saying he was the true champion.

Meanwhile the Canadians were very unhappy about the decision not to award their athlete, Kyle Shewfelt, a medal in the vault, where he had landed both his efforts, considering that bronze went to Romania's Marian Dragulescu, who fell on his second vault. And the Russians were beside themselves over the low score given to their man Alexei Nemov after what many considered to be a breathtaking performance in the high bar final, a judgement which led to a fifteen-minute break in competition due to the strong and noisy reaction of the audience.

Evgeny Marchenko, coach of the US winner of the 2004 all-around title, Carly Patterson, said in the aftermath of the Athens Games: 'Because it's a subjective sport, that will always be a problem. There is always room for improvement. More educated judges and more independent judges would probably be helpful. But I think the problem will always be there.' No amount of manipulation, it seems, will be able to expunge the possibility that judged events may be subject to manipulation.

Mind games

'There is only one rule: BREAK THE FLOW.'
– Stephen Potter

The world between the ears

In a sporting world where physical and technical preparation is becoming ever more efficient, the key area for any competitor, increasingly, is the bit between the ears. The incremental advantages that can be gained by honing one's own mental approach for competition can be decisive. Even more so if those advantages can also result in one's opponent suffering disadvantage. Mind games are played throughout sport, sometimes hovering on the borderline of legality, sometimes hopping over into what most right-thinking people would regard as foul play – mental foul play, if you like – and hoping not to become obvious. Mind games are crucial and, it seems, universal.

'Kindly say clearly, please, whether the ball was in or out.' A simple enough request, polite, delivered in an even tone. In Stephen Potter's artful 1947 book, *The Theory and Practice of Gamesmanship (or the Art of Winning Games without Actually Cheating)*, these words are delivered by his tennis partner, the philosopher C.E.M. Joad, during the first game of a match against younger, fitter and clearly superior opponents. What makes the request surprising is the fact that, a second or two earlier, Joad has barely managed to get his racket on to a powerful serve, sending the ball straight into the stop-netting twelve feet behind the server.

The effect upon the 'charming, well-mannered young men, perfect in their sportsmanship and behaviour' is dramatic. Which is why the masterful humorist uses this interaction as the template for his wide-ranging, tongue-in-cheek advice on how to gain the upper hand in sport, and life. 'I'm so sorry – I *thought* it was out,' ventures one of the youngsters. His partner agrees, and both immediately offer to play the point again. 'No,' replies Joad. 'I don't want to have it again. I only want you to say clearly, if you will, whether the ball is in or out.'

Joad truly doesn't need the point to be played again. He knows a larger point has already been won and that his scrupulous questioning of the young men's etiquette and sportsmanship has already begun its corrosive work on their morale. Amid a flurry of double faults, the two superior players duly gift the match to their middle-aged opponents.

There is always a way to turn the tide. It is never too late to start loosening the nuts and bolts of your opponent's confidence. As Potter puts it: 'There is only one rule: BREAK THE FLOW.' The impulse to gain the upper hand by devious means has always been present in sport. Potter, however, was the man who defined that impulse with his urbane variant on the term 'sportsmanship'.

For instance, Potter would have recognised and respected some, if not all, of the competitive strategems England's multiple world champion bowler Tony Allcock identified in his 1988 book with David Rhys Jones, *Bowls Skills*. Of course, many of the efforts of Allcock's opponents to plant misplaced confidence into his head before a match starts – 'I only entered this competition for the practice'; 'I'm not very well... I don't know if I'll be able to play'; 'I only hope I can make a game of it' – would be recognised as beginners' stuff by the master.

Allcock and bowls

Allcock maintains that such pleas had no effect on him. His recollection of tactics employed during games with the intention of distracting or annoying, again, would fall into the class of crude efforts: 'ill-timed talking, coughing, sneezing, singing or whistling, or kicking bowls "absent-mindedly" behind the player on the mat'.

Other tactics, such as over-exuberant celebration of one's own or a partner's success, or deliberately slowing down a game, are also employed to good effect in bowls – as in so many other sports. All pretty basic. Efforts which perhaps fall into a higher category of effectiveness include standing just that little bit too close to an opposing bowler so as to engender feelings of intimidation, moving just as the opponent is ready to bowl, or causing a distraction such as using a handkerchief or tying a shoelace at the far end as the bowler is launching into his delivery.

As Allcock says, it's all been done, although not too often at the elite level. There, he adds, is where you will find more subtle and effective ploys intended, in his phrase, to psych opponents out. Comments such as, 'What bad luck you are having today!' or, 'I don't think your bowls are helping you' – both of which, Allcock recalls, have been made to him 'in such a sincere and charming manner that no one could possibly take exception' – are much closer to the heart of the territory Potter marked out with such relish.

But it is when he recalls the manner in which his old partner and rival David Bryant operated that we are at the very centre of Potter's imaginary world. Bryant, who habitually played with a pipe clenched between his teeth, might have been a figure out of Potter's imagination – someone who managed to quietly amass six world titles and four consecutive Commonwealth golds without coming across as anything other than a West Countryman quietly enjoying his favourite pastime. He was the same whether he was playing in a world final or an exhibition match at a local club. When this god of bowls turned up to Bishop's Stortford Bowls Club in 1980, for example, he put on a masterly exhibition of winning as if by accident, while giving the impression that something of far greater importance was playing on his mind.

'Talking of behaviour that saps confidence,' Allcock says, 'I have always thought that David Bryant's generosity when applauding a good opposition delivery is so sporting it is almost intimidating.' Now there is brilliance: turning sportsmanship into a weapon. And as Allcock goes on to point out, such artless generosity would more often than not be followed by a ruthless response which would leave no avenue open to an opponent. Beaten by the nicer man. Where do you go with that?

Jeopardising Jimbo at Wimbo

Potter would have loved Bryant's nicemanship. He would also have exulted in the victory which earned the late Mr Arthur Ashe the Wimbledon gentlemen's singles title in 1975. Ashe, by then thirty-two and moving towards the end of his career, was up against his brash fellow countryman Jimmy 'Jimbo' Connors, ten years his junior, who was ranked World No.1 after winning the Australian, US and Wimbledon titles in 1974.

In the previous year's final, Connors had brutally disposed of the much-loved thirty-nine-year-old Ken Rosewall 6–1, 6–1, 6–4. It was the fourth and final defeat in a Wimbledon final for the Australian who had won the US, Australian and French Open tournaments. But Jimbo didn't care about that.

Not many people expected Ashe to win. But he arrived for his match with a strategy he had devised with some of his fellow US Davis Cup players in light of the few weaknesses in Connors' game – in terms of both technique and psychology. The key points were listed on a piece of paper which Ashe calmly consulted at each changeover as his surprisingly good start began to transform itself into an astonishingly good middle and then a gloriously fine finish.

For the first time, Ashe did not attempt to 'trade blows' with his heavy-hitting opponent. He was boxing clever, sending his serves out wide to Connors' two-handed backhand – heavy artillery which could not always be wheeled into place in time – and consistently playing shots which exploited one of his opponent's few weak shots, the low forehand. Throughout, Ashe approached the match in a measured fashion, something which became increasingly vexatious to Connors, who loved to play his tennis on a roaring roll. And throughout, Ashe took the pace off his returns, again frustrating the champion.

Confounded, Connors lost the first two sets 6–1, 6–1, and although he rallied to take the third by 7–5 and got to 3–0 up in the fourth, Ashe – discarding the fleeting temptation of straying from his game plan – endured to take the decisive fourth set by 6–4 and become the first black player to win the men's title. The Wimbledon gentlemen's singles title had been won by a gentleman. A gentleman who had ruthlessly messed up his opponent's psyche. Just to re-emphasise the point – this was not foul play, but a shade of grey; in short, smart play. But a weapon just the same.

Watching victory go with the flow

Bryant and Ashe produced mental strategies as pure and perfect as a Roger Federer forehand. Much as it might pain Potter, however, mind games in sport do not generally tend to operate at such a celestial level. We have already heard from James Willstrop about the way in which the normal argy-bargy of the squash court can escalate into something more obviously illegal, but as the Yorkshireman readily admits, darker arts are also employed within the game with the aim of undermining the mental resolve of an opponent – and he confirms the validity of Potter's 'break the flow' dictum. 'In all sports, particularly individual sports, it is very, very difficult if you lose your momentum,' he says. 'It is a major thing. If you break someone's momentum it is incredibly destructive. You see it all the time in sports like tennis. I always remember the Wimbledon semi-final which Tim Henman played against Goran Ivanisevic. On that occasion the disruption was nothing to do with Ivanisevic – it was simply the rain. But people who watched that match certainly felt that Henman had the momentum, and after the rain he had lost it.'

But the efforts Willstrop has witnessed at first hand to break his own flow have been about function rather than flourish – artisanship rather than artistry. 'Timewasting, through tactics like getting involved in a conversation with the referee – this does happen,' he adds. 'Most of the time the discussion will be for good reason, but sometimes you will get a bit of gamesmanship as players try to disrupt your rhythm, and also to give themselves a chance of a breather. Delaying service, for the same reasons, is also a big issue. It can happen. I've never known anybody to be timed out, but I actually don't know if there is an official limit to the time you can take. However, in squash, play is meant to be continuous.

'Sometimes you might find a player spending time doing up his shoelaces. It's a hard one to call, because if your shoelaces are a bit slack you need to tighten them. But sometimes people take a bit longer than they need to regain their mental focus. Feigning injury can also be a bad one. There have been times when I have suspected that an opponent is feigning injury. Sometimes you make that judgement because you know the player and you know what he is like as a person. Certain players are inclined to do this sort of thing. You get a bit of a clue when they come back on to court five or ten minutes later and start running around like greyhounds.

'You can also get players diving full length to get shots when maybe they don't need to. If that happens, the court can get wet with their sweat, and the other player has the right to ask for it to be cleaned on safety grounds. But again, it can be a disruption to the flow of play. Sometimes people do do things for the wrong reasons, and I can recall instances where it has certainly contributed to me losing, no question, even if it wasn't the sole reason.'

The stratagems Willstrop has experienced, however, are refined in comparison to the activity on sporting fields far and wide which has come to be known as 'sledging'. The word itself began to be used in Australian cricketing circles, for reasons that remain obscure, to describe the process of verbal goading which – like gamesmanship before the word 'gamesmanship' was coined – had always existed in the game.

Sledging – when mind games turn bad…

One explanation for the term ascribes it to an occasion in the mid-1960s when a fielding team, hearing a rumour that one of the visiting New South Wales players' wives was having an affair with a teammate, decided to act upon the information. When the 'cuckold' came in to bat, the fielders all began to sing Percy Sledge's 1966 hit 'When a Man Loves a Woman'.

If that piece of mental goading did indeed mark the arrival of 'sledging' as a term, the activity has been present in competitive endeavours for as long as human beings have had opposable thumbs. A fair few years after that particular evolution, but a fair few too before the Percy Sledge moment, the finest cricketer in Victorian England, W. G. Grace – himself not noticeably averse to working on the minds of his opponents – was the target of what would now be recognised as a classic sledge when the Essex fast bowler Charles Kortright, repeatedly frustrated in his efforts to get Grace out by an umpire who refused to dismiss him, finally accomplished the deed unanswerably by knocking away two of the great man's stumps. As W. G. made his reluctant way to the pavilion, Kortright called out to him: 'Surely you're not going, doctor? There's still one stump standing.'

An element of genuine wit also animated the reported exchange between Australian bowler Merv Hughes and Graeme Hick, the hugely talented Zimbabwean batsman who always struggled to realise his potential in Test matches: 'Mate, if you just turn the bat over, you'll find the instructions on the other side.'

But sledging is not always playful and witty. At its acceptable end, sledging is humorous banter; in the middle, it is the kind of humour which induces a fixed grin; and at the other extreme it is, as former Australian Test captain Steve Waugh once described it, a tactic of 'mental disintegration'. On many occasions, all wit has drained out of this sporting exercise, to be replaced by crude abuse and insult. It's verbal bullying, applied directly to the object of the exercise – the verbal equivalent, in fact, of pulling out someone's brain and pummelling it.

One sportsman who managed to span the full range from humour to humiliation was Muhammad Ali, the former world heavyweight boxing champion. Ali used to operate at a variety of levels as he tormented his rivals in the days and weeks before their bouts. Calling Joe Frazier 'ugly' was not witty or delightful. But some of Ali's poetic offerings occasionally zigzagged into genuine comedy.

As in the ring, Ali showboated and hurt at the same time. When he arrived in the sport, many observers were taken aback by his attitude and predictions of success, which he would deliver like riffs from a stand-up comic. It took some parts of the boxing world a while to warm to him. Ali admitted that in the early part of his career he had based his approach on a flamboyant wrestler from the Los Angeles district who called himself 'Gorgeous' George Wagner.

Before his first heavyweight title fight with Sonny Liston, who was known as the Big Bear, Ali – then plain Cassius Clay – subverted the fearsome name with one word. He called Liston the Big Ugly Bear. Ali would drive out with some of his camp to Liston's training venue in Surfside, Florida and call out his new name for the champion from the side of the ring, adding in other details such as: 'After the fight I'm going to go build myself a pretty home and use him as a bearskin rug. Liston even smells like a bear.'

It was before this fight, too, that he announced his intention to 'float like a butterfly, sting like a bee', a comment which perfectly described his method of operation. It also contained further advice for Liston: 'Your hands can't hit what your eyes can't see.' At the weigh-in, Clay supercharged his performance, rolling his eyes and acting like a man possessed. His heart rate was measured at 120 beats per minute. And he was pressing on a nerve with Liston, who was genuinely alarmed at the idea of fighting someone who was unhinged.

Liston eventually conceded his title in refusing to leave his corner for the seventh round of a fight that was being run by the brash young challenger. Demoralisation appeared to be playing a large part and it was surely a process that had begun before both men entered the ring in Miami Beach on 24 February 1964.

Ali's challenge against defending heavyweight champion George Foreman in 1974 – in the fight known as the Rumble in the Jungle, given its location in the former African state of Zaire – was an all-time demonstration of the power of mind games, allied to strategic manipulation. Ali's tactic was to prepare himself in training for heavy punishment by encouraging his training partners to rain in heavy blows as he covered up and backed up on to the ropes, absorbing and absorbing, before striking back. In order to assist his efforts his trainer, Angelo Dundee, was seen to adjust the tension on the ropes around the ring before the fight. 'If it hadn't taken place in a jungle, he would never have got away with it,' said one British observer who covered the fight.

But the manipulation was merely the means to the end, which was to exploit the vast champion's tiny area of mental weakness. The whole tactic was designed to get the larger man angry, to make him pour out all his energies in trying to despatch the source of his frustration to the ground. It was, essentially, about mental rather than physical disintegration. And then it was a case of striking back, to send him to the canvas himself, which Ali did to claim back his title.

When Ernie Terrell tried to play his own mind game on Ali before their fight by refusing to acknowledge his opponent's change of name from Cassius Clay – and his accompanying change of faith – he found himself being brutalised both physically and mentally as a result. It was indeed one of the most excruciating cases of When Mind Games Go Wrong.

Ali punished his opponent for the full number of rounds, never delivering the *coup de grâce*. At one moment the champion appeared to grab the challenger's head in an armlock and, as one veteran observer of the fistic arts put it, 'rub his eye along the rope'. Ali interspersed his blows with the same, taunting question: 'What's my name?' This was the realpolitik of the mind game.

By insulting Ali's new name, and with that, his religion, Terrell was insulting everything his opponent stood for and taking their opposition outside the sporting realm. In so doing he transcended a barrier of acceptability and the punishment he received, while cringe-inducing, was regarded by many experienced observers of the game as no more than his due. He had tried to mess with more than he should have done.

The balance of opinion with regard to this fight was arguably that, harsh as Ali's tactics were, they were also commensurate with the degree of serious offence he had been offered. There is in all such cases a kind of sliding scale of judgement employed by sporting followers which reveals a primitive sense of justice.

Words that harmed Zinedine Zidane and France

Ten minutes before the end of extra time in the 2006 World Cup final, with the score at 1–1, France's touchstone, Zinedine Zidane, stopped, turned, walked back to the Italian defender Marco Materazzi and headbutted him in the chest. The French playmaker was subsequently sent off and Italy went on to lift the Cup by winning the penalty shoot-out 5–3.

The question afterwards was: why had Zidane, one of the most experienced players in the park, who had stepped up to the challenge of putting France ahead from the penalty spot after just seven minutes, reacted in such a way? And broadly speaking, the answer was: it was something Materazzi said, although it has never been satisfactorily explained what that was.

The curious sequence of events had begun as the two players were simply running up the field together. Words were exchanged briefly after Materazzi, who had headed Italy's equaliser from a nineteenth-minute corner, tugged at the Frenchman's shirt. At which point Zidane did what he did, and the defender dropped to the turf. Job done?

Zidane subsequently told Canal+, the French TV channel, that the provocation had been 'very serious', adding that the words concerned his mother and his sister. 'I heard them once, then twice, and the third time I couldn't control myself,' he said. 'I am a man and some words are harder to hear than actions.'

What may have been the most important factor in all this was that Zidane's mother had reportedly been taken into hospital on the day of the final. Materazzi, for his part, admitted insulting Zidane, but strongly denied he had made any reference to his mother, adding: 'I lost my mother when I was fifteen and still get emotional when I talk about it. Naturally, I didn't know that his mother was in hospital but I wish her all the best.'

Whatever was said, it proved to be a calamitously effective piece of sledging in one of world sport's highest profile events – and, sadly, the main recollection of the final for many people.

Destroying the Soviet mentality

One historic occasion at which sledging was employed to serious and deeply motivated purpose was the Olympic water polo semi-final between Hungary and the Soviet Union, just days after the latter had invaded the former and restored the rule of Communism by putting down a populist revolution.

Ervin Zador, twenty-one at the time and one of the most talented of the Hungarian team, recalled in later years how he and his teammates had already put one mental ploy into operation during their campaign at the 1956 Melbourne Games. 'We double-marked the most dangerous opponent and chose one player to leave free,' he said. 'We shouted to him: "OK, go ahead, shoot!" No one expected to be given the choice to shoot against us. But we had a very good keeper, and these players became very nervous, and then they were never going to score. It was totally a mind game.'

When the Hungarians met the USSR, however, they decided to ratchet up the effectiveness of their mind games by taking every opportunity to get under the Soviet players' skin.

'We had decided to try and make the Russians angry to distract them,' Zador recalled. 'The plan was: "We play, they fight." We spoke their language – back home we had all been made to learn two hours of Russian every day – and so we were able to tell them how much we disliked them, and their families. And soon they were fighting.'

This, however, was a particularly volatile version of a mind game, and pretty soon the Hungarians were responding in kind as hundreds of expatriates in the stands waved the flags which had briefly waved, free of the Soviet emblem, in Budapest, surging down towards the pool and chanting '*Hajra Magyarck!* (Go Hungarians!)'

The players responded by taking a 4–0 lead which the Soviets were unable to overturn, but it was towards the end of the game that Zador suffered the blow captured in the emblematic shot of him emerging from the pool with blood streaming down his face and body from a cut eye – Hungary wounded by the Soviet Union.

Zador explained that the injury was caused by a momentary lack of concentration as he marked one of the Soviets' strongest players, Valentin Prokopov, having taken over from a teammate who had been hit in the ear and suspected his eardrum might have been ruptured. 'I looked after Prokopov for the last few minutes,' Zador said. 'And I told him he was a loser, and that his family were losers, and so on. There was no problem until I made a huge error. I looked up to question why the referee had blown his whistle.

'I shouldn't have taken my eyes off Prokopov. The next thing I saw he had his full upper body out of the water and he was swinging at my head with an open arm. I could imagine he wasn't very happy because the game was won and lost. All he had was anger. After he hit me I was seeing about forty-eight stars. Man, oh man, I was just like a stuffed pig.'

As his blood clouded the pool, the crowd grew enraged and the referee halted the game a minute early. The Soviet players were given a police escort from the pool. 'We were playing not just for ourselves, but for every Hungarian,' Zador said at the time. 'This was the only way we could fight back.' Hungary went on to retain their title with a 2–1 win over Yugoslavia, although Zador's eye swelled up so badly he was unable to play. But while the Soviets may have injured Zador, he was the one who had inflicted the greater damage on them.

This sledging was a world away from the comic-strip chat of Botham et al. Here was a mind game that was won game, set and match. As with Ali, the general view – certainly in the West – was that this was an acceptable violation of the spirit of the rules, in that it was commensurate with the deep anger on the part of the Hungarians about what had happened to their country, and many of their fellow countrymen and women, while they had been en route to Melbourne.

But when sledging is bereft of either wit or perceived justice, it is indeed a sorry thing to behold. Take the example of the 2011 world heavyweight unification title fight in which the Ukraine's Wladimir Klitschko defeated David Haye.

Haye, by his own later admission, attempted to unsettle his larger opponent to the point where he was so angry that he would lose his habitual defensive discipline against him. But when these tactics included having T-shirts printed with Haye holding the 'heads' of Klitschko and his elder brother, Vitali, who held all the world heavyweight titles between them, many people's instinct was to turn away in weariness.

On his way into the ring in Hamburg, Haye and his entourage had a bumpy ride, being jostled as they made their way through crowds of spectators. After the fight Haye's camp insisted that they had been deliberately left unaware of the arrangements so that their man would endure an unsettling pre-fight experience. But then that same man had previously attempted to bring about a final disconcerting manoeuvre himself by refusing to leave his dressing room for quarter of an hour. And of course, after the fight, all the supposed animosity dropped clean away.

It felt as if an empty commercial exercise had come to an empty commercial conclusion. The experience was akin to a bad film – whether it's the direction, or the lighting, or a scrap of dialogue, you know it's bad within three seconds. But there are worse things in sledging than empty threats, as a series of cases involving alleged racism between sportsmen have proved in recent years. Here we are truly at the low end of the scale.

Something else, however, that should arguably be included in that bottom end of the scale is the grunting which has become a notorious part of international tennis over the last twenty years – after all, what is grunting other than terminally inarticulate sledging? Oh, it's a necessary part of some players' game, is it? Then how come such players have been known to operate effectively with the volume control turned right down?

Habitual grunting in tennis came to wider notice in the 1970s with our old friend Jimmy 'Jimbo' Connors and, in more recent years, Monica Seles. It has since been practised by a host of current players including Serena and

Venus Williams, Maria Sharapova, Rafa Nadal and Novak Djokovic. It is often annoying. But is it cheating?

No less a figure than Martina Navratilova, winner of a record-breaking nine Wimbledon singles titles between 1978 and 1990, believes so. At the 2009 French Open the constant shrieking of sixteen-year-old Portuguese player Michelle Larcher de Brito caused her opponent, Aravane Rezaï, to complain to the umpire. To little avail. In the aftermath of this incident, Navratilova declared: 'The grunting has reached an unacceptable level. It is cheating, pure and simple. It is time for something to be done.'

Nothing much has been done, however. Whether it is primarily a means of putting off one's opponent, or merely affirming to the players themselves that they are operating at peak efficiency, the problem continues to shout for attention.

On-track minds

By their nature, mind games push acceptable practice up to and on occasion beyond the borderline of what is generally deemed acceptable. And sometimes that borderline looks very much like a starting line. Mary Queen of Scots – 'in my end is my beginning' – always misunderstood the 100m. T. S. Eliot – 'in my beginning is my end' – was clearly more attuned to the eternal verity of the event: if you want to win, you need a good start.

Armin Hary, the German who won the 1960 Olympic 100m title, was renowned as a sprinter who would occasionally get away to 'a flyer'. This was before electronic timing was introduced in 1977. In the year he won his Olympic title, Hary had to rerun a race in which he set a world record of 10.00 seconds after being accused of beating the gun. He won the second race in the same time. In the final, Hary beat the gun and was penalised. Under the rules of the time, any runner getting off to a second false start would be disqualified, so Hary had no more leeway. But he got a perfect start second time around before winning with an Olympic record of 10.2 seconds.

Some time afterwards Hary explained how he legally manipulated his starts through what he described as a 'trick' – effectively a mind game involving the official in charge of the start. When the starter called 'set', Hary would make sure he was the last to rise to the set position, anticipating that the starter would fire the gun as soon as he had completed the movement. He would therefore pause for a fraction before setting off in expectation of the starting pistol. This was, to be sure, a case of being smart to gain an advantage – using knowledge of an official's likely mindset. Is it cheating? His opponents might have felt that was a debatable point.

Usain Bolt – when mind games go wrong

By the time another Olympic 100m champion, Usain Bolt, went to his blocks in the 2011 World Championship final, the rules had changed so that no false starts were allowed. So when Bolt, the defending champion and world record-holder, found himself disqualified for moving too quickly at the start, it caused a commotion that rumbled out from the host city of Daegu in South Korea and all around the sporting world.

It seemed to many observers that a minor twitch from the runner in the next lane, Bolt's twenty-one-year-old training partner Yohan Blake, might have set the champion off. After Blake won the gold in his senior partner's absence, Bolt denied that he had been affected in this way. But you still had to wonder.

Just possibly, Bolt may have been the victim of a little mind game here. And just possibly his vulnerability at that moment was the consequence of mind games he himself had been playing in effective collaboration with a stadium and a world full of spectators.

In the space of the previous three years the six-foot five-inch phenomenon from Trelawny, Jamaica had done terrible things to the minds of his opponents, playing to the gallery and thereby diminishing confidence among his would-be rivals.

Bolt's adoption of the 'Lightning Bolt' stance he introduced at the 2008 Beijing Games – forefinger of the left arm extended into the air while the other arm is cocked back as if drawing the string of a bow – has become his trademark. But there are two strings to this bow. The performance is partly commercial, and partly inimical to his rivals' psyches.

As Bolt prepared to defend his 100m title in Daegu the crowd seemed to be getting even more of a performance than usual. What has made this amusing, rather than grating, over the years is the fact that Bolt's clowning has a natural charm, as opposed to some of the strenuous efforts employed by others at 100m start lines down the years to gain a mental edge over their opponents.

Former world and Olympic champion Maurice Greene would growl and bully, cock of the walk. On one occasion, as he beat his rival Tim Montgomery to the line at the US Championships, he shouted across to him: 'This is for real!' His US teammate Jon Drummond used to jape around. Another of the US sprinters of the 1990s, Dennis Mitchell, would stomp up and down near his blocks, shouting and roaring to himself and all around him.

By contrast, Britain's 1992 Olympic champion Linford Christie decided that, when it came to the stadium, less was more. He would stand at the start line, staring silently and intently down his lane, like an Easter Island statue amid hyperactive tourists. Different mind games, employed to the same effect – to unnerve rivals.

The effect of Bolt's antics on his fellow sprinters as he engages with the watching world is varied. But it has its effect on most as they seek to eradicate the impact by developing strategies of their own. Some affect disdain. Others seem to feel compelled to bring a little of Bolt into their own pre-race demeanour. Even Bolt's friend and teammate Asafa Powell, quietly funny but never showy, has begun to exhibit some comedy moves before races, complete with winks and smiles.

Such pre-race activity by Bolt says one clear thing to his competitors: 'I am the star. You are the bit-part players.' But Bolt's demeanour in the minute or so before the 2011 World Championship 100m final went significantly beyond anything he had ever done before. Standing in front of his blocks with the camera on him, having played to the crowd by smoothing his hair and admiring his visage on the big screen, he then pointed a finger to his right and then to his left, shaking his head on each occasion, before pointing both fingers down his lane and nodding his head with a grin.

The crowd in the Daegu stadium loved it. As the man who had recently been assessed as the most marketable sportsman on the planet – move over LeBron James – Bolt was bringing off yet another piece of mass communication without the need for words. However, to some observers, this bordered on insulting behaviour to his fellow runners, not least the man to whom one of those wagging fingers was most immediately pointing: Blake.

The fact that Bolt then, calamitously, earned himself disqualification through a false start might almost have been seen as the nemesis that Greeks believed followed hubris. As the ex-champ wandered, distracted, around the infield, he seemed not to know what to do with himself. It was a stunning example of a mind game backfiring, transforming him in an instant from Man About To Win into Man In Hyperactive Torment.

To understand how Bolt reached this point you have to go back to the Olympic Games of 2008, where the twenty-one-year-old effectively announced himself as a sporting superstar. Many minds were messed with at those Beijing Games – and much of the mental damage was down to this very tall sprinter. When the bus set off from the Olympic Village carrying the sprinters due to take part in that evening's 100m semi-finals at the Bird's Nest stadium, Bolt was among them. Previously known as a 200m specialist, a couple of months earlier he had run a 100m world record of 9.72 seconds on a rainswept evening in New York in what was only his fifth serious race at the shorter distance.

That event in itself would have been enough to leave the psyche of even his most serious challenger quivering on the edge of reason. But Bolt had more in store on this day as he asked the driver to stop off at the obligatory McDonald's restaurant within the compound and proceeded to order a cheeseburger and fries, which he consumed with relish in front of his fellow sprinters as the bus made its way towards the stadium.

Such wanton disregard of all accepted nutritional behaviour on the eve of competition was enough to mess with the minds of all those who witnessed it, sipping on their isotonic drinks or perhaps allowing themselves the luxury of an energy bar. Bolt won his semi-final with what appeared to be a jog. It was like watching someone in a slow bicycle race.

He went on to win the Olympic final in what was, from any opponent's point of view, the most demoralising fashion imaginable. Not only did he decelerate from thirty yards out – nobody consciously decelerates in world or Olympic 100m finals, but he did – the lanky Jamaican also found the time to beat his hand across his chest and skip into the air as he crossed the line. In a world record time of 9.69 seconds. As one observer remarked at the time: 'What could he have run if he'd tried?'

A year later Bolt demonstrated the answer to that question as he lowered the record to 9.58 seconds at the IAAF World Championships, concentrating throughout. But his Beijing breakthrough was a shattering blow, mentally, to every one of his opponents. Now, however, in Daegu, it was Bolt who appeared in danger of being shattered after messing up his mind game.

It took someone of Bolt's charisma to manoeuvre successfully away from that high-profile nightmare. By winning the subsequent 200m in fine style, and capping the Championships by bringing home the baton for the Jamaican relay team in a world record, Bolt offered the best possible response.

There was no doubt that the charm which allows him to communicate so easily with an adoring public also worked in his favour in the aftermath of his 100m debacle, insulating him from some of the harsher judgements that might have been made. Bolt is in some ways a successor to Ali, in that his riffs and games appear to spring quite naturally from him. People love this, and will forgive much from those who offer it. While George Best's transgressions were of a totally different nature to Bolt's momentary misjudgement, he enjoyed the same extra leeway through a combination of the same qualities.

Bolt successfully plastered over his faux pas. It was readily forgiven, but could it ever be forgotten, not least by Bolt himself? Who knew how corrosive the memory might prove to his ambitions, particularly as Blake then finished the season so full of confidence that he ran the second fastest ever 200m – beaten only by Bolt's world record of 19.19 seconds – and spoke in eager terms about challenging his mentor in the forthcoming Olympic year. Beware the Curse of the Inverted Mind Game… And yet Bolt prevailed again at the London Games, winning three more golds for his collection. The pre-race antics were noticeably toned down, however.

'Do you think you can beat me today?'

On occasion, competitive sportsmen and women will attempt manoeuvres which play even more directly upon the psyche of their opponents. You could call it bullying. Sometimes it works. Before the 1993 World Athletics Championships in Stuttgart, Linford Christie, who had won the Olympic 100m title in Barcelona the previous year, was up against two Americans who were determined to show that, while he may have been an Olympic champion, he wasn't the world's No.1 sprinter.

Andre Cason was a small, squat athlete who had previously excelled at the 60m event, run indoors, but his 100m times heading into Stuttgart were swifter than those of Christie. The second American had already established himself as a legendary figure within the sport, having equalled the achievement of his compatriot Jesse Owens by winning four Olympic titles in a single Games in 1984. He was Carl Lewis. Although he had failed to do well enough in the US Olympic trials to earn an individual 100m place in the Barcelona Olympics, Lewis had anchored the victorious American relay team. One year on he was keen to suggest that Christie's win in Barcelona had had much to do with the fact that he had not contested the race.

Christie won in Stuttgart, stopping the clock at 9.87 seconds. It was the best time of his life. But the powerful Briton had put in a little groundwork before he got out on to the track. At the warm-up arena, Christie had made a point of rolling his running vest down so that his opponents were fully aware of a torso that had been honed to intimidating proportions.

Then the west Londoner moved things on a stage by simply taking over the lane in which Cason, who was perhaps five foot seven inches on tiptoes, was operating. Simple and effective. The American's cool was compromised, his mojo messed up. He ran disappointingly.

An athlete on the eve of competition is a mentally fragile creature, and in track and field events these creatures are rounded up into a little pen called a warm-up room before competition, where they must co-exist for several minutes before being allowed to scamper off to the business part of the arena. During this time much mental damage can be inflicted or suffered. Some athletes give themselves away by talking too much. Others offer clear evidence of their inner tension with a stiff unwillingness to engage in any way with their imminent opponents. As a rule, everyone aims strenuously for relaxation. But composure can be up and out of the blocks in a moment, given the required stimulus.

Before the 1990 Commonwealth Games 400m final, Darren Clark decided on some pre-race tactics. The Australian had risen swiftly through the international ranks four years earlier, and had been favourite to take the Commonwealth title at Edinburgh in 1986, only to find himself gazumped by another bright young thing: England's rugby-player-turned-runner Roger Black, whose victory in Scotland came a year after he had secured the European junior title.

By the time of the Auckland Games, Clark had proven himself as a stayer, with fourth place at the Olympics in an area record of 44.38 seconds. But he was still after a big gold medal. And so, in the minutes before the field took to the track, he went round to every opponent in turn, stared them straight in the eye, and asked them the same question: 'Do you think you can beat me today?' As it turned out, none of them could. Or at least, none of them did. Which may not have been the same thing.

The mental vulnerability of elite athletes was further demonstrated during the 2011 World Championships in Daegu when, purely – surely? – by chance, a sequence of competitors featured on the front cover of each day's official programme came to grief.

The first day's subject, Australia's world and Olympic pole vault champion Steve Hooker, failed to register a height in qualifying. On day two the featured athlete was Usain Bolt: disqualified from the 100m final. Day three saw Cuban high hurdler Dayron Robles on the cover – he was disqualified for obstruction after apparently winning gold. The following day's victim was world pole vault record-holder Yelena Isinbayeva, who failed to get onto the medal podium.

By this time athletes were running scared. Of course it was all just coincidence. What else could it really be? But the power of the superstitious mind was made evident as several agents contacted the administrator's office to insist that their athletes should not be featured. Agents resisting publicity for their clients at a World Championships – you don't hear of that too often. It was not a deliberate mind game, but minds were clearly being affected.

Eventually the sequence of woe in the stadium was broken by Hooker's compatriot Sally Pearson, who won gold in nigh-on perfect fashion in the 100m hurdles before brandishing her image on the front cover of a programme which had been thrown on to the track along with the obligatory national flag. It didn't quite match winning a world title, but such was her capering glee that beating the hoodoo appeared to have come a close second.

Not trying too hard, are you?

Steve Cram, Britain's former 1500m and mile world record-holder, remembers how some of his competitors tended to try a bit too hard before races – even John Walker, New Zealand's 1976 Olympic 1500m champion and former mile world record-holder. It was a mental thing. 'You could never shut John up,' he said. 'I think runners like John couldn't help but tell you about the sessions they had done recently. But I used to be immune to all that. To some extent, I think it was a process which was designed to build up their own confidence rather than to worry their rivals.

'And very often before a championship you will get runners coming together and saying, "So and so's done this time, so and so's done that time." But all the talk very rarely got translated into results on the track.'

Steve Backley, the former British javelin thrower who won Olympic and world silver as well as European and Commonwealth titles, tends to agree with his old international colleague. 'You do see athletes who talk themselves out of success,' he said. 'They end up putting too much pressure on themselves with predictions, and then find they can't live up to it.'

Backley also recalls opponents trying ever so hard to undermine his equilibrium before events. 'Someone would only be able to manipulate what I thought and felt if I let them, and I would never give someone that ability,' he said. 'Medals are won and lost at the warm-up track. You will find athletes who look fantastic when they warm up, but when they get inside the stadium they can't translate it. They've left their best performances at the warm-up facility. Sometimes during javelin warm-up throwers try to lure you into a competition. Once or twice I've found myself getting dragged into it, but then I stopped myself. But that's the sort of thing which can see you draining your energy levels before you get to the real thing.'

The Psyching of Ryan Brathwaite

They say that laughter is often the best cure. But that might not have been the case for the 2009 world 110m champion Ryan Brathwaite when he raced in the 2010 Samsung Diamond League meeting in Shanghai. Speaking at a press conference the day before the meeting, the quietly spoken young man from Barbados explained that he was trying to recover from cutting his knee in a recent fall, adding: 'I'm just going through a little depression.'

His glum demeanour prompted a little ripple of amusement among the other athletes on the stand. Asked to say a little more about his little depression, Brathwaite looked just a little uncomfortable. 'Obviously it's just because I had a bad fall,' he said, as the other athletes tried to suppress laughter. 'And it just takes my mind off running faster, but now I'm back to how I was last year, so there's going to be some good showdowns this weekend.'

So there he was, already on the mend. And by the time he had been asked a question about the forthcoming competition by Shanghai TV he was back on top of the world. 'I'm not depressed any more, I'm ready to go,' he insisted.

But Brathwaite's secret torment had obviously registered with his fellow athletes. Talking about their forthcoming race, Brathwaite's high hurdles rival David Oliver mused: 'You've got ten barriers you've got to get over, and you could fall or something, and, you know, fall like, into a depression. But if you don't get it done this time you've got plenty of other races to get it done, so it's all right.'

Norway's Olympic javelin champion Andreas Thorkildsen too seemed to be mindful of Brathwaite's plight when he discussed how travelling to Diamond League meetings outside Europe presented a lot of different challenges: 'Travel and jet lag. Um, depression and all that stuff.' By now,

Brathwaite was laughing along with his fellow athletes. But you had to wonder if all the hilarity at his expense had affected him when he failed to finish his race the next day… or indeed if his state of mind had significantly altered by the time of the following year's World Championships, where he relinquished his title with a whimper rather than a bang, failing to qualify through the rounds. In retrospect, witnessing The Psyching of Ryan Brathwaite seemed less funny than it appeared at the time.

Crossing the borderline at Brookline

While Brathwaite's trials and tribulations passed largely unnoticed, the mind games which took place during the 33rd Ryder Cup match in 1999, played at the Brookline Country Club in Massachusetts, evoked a huge public reaction – and in particular the behaviour of many in the US camp at the crucial point of the competition.

The US team felt they had a good chance of winning the biennial tournament for the first time since 1993, and many present at the course went beyond what most golf followers felt was acceptable in terms of support during a closely fought contest. Sam Torrance, of the European team, described the behaviour in the galleries during play as 'disgusting', while his team captain, Mark James, later compared the atmosphere to being in a 'bear pit'.

However, it was the manner in which the home team sealed an unlikely victory that was to earn a dishonourable place in the game's history. Having embarked upon the final day 10–6 down, they recovered to the point where Justin Leonard, playing in his final-day singles match against José María Olazábal, had the opportunity to win the Cup for them by either beating his opponent or halving the match.

The two men were level at the seventeenth green, but the odds seemed in Olazábal's favour as his ball was only about twenty-five feet from the hole, whereas the American's had drifted to almost twice that distance away. Leonard putted first, however, and when the ball travelled and travelled all the way into the hole there was an uproar of jubilation all around the green, with US players and their wives cavorting in premature triumph.

What seemed to have been forgotten in all this was that Olazábal had yet to attempt a putt which, had it gone in, would have halved the hole and at least given him an opportunity to try and deny Leonard and the host team by winning the eighteenth. It was hardly surprising, however, that the bedlam around him should affect the Spaniard's mental equanimity, try as he might to remain aloof. His putt missed, Leonard won the hole, the US took the Cup. But at what cost?

There was huge criticism of the US behaviour in the European media, and in particular for their patent failure to attend to the spirit of the game, even if no one – except perhaps a TV cameraman intent on capturing the scenes of premature celebration – had crossed the line of Olazábal's putt. Nevertheless, after the competition was over a number of the US team felt moved to apologise for their behaviour.

Football – very superstitious

Football is riddled with superstition. Gary Lineker would never shoot at goal during the warm-up, for instance, as he didn't want to waste any potentially goal-scoring efforts. John Terry, the Chelsea captain, claims to have 'about fifty' superstitions, which include using the same urinal at Stamford Bridge, taking the same seat on the team bus, and listening to the same CD before every game (it's by Usher; could be worse). More bizarrely, Liverpool's goalkeeper Pepe Reina has revealed that before each game he has to fill up his car with petrol he doesn't need.

So what? These aren't mind games, are they? Well, not exactly. But they indicate the curiously delicate cast of mind belonging to some of our robust national footballing figures. Which, you would argue, makes them vulnerable to mind games. Take the case of West Ham and England's incomparable Bobby Moore, a byword for poise and mental strength. This was the man who, after captaining England to the 1966 World Cup, had the presence of mind to wipe his hands before accepting the Jules Rimet trophy from the Queen. But Moore had his own little quirk of being the last to put on his shorts before the team left the dressing room. And occasionally, purely in the cause of mischief, Moore's weak mental link was played upon by his West Ham and England colleague Martin Peters, who would remove his own shorts at the last minute, causing Moore to drop his shorts. And so it went on. As kick-off loomed, it was a question of who would fall short of nerve.

Footballers' minds – they can be strange and wobbly things. Which means other footballers can work on them. In a column for the *Guardian* newspaper towards the end of 2011, The Secret Footballer observed that one of his former colleagues liked to use the pre-game handshakes which have become a ritual before Premier League matches to remind particular opponents that they had better not take him on if they wanted to avoid a nasty injury. All done in a spirit of fun, no doubt. Or not, as the case may be.

Tommy Gemmell, Celtic's left back during their glorious years of the late 1960s and early 1970s, revealed after his playing days how such bullying on behalf of defenders could be counteracted. Gemmell recalled how, every time Celtic's small and endlessly tricky winger Jimmy Johnstone was hacked down, the instruction from Celtic's wily manager Jock Stein was to play the free kick swiftly to Johnstone again so he could run at the offender, who would have in mind that another foul challenge could see him booked or dismissed. It was a tactic of playing on the mind, turning the weapon round on the aggressor, and has been widely used since those days.

More and more frequently nowadays – or so it seems – attempts are made to influence the minds of officials rather than opponents. Pressurising referees, often in groups, has become an unpleasant feature of football in recent years, and it is something for which some teams have earned an unfortunate reputation.

Towards the end of the 2010–11 season, Arsenal's young England midfielder Jack Wilshere suggested that his team needed to emulate their old rivals Manchester United in this respect. 'You just see other teams do it and you think, "We need to do it as well." Man United are the best at it. They get round the referee.'

Such a comment might well have generated a good deal of hollow laughter around Old Trafford, however, given some of Arsenal's excesses in this respect during the days when Wilshere was just a talented schoolboy with a dream. The fact is, orchestrated attempts to influence the mind and judgement of match officials are part of football all over the world.

Hit them with the stick, then hit them with the carrot

As indeed are attempts by managers to influence officials – and it could be argued that nobody does this as well as United's manager Alex Ferguson. Over the years Ferguson has used both carrot and stick on referees. After hitting them with a stick, he has hit them with a carrot.

Ferguson's comments about referee Martin Atkinson's handling of United's league match at Chelsea on 1 March 2011 – where the home side won 2–1 through an eightieth-minute penalty after the visitors' central defender Nemanja Vidic was sent off – earned him a five-match ban from the touchline and a £30,000 fine from the Football Association.

The severity of the punishment had something to do with the fact that it was not the first incident of this kind for which the Scot had been called to account. In October 2009 he had incurred a two-match suspended touchline ban after claiming that Alan Wiley was 'unfit' to referee, and that was activated along with an additional sanction.

Likewise, the fine followed an escalatingly large series of similar punishments. Ferguson chose not to appeal, but was clearly very angry about the decision. 'It's disappointing,' he said. 'It is the only industry where you can't tell the truth. It is in the past and it is not worth it.' Ferguson had told the official Manchester United channel, MUTV, after the match: 'We need a fair referee and a strong referee and we didn't get one.' He added that he had 'feared the worst' when he heard that Atkinson would be refereeing the match. (That said, Ferguson's mind games have on occasions been at the other end of the scale compared to his comments on Atkinson. It has been remarked upon that he has, from time to time, conspicuously praised referees who will soon be officiating in matches against his team. He can play hardball. He can play softball.)

Five days after that match at Chelsea, when United were due to play Liverpool at Anfield, Liverpool's then current and former managers, Kenny Dalglish and Rafa Benitez respectively, both made pointed comments about the need for the authorities to act strongly against managers who persistently criticised referees, particularly in light of the FA's recently established Respect campaign, designed, as it implies, to improve levels of respect within the game for match officials.

'I was made aware of the Respect campaign for referees when I came back to management,' said Dalglish. 'It's something we've adhered to. Referees make mistakes, it is difficult for them not to. But we make mistakes as well. If we adhere to the campaign, though, I just hope we are not the ones to suffer. Sometimes you think the ones who shout loudest get the more beneficial decisions and that would be totally unfair.' Benitez added: 'The people who are doing the right things have to have some benefit. And to the people who are not doing this, someone has to say: "Enough is enough."'

But six months later Dalglish's fears about his club being the ones to suffer appeared to be confirmed. Apparently deciding that he needed to fight fire with fire as far as defending his club's interest was concerned, he said in the wake of a 1–0 defeat at Stoke – in which he felt his team had been denied a valid penalty and that the decisive penalty given against them had not been valid – that he would be talking to his club's owners about future strategy over how to deal with refereeing issues.

The inference was that he was considering more pro-active tactics in talking about referees to the media – doing something more akin to what Ferguson has done, in fact. 'The first four games have had contentious decisions in them and every one has gone against us,' Dalglish said. 'We would like to be respectful to referees but more important is having respect for my football club. If I feel the club is suffering in any shape or form I will need to go the same route other people go and see if we can gain some benefit from that… If we continually get battered by things outside of our control we are not going to get much chance.' If managers were referees, Dalglish had just waved a yellow card.

Former Premier League referee Graham Poll speculated in September 2011 on the prevailing mindset of referees given the amount of criticism they risk in giving penalties against the 'big' teams. He said that, although he didn't believe any referee went out to give soft penalties against small teams, 'they only give stone wall penalties against the biggest ones'. Poll added: 'One of the reasons for this is that they know the fallout, from the managers and the media, if they give a soft penalty against one of the big teams, and the subconscious mind kicks in to afford referees a level of protection, quite naturally.'

Other deep instincts governing the behaviour of referees lay them open to mental manipulation by opportunistic team tactics. It has long been a given in footballing circles that if you are going to kick an opponent, then the earlier the better. Referees, understandably, are loathe to upset the parity of eleven men versus eleven at such an early stage of what is, after all, meant to be an entertainment and diversion for those who have paid to watch it, either via the turnstiles or via the direct debit.

Picking the weak links

'Let him know you're there early on' has been the broad instruction offered to generations of the game's more abrasive characters. Celtic's Tommy Gemmell offered an assessment of the operation which is typical of the calculations made by many defenders down the years.

Gemmell was never known as a clogger. His manager, Jock Stein, would certainly never have described him as the finest left back in the world had he not had a combination of strength, speed and skill. But he was a tough lad from Lanarkshire and well capable of applying a little well-timed muscle.

As he recalled, Stein would often pick out members of opposing teams and tell him, 'If you get in about him he will disappear from the game.' Gemmell recollected how one of his more skilful opponents could be annulled – 'I knew that, if I hit him hard and early, he would give me a quiet afternoon.' Certain wingers were made of sterner stuff, however, such as the Rangers pair of Willie Henderson and Willie Johnston. 'George Best, too,' Gemmell added. 'You couldn't intimidate him.'

Knowledge of your opponent's mental weakness means you can split his composure apart with the ease of an axe splitting a log. It's all about applying force at the right angle.

As well as exerting force on referees, Alex Ferguson has been known to wreak mayhem within the heads of rival managers, most notably over the years Arsène Wenger, whose Arsenal side were his team's main challengers before Chelsea got rich. In 2005 it got to the point where Wenger hissed: 'I will never answer to any provocation from him any more. He doesn't interest me.' But within a year Wenger admitted: 'Our mental duels keep me awake.'

The target of Ferguson's most effective action against another manager was Kevin Keegan, when the latter's exuberant Newcastle United team were seriously challenging United for the Premier League title in the final stages of the 1995–6 season.

Newcastle had held a ten-point lead coming into 1996, but by the time of their visit to Leeds United on 30 April they were in second place. On the eve of the match Ferguson had suggested that most teams, and particularly Leeds, tried harder against his team than against others.

Leeds had beaten United 3–1 at Elland Road on Christmas Eve, and had given them a real run for their money in the return on 17 April before losing 1–0 in a match that came just twelve days before their home game against Newcastle. As Ferguson said afterwards, it had been a comment deliberately aimed at safeguarding his team's interest by inviting the Leeds players to prove him wrong against Newcastle.

Leeds played hard, but Newcastle still managed to earn a 1–0 win which maintained their title hopes with two matches remaining. However, an agitated Keegan lost control of his emotions in a live interview with Sky TV, as it was put to him that what Ferguson had done was 'part and parcel of the psychological battle'.

Wagging his finger at the camera, giant earphones clamped over his already greying hair, Keegan responded with an extraordinary, and only partly coherent, outburst: 'No! That's, when you do that with footballers like he said about Leeds... I'm, I've kept really quiet, but I'll tell ya something: he went down in my estimation when he said that. We have not resorted to that. But I'll tell ya – you can tell him now, he'll be watching it – we're still fighting for this title, and he's got to go to Middlesbrough and get something, and, and I'll tell you honestly, I will love it if we beat them – LOVE IT!... It really has got to me... but the battle is still on, and Man Utd have not won this yet...'

But Newcastle only managed to draw their final two games, while Manchester United did get something at Middlesbrough in their last match – a 3–0 win, and the title. It appeared that Alex Ferguson got a result all round. Did Keegan really get hold of the wrong end of the stick? Or did wily Ferguson know that this most formidable of players and most strangely brittle of managers would do just that?

Cristiano Ronaldo 1, Wayne Rooney 0

Knowing how to destabilise an opponent to the point where they self-destruct is a fine art. It appeared to be demonstrated to good effect in the 2006 World Cup quarter-final between England and Portugal – eventually won by the latter team on a penalty shoot-out – when Wayne Rooney responded to being hounded and hassled by two Portuguese players in midfield, with Ricardo Carvalho being particularly zealous. As the defender ended up entangled in the Englishman's legs, Rooney appeared to put his foot down directly into the Portuguese player's groin, although he maintained there had been no intent.

Immediately several Portuguese players raced to the referee, who was standing right next to the incident, and foremost among them was Rooney's Manchester United colleague Cristiano Ronaldo, who appeared to be appealing very urgently to Mr Horacio Elizondo for something or other.

Rooney twice tried to push Ronaldo away from the referee before being moved aside in the general melee. Ronaldo continued to talk animatedly to the referee and, once Rooney had been shown the red card, was seen on a TV close-up winking to his bench.

Of course, the PR machines got busy after the match, with Rooney insisting he bore no grudge against his good friend Ronaldo, who insisted in turn that he had not tried to get his good friend Rooney sent off, and the referee insisted he had had no hesitation in sending Rooney off for violent conduct, although he did miss the opportunity to say what a good friend he was of either player.

It looked as if the Portuguese were well aware of Rooney's short fuse, and it was a legitimate tactic to test it. It also looked as if Ronaldo had been making the case for punishment. Certainly Rooney's England teammate Steven Gerrard, notwithstanding his club allegiance to United's bête noire, Liverpool, thought so judging by his post-match comment. 'If it was one of my teammates I'd be absolutely disgusted with him because there's no need for that,' Gerrard said. 'I've seen Ronaldo going over giving the red card and I think he's bang out of order.'

What stuck in the throat of many, however, was not so much Rooney's rashness but Ronaldo's calculation, a perception that cohered around that wink the Portuguese player gave to his bench. For most English fans that confirmed a cynical job well done.

Mind games of a more humorous but equally effective kind were played by Liverpool's eccentric goalkeeper Bruce Grobbelaar, during the penalty shoot-out between his side and AS Roma to decide the winner of the 1984 European Cup in a final being played, as fortune had it, at Roma's home ground of the Stadio Olimpico.

As Roma's Italian international Bruno Conti prepared to take his kick, Grobbelaar marched, smiling, towards the cameras trained upon him from behind the net, which he proceeded to bite with a crazed expression, as if eating strands of spaghetti. Conti sent his effort over the bar.

The keeper then produced another moment of slapstick before Francesco Graziani took his kick, repeatedly wobbling his legs as if shaking in terror. If you wanted to maintain a theme, you could have described them as waving around like two strands of spaghetti. But anyway. It was a highly pressurised situation for the Italians, and maybe they found the weight of home expectation too great. But maybe they were also discomposed by the loony between the posts. Whatever the case, Graziani missed and Liverpool went on to win the shoot-out 4–2. Job done.

Taking the mickey out of Rafa Nadal: worth a try

Knowing your audience is a powerful weapon for the sporting protagonist wishing to apply mental pressure to an opponent, and it can have correspondingly profound effects. Tennis, with its fluctuating individual dramas played out in front of closely packed spectators, lends itself particularly well to this kind of interaction.

Let's examine a couple of instances where players attempted to use the audience – to rope us in – as a potent weapon against their opponent's mental equilibrium. Robin Söderling of Sweden is a fine player and a massively determined and intelligent competitor, as he demonstrated in his third-round match at Wimbledon in 2007 when he took on the game's coming man in Rafael Nadal.

Nadal habitually comes to the tennis court in the manner of a boxer, but it was the twenty-one-year-old's credentials as a fighter that were thoroughly examined by an opponent who threw everything at him, including ridicule. Having missed a chance to land a knock-out blow on Söderling when he held match point at two sets up and 7–6 up in the tie break, Nadal, who had won his third consecutive French Open earlier in the year, saw the balance of this rain-interrupted contest tip away from him as Söderling went on to level the match at two sets all.

As Nadal stood ready to serve at the start of the final set, Söderling kept him waiting as he fished in his bag for another racket, and his belated arrival drew a comment from Nadal which sent a ripple of amusement through the crowd. At which point Söderling called for more time to prepare himself and went into a clear parody of the Spaniard's habit of picking at the back of his shorts between points. Smiling mischievously, the Swede seemed set on disturbing the concentration of the man who was seeking to match the achievements of Rod Laver and Björn Borg in winning French Open and Wimbledon titles in the same year.

By the time play was abandoned for the fourth and final time on a day of frequent downpours, Söderling's initiative had flagged, and the Spaniard went on to reach a final in which he was narrowly beaten by Roger Federer. But Söderling had given it a real go, and for those few moments in the final set had managed to access and direct the energy of the crowd against his opponent.

A capacity for mimicry, on and off court, is also a talent of Novak Djokovic, the Serbian player who established himself as the world No.1 in 2011, when he won the Australian, Wimbledon and US Open titles. It was the manner in which he progressed to the final of the latter grand slam tournament, however, which demonstrated his ability to harness the Power of Us against that most popular of players, Roger Federer.

Coincidentally, the two men had met at the same stage of the US Open the previous year, where the older player held two match points with Djokovic 5–4 down on his serve. But the young Serb saved both before rallying to win the final set 7–5.

One year on, however, Federer appeared to be on the brink of revenge. Although Djokovic had managed to level the match after falling two sets down, he found himself once again needing to save two match points as the Swiss player, 5–4 up in the fifth, served to reach 40–15. Dramatic action was required from Djokovic, and he supplied it with a spectacular gamble of a cross-court forehand return that sent the ball flashing back past the astounded Swiss.

It was at this point, however, that the mental action began to become relevant, as the exultant Serb, arms aloft, encouraged and milked the hysterical applause, raising his palms, and eyebrows, higher. It seemed clear that he was encouraging all present at the Arthur Ashe Stadium in Flushing Meadows to believe he could repeat recent history, that he could do it again. He was excited about that prospect, and he duly got the crowd excited. The message to his opponent was clear: 'I did it last year, now I am going to do it again. Look at these spectators. Listen to them. They believe it too.'

Djokovic's rousing efforts left Federer feeling… well, there's no way of knowing from his face what Federer is feeling, which has been part of his abiding mastery on the court as he has amassed his record total of grand slams. But the Swiss player's next action clearly indicated his mental state: he lost the game on a double fault, after which the Serb accelerated to victory and a final which he would win against Rafael Nadal, leaving him with three of the four 2011 grand slams. The new kidder in town.

It was a demonstration of fearsome mental power, almost cruel in its effectiveness. There was something almost gladiatorial about the whole thing, something of the new pack leader killing the old. Primitive stuff – and we, the spectators, were profoundly complicit.

How to handle a haka

Handling the pre-contest manoeuvres of a potential rival is one thing. But how do you handle a haka? The synchronised Maori dance which, with its chanting, chest-beating and eye-rolling, gets the All Blacks into a nice competitive mood before every match poses a major mental challenge to any team they are facing. The question is, what's the best reply?

New Zealand have been posing this problem for the opposition since 1894. Mostly they have performed the version of the haka known as the Ka Mate, but in 2005, before beating South Africa 31–27, they unveiled a controversial new model, the Kapa o Pango, which included what looked like a 'throat-slitting' action.

The haka, whichever version it may be, leaves the fifteen big, strong men in the opposition team standing the regulation fifteen metres away with the dilemma of reacting or not during the couple of minutes the 'dance' takes. In 1905, on the All Blacks' first tour of the UK, the Welsh crowd – led by its team – responded by singing the Welsh national anthem. Since then the Australian crowd have drowned it out with 'Waltzing Matilda'.

Other responses have been to ignore it – the Australians famously performed their warm-up drill during the haka in 1996 in Wellington. But this ploy didn't bring the Italians much success in a 2007 World Cup pool match, as it spurred the New Zealand team on to a 76–14 win.

Irish captain Willie Anderson and his team chose to edge towards the haka in 1989, with Anderson ending up inches away from his New Zealand counterpart Buck Shelford's face. Englishman Richard Cockerill performed a similar stunt in 1997, as did the French team in the 2007 World Cup quarter-finals. In the 2008 Rugby Autumn Tests, Wales responded by standing on the pitch, refusing to move until the All Blacks did. This resulted in the referee Jonathan Kaplan berating both teams for a full two minutes after the haka had ended.

It's a continuing mental puzzle, but the French team that played the All Blacks in the 2011 World Cup final at Auckland's Eden Park nearly found the final piece as they approached the hunched and chanting home team slowly from a distance, forming an arrowhead, then lined up to face their opposite numbers. The French lost with honour, 8–7, but it was at least honours even as far as the haka contest was concerned, as their ominous actions confirmed that they, too, had come prepared for battle.

The difficulty involved with combating the haka is that it is not just some pushy manoeuvre, but a sacred part of the Kiwi culture. So while teams strive to oppose it, they have to be careful not to insult it. Such a balance was not maintained, most Kiwis will insist, when the England team turned up to the 2011 Rugby World Cup in New Zealand with a controversial choice of change strip to their traditional all-white – that is, all-black. And Martin Johnson's men were sporting their all-black in the home of the All Blacks during their first pool match against Argentina.

This turn of events certainly stirred up feelings of anger, even outrage, in their host country, where, in this context, black is not even a colour in the spectrum, but a statement of national identity. Thus, for many in New Zealand, it was as if England had stepped up nose-to-nose with their haka warriors and stuck their tongues out at them.

Even New Zealand's prime minister, John Key, was drawn into the controversy, commenting: 'There's only one team that wears black with pride and that's the All Blacks.' Keith Quinn, the New Zealand rugby commentator, asked: 'Of all the colours in the rainbow, why would they choose the colour of the host nation? They are thumbing their noses at a New Zealand tradition. It's bizarre.'

There was also a school of thought in New Zealand that the move should be taken as a compliment to the home nation, on the basis of imitation being the sincerest form of flattery. And indeed there was a school of thought in England that this was disrespectful to the English tradition.

No disrespect would have been intended to either shirt from Johnson, England's manager and former captain, who had learned his rugby in New Zealand and played for their under-21 side and later wrote that he would have been 'honoured and proud' to have won the shirt of the full All Black side.

But then Johnson had not made the marketing decision about the colour of the shirt. That deal had been done by the Rugby Football Union, which insisted its New Zealand counterpart had 'no issues' with the choice. It was, nevertheless, a transparent breach of etiquette – no doubt designed as a kind of mind game. Anyone who knew the game would know it would upset the hosts. The question perhaps being asked was: would it upset the All Blacks enough to put them off their game?

To judge by results, the answer to that question was no. The All Blacks duly secured their second World Cup victory, and at the point in the tournament where England's daring dark arts were being employed, the eventual winners were doubtless more concerned about the rate at which their fly halves were dropping out of the action.

There were other more cynical observers who saw the whole controversy as being manufactured by the shirt sponsors on the basis that no publicity is bad publicity. On that hypothesis, let's not name them here.

Moral maze

'I need to do it. I can't do it. I have to do it.'
– Leonardo Piepoli

Honour among dopers

Athletes shouldn't dope. This we know. And if a national team strengthens itself by recruiting someone with no national connection, that's wrong. This, too, we know to be foul play. But sometimes the details can give us pause, can present us with judgements which are not clear and straightforward. Sometimes, in other words, we can find ourselves in a moral maze.

Let's take an example from cycling. When Floyd Landis was stripped of his 2006 Tour de France title for doping abuse, the moral position was clear. A bad thing had been done, and Landis, despite his protestations of innocence, was duly punished. But when, in 2010, Landis admitted his wrongdoing and named other riders whom he alleged were guilty of similar offences – in his words, to 'clear his conscience' – there was a huge backlash against him within the sport. The American was accused of being bitter, and of betraying fellow riders. In January 2011 he was unable to find another team to ride for, and called a halt to his career.

Landis might justly plead that he was victimised for speaking out on behalf of his sport. What's wrong with that? And yet the reaction of so many of his fellow riders, and many of the sport's observers and followers, gave evidence of another deep instinct operating – a sense of solidarity. Landis was regarded as 'shopping' his fellow cyclists. So was Landis disloyal? Or was he right to speak out? Not an easy question to answer.

A similar moral question was raised recently by the testimony of a less successful but still very talented cyclist, Leonardo Piepoli. *The Peloton*, a book of cycling portraits taken by the photographer Timm Kölln plus additional text, offers an illuminating insider's view on doping from this Italian rider, who won mountain stages on all three major Tours – France, Italy and Spain – but who was on the whole a *domestique* rather than a team leader throughout his career.

Piepoli tested positive for CERA, an advanced version of EPO, during what he had decided would be his last Tour de France, at the age of thirty-six, in 2008. He was one of the team riders supporting fellow Italian Riccardo Ricci, who also tested positive. Piepoli explains how, earlier in the year, he had had a punishing experience in the Giro d'Italia, crashing three times and fracturing two ribs before having to abandon the race on the seventeenth stage and taking three weeks off to recover.

Then, he recalls, he was asked to do the Tour (de France) 'to help Ricco', adding: 'He had ridden a great Giro and people regarded him as some new god of cycling. I knew it could be my last Tour so I said I'd go. I also knew that to be of any use I'd have to be in really good condition, so you know... that combination of things.

'Somebody I thought was a friend made it obvious that they could "help" me and then you're thinking about it all the time, day and night, day and night. "I need to do it, I can't do it, I have to do it." And I did it. The positive test changed my life. It changed Leonardo Piepoli the man... suddenly you're not in a position to decide for yourself any more. I made a mistake when I was thirty-six, too old to come back as a rider. I doped and that's that. I'm finished.'

Piepoli's testimony offers another take on doping in cycling. In his case, and perhaps in the case of many other talented riders who were never going to be champions, doping was part of surviving, and earning a living, in one of the most gruelling of sporting tests. Poignantly in his case, there was the overriding desire, as it were, for one final hurrah on the Tour of all tours. But his decision was clearly compounded by the desire not to let down his teammates and to maximise the impact of the star man, Ricci. It was, at least partly, about loyalty.

The team ethic – sticking with your mates through thick and thin, being greater than the sum of your individual parts – is intrinsic to so much of sport, as it is to so much of life. And yet how exactly does loyalty operate in sport? Even in the case of Piepoli, we see it is not a simple matter. How is he to be judged? He is disloyal to other non-doping riders in the sport he patently loves. But he is loyal to his star rider and his team.

Lance Armstrong's mighty fall from the saddle

In 2012 the unspoken code of silence which Landis had broken was smashed to pieces, releasing a torrent of evidence which precipitated one of the most serious doping accusations in the history of not just this sport, but sport itself. This resulted in Lance Armstrong, winner of a record seven Tour de France titles, being stripped of every one.

On 10 October a thousand-page report was released by the United States Anti-Doping Agency concluding that Armstrong's United States Postal Service (USPS) Pro Cycling Team 'ran the most sophisticated, professionalised and successful doping programme that sport has ever seen'. Travis Tygart, USADA's (US Anti-Doping Agency) chief executive, said in a statement that there was 'conclusive and undeniable proof' of a team-run doping conspiracy after hearing the evidence of eleven of the retired champion's former teammates. Armstrong, who had not been shown to have failed a doping test and who insisted he had not been involved in doping, nevertheless refused to contest the charges. Nor, after the international cycling body, the UCI, had confirmed the forfeit of his titles later in October, did he take up his right to appeal. In August Armstrong had announced he would not fight the doping charges filed against him by USADA, saying in a statement he was 'finished with this nonsense' and insisting he was innocent.

Tygart said the evidence amassed contained 'direct documentary evidence including financial payments, emails, scientific data and laboratory test results that further prove the use, possession and distribution of performance enhancing drugs by Lance Armstrong and confirm the disappointing truth about the deceptive activities of the USPS team, a team that received tens of millions of American taxpayer dollars in funding'. Tygart also claimed the team's doping conspiracy 'was professionally designed to groom and pressure athletes to use dangerous drugs, to evade detection, to ensure its secrecy and ultimately gain an unfair competitive advantage through superior doping practices'.

USADA confirmed that two other members of the USPS team, Dr Michele Ferrari and Dr Garcia del Moral, accused of helping Armstrong and other riders remain a step ahead of the doping testers, also received lifetime bans for their part in the doping conspiracy. Tygart added: 'We have heard from many athletes who have faced an unfair dilemma – dope, or don't compete at the highest levels of the sport. Many of them abandoned their dreams and left sport because they refused to endanger their health and participate in doping. That is a tragic choice no athlete should have to make.'

In ratifying the USADA conclusions, the UCI president Pat McQuaid – whose own position had been widely questioned in the press following the emergence of evidence in the case – declared, 'Lance Armstrong has no place in cycling… he deserves to be forgotten in cycling.' Which was true up to a point. It could just as well be argued, however, that Armstrong should never be forgotten in cycling.

Twenty-six people in total, Tygart said, gave sworn testimony. Among the former teammates who did so were Landis, Tyler Hamilton and George Hincapie. Tygart praised those riders involved in the 'doping conspiracy' for having the 'tremendous courage' to come forward and 'stop perpetuating the sporting fraud'. Which was true up to a point. But as Hamilton made clear in his subsequent book, *The Secret Race* – which won the William Hill Sports Book of the Year award for 2012 – the testimony was not exactly offered spontaneously.

In an interview with Sky Sports the day after his book prize win, Hamilton was asked, 'What made you take this decision to tell the truth?' To which the blunt answer was: 'I had a subpoena.' The man who had ridden alongside Armstrong in the US Postal team had an unavoidable appointment with a federal grand jury. It had taken an offer he couldn't refuse for him to break the cycling *omertà*. It emerged that the man behind this 'offer' was Jeff Novitzky, the former special agent for the Internal Revenue Service who had masterminded the investigation into the BALCO doping web in which so many athletes from track and field and baseball were implicated. In his book Hamilton wrote that Novitzky – whom some have compared to his legendary predecessor in the IRS, Eliot Ness – had driven a 'bulldozer' through the sport of cycling in his efforts to uncover evidence of doping.

Hincapie, a close friend of Armstrong's who was in the USPS team from 1997 to 2007, also made it clear in the aftermath of the USADA revelations that his experience had mirrored that of Hamilton: 'About two years ago, I was approached by US federal investigators, and more recently by USADA, and asked to tell of my personal experience in these matters. I would have been much more comfortable talking only about myself, but understood that I was obligated to tell the truth about everything I knew. So that is what I did.'

Although Hincapie said he had competed clean for the past six years, he added: 'Early in my professional career, it became clear to me that, given the widespread use of performance enhancing drugs by cyclists at the top of the profession, it was not possible to compete at the highest level without them. I deeply regret that choice and sincerely apologise to my family, teammates and fans. Quietly, and in the way I know best, I have been trying to rectify that decision.'

In January 2013, Armstrong admitted for the first time that he had used performance-enhancing drugs in his career, adding that when he heard that his friend and former colleague George Hincapie had added his testimony to the evidence against him, he felt the game was up.

The disgraced cyclist chose to make his confession in a televised interview with Oprah Winfrey recorded near his home in Austin, Texas. Armstrong may have chosen the setting, but he was unable to control the content of the interview as Winfrey jumped straight in with three hard questions, each eliciting the same measured response: 'Did you ever take banned substances to enhance cycling performance?' 'Yes.' 'Was one of those substances EPO?' 'Yes.' 'Did you use any other banned substances?' 'Yes.' Result, times three.

But Winfrey, in the pre-broadcast trailers to her show, had said that Armstrong 'did not come clean in the way I expected'. Perhaps that was a reference to a statement of his which followed this startling opening salvo: 'I looked up the definition of cheat,' Armstrong said. 'The definition of a cheat is to gain advantage on a rival or a foe. I don't view it that way. I viewed it as a level playing field.'

And there it was. The classic doper's defence. It might have been Ben Johnson speaking.

Earlier in the week, looking ahead to the broadcast of the Armstrong interview, Johnson had been interviewed by the *Toronto Star* for his thoughts on the matter. 'Confess it all, get it out of the way and move on,' Johnson advised Armstrong. 'People don't like liars – once you tell the truth you can move on.'

By the by, you had to wonder just how candid this advice was, coming as it did from a man who had only admitted his doping when called to account for himself under oath at the Canadian Government enquiry headed by Chief Justice Charles Dubin the year after his Seoul 'triumph'. And given also that, having confessed and served his ban, he subsequently incurred a life ban for further doping offences.

But it was Johnson's take on the overall moral position of the infraction in which he pre-figured that of the disgraced Texan with eerie exactitude.

'It's only cheating if you're the only one doing it,' said the fifty-one-year-old former sprinter, who had always insisted that cheating was rampant at the Seoul Games. 'I've been trying to say it for 24 years. Almost every professional athlete does something.'

Pressing Armstrong on the subject of his doping, Winfrey asked: 'Did it feel wrong?' Armstrong's reply: 'No. Scary.' 'Did you feel bad?' 'No. Even scarier.' 'Did you feel that you were cheating?' 'No. The scariest.'

Presumably Armstrong did not mean that, while it didn't feel wrong to be doping, it felt 'scary'. Presumably the scary element only exists now that he looks back upon his actions. It is a judgement meted out retrospectively. And what, then, is the scary thing? Again, presumably, the recognition of a state of mind in which morality is simply absent.

Plastic Brits?

Loyalty requires common cause, and one of the most basic of those is nationality. But in recent years that criterion has become increasingly hard to define. It sounds straightforward, but it isn't. Another subject for moral debate.

In 2011, amid ambitions to excel at the home Olympic Games looming up a year later in London, UK Athletics (UKA) introduced some competitors to its team who had lately competed for other nations – a circumstance which earned them criticism from some quarters of the media for being 'plastic Brits'.

The man charged with this offence against righteousness was Charles van Commenee, the Dutchman appointed as head coach of UKA in 2008. What prompted this particular outcry was the arrival of three new female athletes in the British ranks, two of whom – 400m runner Shana Cox and 100m hurdler Tiffany Porter – were born and raised in the United States. Cox gained a British passport through having British parents, Porter through having a British mother. Britain's team also gained long jumper Shara Proctor, born and raised on the Caribbean island of Anguilla, but gaining a British passport because Anguilla is a British overseas territory which, incidentally, has no Olympic affiliation.

What van Commenee was doing was quite legal and, as far as he was concerned, quite logical. As he stated plainly, the newcomers were better than any homegrown competitors in those events. It was not as if this had never happened before in the British athletics team. Only a year earlier Michael Bingham – born in Sylva, North Carolina and whose hometown of Winston-Salem gave the world the Krispy Kreme doughnut – had become part of the British team thanks to the fact that his father came from Nottingham.

At the 2011 World Championships in Daegu, thirty-nine-year-old Yamilé Aldama, born and raised in Cuba, competed for Britain in the triple jump having belatedly earned a passport through marriage to a Scotsman in 2001. Her plan to earn British citizenship in time to compete in the 2004 Athens Olympics failed to work, and – having been categorised as a defector by Cuba – Aldama became effectively stateless. In the end she took up Sudan's invitation to compete for them in Athens.

The *Daily Mail* headlined Aldama's triple representation as a 'farce'. And when Tiffany Porter broke Angie Thorp's fifteen-year-old British 100m hurdles record, the *Mail* reported Thorp as saying, 'When I heard who had broken it, I was absolutely distraught,' describing Porter as 'a plastic Brit who is using Team GB to fulfil her own Olympic ambitions'.

A year later Porter was placed at the centre of another feverish debate when, at a press conference ahead of the World Indoor Championships, she was challenged to sing the national anthem by a reporter. Many newspaper columns were subsequently written on the question of whether Britain should expect its sporting performers to know the words and tune of 'God Save the Queen'. And if Porter had, would that have proved she was British?

There is an uncertain swirl of response to these circumstances within Britain – it is similar to the kind of debate which took place when Swede Sven-Göran Eriksson became the first foreigner to take charge of the England football team. Eriksson's foreignness faded almost into the background when England enjoyed a superlative 5–1 win over their ancient rivals, Germany; but as the Eriksson momentum failed, usually around the quarter-final stage of any tournament worth winning, he became a foreigner once again.

There was a similarly ambivalent attitude to England's midfielder Owen Hargreaves, who earned his second cap in that 5–1 win and went on to become a part of the squad at the 2004 European Championships and the 2006 World Cup. Hargreaves had a Welsh mother and an English father. But he had been born and brought up in Canada and hence, regrettably, had a trace of a Canadian accent. Also, even more unfortunately, he spoke fluent German, having played much of his football in that country. The fact that he was one of the few England players to perform with merit at the 2006 finals helped his case, however, to the point where some of his more vociferous critics at least shut up.

For some English tennis followers, until the blessed appearance of Tim Henman in the late 1990s, there was the faintly disturbing prospect of having to embrace a man whom many regarded as being about as British as maple syrup – Greg Rusedski, born, like Hargreaves, in Canada.

In the absence of any Brit with a ghost of a chance of doing much at Wimbledon, Rusedski emerged on the scene in the mid-1990s, initially wearing a Union flag bandana – a quintessentially un-British way of affirming Britishness. One of the affable and able Rusedski's parents was English, thus offering him a clear right to represent Britain. Despite some scepticism, he was taken to the nation's bosom to the extent that in 1997, having reached that season's US Open final, where he lost to Australia's Pat Rafter, he was voted BBC Sports Personality of the Year.

Plastic Terry Butcher?

What is it, then, that determines 'acceptable' nationality within sport? Does the ingenuity occasionally employed to 'claim' a sportsman or woman constitute foul play? Let's think for a moment of one of the lasting images of English football: Terry Butcher, captain and central defender, leaving the pitch after helping England earn the goalless draw against Sweden in Stockholm that ensured qualification for the 1990 World Cup, his face, shirt, shorts and socks all showing evidence of blood that has poured from a bandaged head wound. Having had stitches inserted, Butcher had returned to the fray and made a conspicuous number of defensive headers. In times of despair – and there have been a few – England supporters have loved to recall this iconic devotion to the cause of the Three Lions. But Butcher, like Hargreaves, was not born in England. He was born in Singapore. So why the different treatment? Can it really come down to an accent? Or is it the fact that Hargreaves, until later in his career, did not play his football in Britain?

If that is to be regarded as a criterion, then David Hemery's 400m hurdles victory in a world record of 48.12 seconds at the 1968 Mexico Olympics should have been howled down back in Britain, as he had learned his running as a schoolboy and college student in the United States. Boo hiss? Well, not really. Hemery was voted BBC Sports Personality of the Year for 1968, and is now regarded as the quintessential English sportsman. Go figure – as he would never say himself. If someone is British enough to be given a passport, you have to ask, why should they not be regarded as British enough to represent a British sporting team?

Plastic Paddies?

Same goes for Ireland, who have recruited a fair few footballers in recent years who would not, how should we say, strike one immediately with their Irishness. This particular area on the sporting borderline was marshalled for many years by the redoubtable figure of Jack Charlton – a very English Englishman, born and bred in the coal-mining area of Ashington, Northumberland.

When he played in the centre of the Leeds United defence in the 1960s and 1970s, Charlton – six feet three inches of stubborn determination – made a habit of testing the rules of the game to their limits, and occasionally beyond, by standing right in front of opposing goalkeepers before corner kicks or free kicks were sent into the box. It was highly unpopular, and hugely effective. A lot like the team he played for, in fact.

As an international manager with Ireland it was no surprise that Charlton should test the flexibility of other rules in the pursuit of results. But now his area of operation was in the ingenious poaching of players who might not appear Irish but were eligible to play through a series of criteria such as family background or place of birth. Or, as some more cynical observers might observe, through other obviously Irish links such as having a green jumper or liking a drop of Guinness. The same observers who came up with the un-PC label 'Plastic Paddies'.

Let's get one thing straight. Charlton, and Ireland, did nothing illegal in building a team that would excel at European and world level for a decade. All Charlton did was push the rule to its logical limit, the rule being a particularly generous construct of the world football governing body. FIFA's Article 18 states that: 'any person who is a naturalised citizen of a country by virtue of that country's laws shall be eligible to play for a national or representative team of that country'.

What came to be known as the 'granny rule' was of particular benefit to Ireland for two reasons. Firstly, the significant migration which had occurred over the years to the United States and mainland Britain. And secondly, the Irish citizenship rules – perhaps framed by a country with a small population to maximise the possibility of maintaining Irish links – which state that no matter where a person is born, anyone whose parent or grandparent is an Irish citizen is entitled to Irish citizenship.

Although he was the manager credited with using this opportunity to its greatest effect, Charlton was not the first Irish manager to exploit the ruling. Manchester United's full back Shay Brennan, whose parents had emigrated to England from County Carlow, was the first 'second generation' player to turn out for Ireland, earning the first of what would be nineteen caps in 1965.

Irish player-manager Johnny Giles also utilised the option in the 1970s, recruiting Liverpool's world-class central defender Mark Lawrenson by dint of the fact that Lawrenson's mother was from Waterford. It was while Giles was in charge that the last 'all-Irish' Ireland team played – in 1975.

During the Charlton years, however, the granny rulers ruled. And after initial resentments, from both inside and outside the camp, the Irish success meant everything was beautiful. They reached the quarter-finals of the 1990 World Cup in Italy, during which they were the only team to have an audience with Pope John Paul II, and the knockout round at the 1994 World Cup, where they beat Italy in their first match.

'Scousers' John Aldridge and Ray Houghton made their debuts in Charlton's first match in charge, and the list of Anglo-Irish players grew from there. Sometimes, however, suspicions that links had become overly tenuous proved to be correct. In his 1996 autobiography Tony Cascarino, who spent many stirring years as Ireland's central forward thanks to an Irish connection through his grandmother, revealed that he was adopted, and thus had no known blood links with an Irish heritage.

But then the previous manager to Charlton, Eoin Hand, had played forward Michael Robinson, who only became eligible because his mother, who was third generation Irish, had taken up Irish citizenship to enable the international career of her son.

Charlton was characteristically blunt about the need to trawl England and Scotland for top players. 'Now, if you don't want me to do that,' he told the Irish media, 'tell me, and I'll fucking concentrate on the League of Ireland and we'll win nothing. But give me the freedom to produce results and I'll produce results.'

Why Graeme Smith doesn't like Kevin Pietersen

Athletics and football are far from being the only sports where these issues have been raised. South Africa's cricket captain Graeme Smith, for instance, has clearly never forgiven his former teammate Kevin Pietersen – who was born and raised in South Africa but has an English mother – for electing to play for his adopted country of England. 'I'm patriotic about my country. And that's why I don't like Kevin Pietersen,' Smith has gone on record as saying.

In rugby, too, there have been periodic outbursts of complaint over players switching to play for different national teams. Shortly before taking England on their ultimately ill-fated journey to the 2011 World Cup in New Zealand as manager, Martin Johnson spoke in surprisingly liberal tones about the whole issue with the sport. Acknowledging the criticisms that had been raised over England squad members such as Manu Tuilagi and Thomas Waldrom, who some saw as operating under a flag of convenience, Johnson recalled his own time as a young player spent in New Zealand, whose under-21 side he played for.

He told the *Independent*: 'People don't understand, talking about our guys born abroad. They've got to come in and prove themselves like anyone else. If we think they're the right people and the right characters then they can play… It's what you do and who you are, not particularly where you are born.'

But then if you waive birthplace as a means of determining nationality, surely you need to retain a blood link? Of course, it's all relative, ultimately, as we reflect on the nomadic history of humankind over time. But the logical end point of Johnson's argument seems to be that you can play for England if you have what the US astronaut programme used to call the 'right stuff' about you – that is, if you have the right kind of 'English' stuff.

Paolo in di right – or Paolo in di wrong?

Like Charlton, Paolo di Canio is a footballing figure who has generated a degree of moral contradiction. Di Canio is, in fact, a one-man moral debate. The Italian has earned censure for offering apparently right-wing salutes to fans in Rome, and, back in England, for pushing over an admittedly wobbly ref while playing for Sheffield Wednesday. But in 2001 he won the FIFA Fair Play Award for his instinctive action in a match against Everton, when he shunned a goal-scoring opportunity from a cross because he saw the opposition's keeper, Paul Gerrard, lying injured on the ground with a twisted knee. The Italian caught the ball to allow the keeper to be treated. Right or wrong? Not every West Ham fan agreed with his action. But you would have to be very cynical to suggest he had spot-betted on such an unlikely turn of events.

However, even if you credit di Canio with all the right human instincts in that instance, the practice of halting play in order to offer swift assistance to an injured player has been manipulated on many occasions since, with the Euro 2012 championships offering numerous examples of its cynical abuse. That's human nature for you. But it still doesn't make the practice wrong, does it?

'Who says doping is unethical?'

Let's return to the subject of doping. Doping is bad. And of course we know this. But doping in sport contains numerous conundrums. For instance, if what you did then was not illegal, but it is now, does that make you a cheat? The obvious answer is no, you didn't break the rules. But then you may still have gained an unfair advantage over others who didn't take the same path – or pill – as you. Which is cheating, isn't it?

As we have already seen, Thomas Hicks, winner of the 2004 Olympic marathon, had been effectively doped on the course with strychnine washed down with some fine French brandy. That would certainly not go down well with the World Anti-Doping Agency nowadays.

Another example. While anabolic steroids remain on the banned list of performance-enhancing substances, there is no such listing for creatine supplements, a legal substance which became widely available in the 1990s and is still widely used today – it mimics many of the effects of steroids in terms of building muscle mass and enabling higher levels of performance in anaerobic work such as weightlifting or sprinting.

So while someone taking steroids is likely to be busted, someone taking creatine is OK. Similarly, if you are found to have taken EPO or one of its related cousins to boost the level of oxygen-carrying blood cells in your body, you will incur a doping ban. And indeed, if you take out a sample of your own blood and store it, replacing it into your system once your body has generated extra red blood cells to fill the gap, you will also be deemed to have committed an offence.

But if you have been able to afford to train at altitude, where the same process takes place naturally as your body responds to the relative lack of oxygen, you will gain the same advantage when you return to sea level without incurring any sanction. Indeed, if you have the money to set up an oxygen tent in your bedroom, you can sleep your way to legitimate extra capacity.

Eric de Bruin, the retired Dutch athlete whose wife Michelle won three Olympic swimming golds at the 1996 Atlanta Games before incurring a subsequent doping ban for manipulating a test, posed a very direct question: 'Who says doping is unethical?' he asked. 'Sport is by definition dishonest. Some people are naturally gifted. Some people are not going to make it without extra help. For me, doping is a list of banned products, that's all.'

His wife, who maintains that she has never taken banned performance-enhancing drugs and who retained her Olympic medals as her doping infraction occurred after the 1996 Games, wrote some years after her ban: 'If you were to ask my views on such substances, then I would say that I believe the same rules should apply to all and that there should be a level playing field.'

But even if such a position were to be widely accepted, it could never work. There are simply too many variables ever to create a truly 'level playing field' for sportsmen and women. Most athletes couldn't afford the expensive drugs. Many athletes can't even afford a good diet, or don't have access to good facilities. It all gets a bit muddied, doesn't it? And what exactly is it that is muddied? Not necessarily a level playing field.

The default position of 'let everyone take anything' has been addressed elsewhere in this book. And yet there is always another question beyond the answer. For instance, what are the ethics of genetic engineering, which many believe may soon be the new field of operation for those wishing to improve sporting performances – and indeed for those wishing to diminish the world's supply of virulent diseases. Will such genetic manipulation be 'illegal'?

The vexed case of the BOA by-law

Clarity, then, is not easily obtainable on the subject of doping. Nor, indeed, on the subject of suitable punishments for doping – although, interestingly, it is competitors themselves who tend to take the hardest line on this matter.

Malcolm Arnold, the coach who guided Colin Jackson through a career which included two world 110m hurdles titles and a world record which stood for fifteen years, offered his own perspective on crime and punishment in a doping context when he spoke about how he and Jackson had offered Mark McKoy, the Canadian who had served a two-year doping ban, a place in their training group in 1992.

'Some people had condemned me without having the courage to say anything to my face,' Arnold said after McKoy had won the 1992 Olympic title. 'I didn't seek any assurances from Mark when he first came. But I know when athletes are up to something, and he's back on the straight and narrow. In the present system it's very easy to condemn people. Perhaps my ethics are a little more Christian. Forgiveness is an important aspect.'

That said, the reactions of many sporting figures, or ex-sporting figures, have tended to view offenders more stringently. This was evident in the debate over the validity or otherwise of the British Olympic Association's by-law, which it adopted independently in 1992, whereby any British competitor found guilty of a serious doping offence was debarred from selection for any future Olympics.

When, in 2011, the Court of Arbitration for Sport overturned a less severe ruling established by the IOC, whereby any athlete serving a doping ban of six months or more was debarred from the next Games on the calendar, the BOA's position appeared to be even more out on a limb and faced a strong challenge from the World Anti-Doping Agency, which had standardised the doping sanction at two years without any extra rulings concerning Olympics.

The BOA position polarised opinion within athletics on the question of how best to address the problem of doping. When Dwain Chambers unsuccessfully challenged his Olympic life ban at the High Court on the eve of the Beijing Games, the sanction was described as being 'like a death sentence' by no less a figure than Ed Moses, the double Olympic 400m hurdles champion and the man who was instrumental in creating the sport's first random out-of-competition drug-testing programme.

Yet many other athletes and ex-athletes are in favour of the ruling. After each of the four Olympics before London 2012, a survey conducted by the BOA Athletes Commission found 90 per cent or more of British athletes in favour of the Olympic life ban. As a member of the formative BOA Athletes Commission, Bryn Vaile – a gold medallist in the 1988 Olympic Star sailing class – was among those responsible for getting the by-law on to the statute books on 25 March 1992. Along with Olympic swimming gold medallist Adrian Moorhouse, he argued its case successfully to the BOA Executive Committee – and he believed passionately that the by-law should remain.

'We looked into the legal position of restraint of trade,' Vaile said. 'But the way we saw it, this was not preventing people carrying on their careers – they could still compete in grand prix meetings or World Championships.' Vaile, however, wanted to see conditions become even more difficult for doping cheats. 'I still believe that if you take performance-enhancing drugs, you should be banned for life,' he said. 'There should be no compromise to it, because that is compromising our futures. Every time a drugs cheat comes back to competition, it doesn't just tarnish the sport, and the people watching. It tarnishes the next generation, and it belittles every other clean athlete.'

Tim Brabants, 2008 Olympic gold medallist in the K1 1000m canoe sprint event, agreed: 'I certainly agree with the BOA by-law and wish it was consistent across all countries.' Brabants, who has combined canoeing with a medical career, added: 'It's so frustrating in my sport to compete against athletes who suddenly test positive, disappear for a two-year ban and return fit and strong competing as fast as before.

'For example, the muscle gained while an athlete is cheating using steroids is not suddenly lost when they stop taking them. They still benefit from the cheating they did, even when they stop. This isn't fair in my mind and the only way to stop it is to have lifetime bans.'

But a couple of months before the 2012 London Olympics, the Court of Arbitration for Sport in Lausanne rejected the BOA's appeal against a WADA verdict that its by-law was 'not compliant' with the WADA code to which Britain had signed up. As a result, the BOA was obliged to give way, and athletes such as Chambers and cyclist David Millar were subsequently selected for the Games.

Many disagreed. But once the decision was made, the BOA went out of its way to insist that Chambers and Millar would receive exactly the same level of support as any of their teammates. We were back to a different mindset here – the mindset of team loyalty and its associated moral conundrums. The mindset, you might even argue, of Leonardo Piepoli....

Which punishment fits which crime?

There have also been recent debates in British anti-doping circles about the justice of punishing those who take so-called recreational drugs, such as cocaine or ecstasy, as severely as those found to have used performance-enhancing drugs such as EPO or anabolic steroids.

Among those who have spoken out strongly against creating any kind of differential, however, is Lord Sebastian Coe. 'There is no place for it,' the double Olympic 1500m champion and chairman of the London 2012 Organising Committee told reporters. 'You can't mix the messages – I am really strong about that. It's about confidence, it's about trust. What am I saying to kids out there? "Well look, we might take a view on ecstasy or cocaine…"'? I'm sorry – it's the morality of the knackers' yard. You've got to fight this and you've got to be clear.' Clearly no moral conundrum for Lord Coe.

Another area of extended discussion in recent years is the justice or otherwise of taking medals from relay teams when one or more of their number is discovered to have been doping at the time of their success.

At the 2006 European Championships in Gothenburg, after the British quartet had won the sprint relay gold, one of their number, Darren Campbell, refused to join his teammate Dwain Chambers on a victory lap because the latter's doping ban had triggered retrospective actions which cost Campbell his relay gold from the previous European Championships, and a relay bronze from the 2003 World Championships. Because Chambers had admitted doping at the time, his relay team's overall performance was deemed to have received an illegal gain.

Similar calculations and revisions have had to be made by more than one relay team because of doping infringements by contributing individuals. In 2004 the United States was stripped of its 400m relay gold from the 2003 World Championships after one of their number, Calvin Harrison, tested positive for a banned substance.

Four years earlier Harrison and his brother Alvin had become the first twins to compete and win Olympic sprint relay medals together as they contributed to victory in the 4x400m at the Sydney Olympics. But that US team was also stripped of its medals in June 2004 when the Court of Arbitration for Sport ruled that Jerome Young, who had won a gold after running the opening heat and semi-final for the team, should have served a two-year ban for a doping infringement in June 1999.

A year later Young's teammates got their medals back, through the Court of Arbitration for Sport – but the medals were forfeited again in 2008 after Antonio Pettigrew admitted to having doped at the time of the final and the IOC withdrew the golds. The gold medal position in the men's 4x400m relay from the Sydney Olympics is now officially void. If doped runners have competed, that is not fair to the teams they have beaten. But it is also unfair to their innocent teammates.

How can 'doped' East German medals stand?

Also difficult – much, much more difficult – was the decision about how to react once information on the extent of the doping regime practised in East Germany came into the public domain. This triggered a huge moral debate in sporting circles about the justice of allowing all those who were clearly implicated in the process to keep the medals they had earned.

British swimmer Sharron Davies, who won silver behind East Germany's Petra Schneider in the 400m medley at the 1980 Moscow Olympics, was among several athletes who petitioned the IOC to strip East German athletes proved to have taken drugs of their Olympic medals.

'All my career I was swimming against Eastern bloc swimmers who were on a drug programme devised for them from above,' Davies said in January 1998. 'How can the world records or medals that were set or won stay in place now the truth is known?'

British sprinter Kathy Cook was another who lost out to East German athletes subsequently implicated in doping. It was Cook's misfortune that her prime should coincide with the prime years of a regime which turned a small country of seventeen million people into the third-strongest sporting nation on earth behind the United States and the Soviet Union.

If one subtracts the performances of retrospectively implicated East Germans in Cook's races, you could argue she would have been European champion in 1982 instead of silver medallist, and she would have had another two Olympic medals to go with the bronze she won in the 400m at the 1984 Los Angeles Games.

Cook was in sympathy with Davies's position. 'I can fully understand how Sharron feels,' she said. 'Just like her, I have been thinking about the question recently. You do wonder if things in your life might have been different if all this had come to light nearer the time.'

There was no simple answer, however. Firstly, as far as track and field records were concerned, the international athletics body – the IAAF – insisted that it was too late to change any of the results as it had a six-year time limit on any such alteration. The IOC's executive committee then announced it had no intention of revising the Olympic record books.

The other factor that militated against a sweeping annulment of East German success was the doubt that had been raised about performances of other nations, not all of them from within the Eastern bloc, over the same period of time. For instance, rumours had circulated for a decade about some less than straightforward activity at the testing laboratory for the 1984 Los Angeles Games. In 1994 it emerged that orders were given to close the lab before competition had finished, and some tests which had showed up positive were not followed up or assigned to the athletes involved.

After the Games, when attempts were made to find out why the positive tests had not been pursued, investigators heard that the files which listed the codes by which the suspect athletes could be identified had been taken away and shredded, and since there was no name on the samples there was no point in carrying out the standard corroborative test on them. Somebody, somewhere, had decided to ensure a drug-free Games...

Over time, Cook – who is married to another former British athlete, 400m runner Garry – has reached her own position on the question. 'Garry and I talk about it when evidence comes out, and we say, jokingly, I was robbed. But I had my fair share of standing on the rostrum, and I think there is too much water under the bridge to change things now.'

Cook's magnanimity was partly informed by simple logic. As she pointed out, if GDR performances were annulled, how could one legislate for all those wrongfully knocked out in the heats and semi-finals, and how could one know how they might have reacted to the challenge of continuing competition?

Cook, who retired from the track in 1987, got to know a number of East German athletes during her ten-year career. 'Sometimes I would have to look at runners twice because their whole shape had completely changed,' she said. 'The most disturbing thing was the way some of the girls' voices had lowered… The idea that the whole team was involved, lock, stock and barrel, is horrifying. Especially when you think that some of them were so young.'

She was especially disappointed to see the evidence implicating Marita Koch, who took gold, two places ahead of her, in the Moscow 1980 400m final. 'Marita was a role model for me,' Cook said. 'She was a really nice person, and she had this charisma. The crowd would go silent because she was so fast. She just destroyed fields. I remember watching on television when she set her world record and I was just speechless. I don't know how I would feel if I ever saw her again. I've no particular wish to. I feel a mixture of sadness and anger about the whole thing.'

Cook's strongest expression of anger was directed not at an East German opponent, but one from Canada: Angela Issajenko, who beat her to the 1986 Commonwealth 200m title and admitted three years later – at the Dubin Inquiry, sparked by the scandal of Ben Johnson's failed test at the 1988 Seoul Olympics – that she had taken drugs since 1980.

'I did feel angrier about what Angela did because she chose to go down that track herself,' Cook said. 'It seems a lot of the East German athletes were taken as youngsters and told what to do without always being given the facts. It is a horrific situation, but you can have more sympathy for people involved in it.'

'I have to live with what went on'

Hugh Matheson was a member of the British rowing eight beaten to gold by the East Germans at the Montreal Olympics of 1976. But he did not embrace the idea of being promoted to gold by virtue of the East German result being annulled.

Matheson pointed out that, ironically, it was only because of the thoroughness with which East German performances were logged that authorities could be in a position to sanction them. Although the pre-event testing prevented any positive tests from occurring in competition, the wealth of information back in the laboratories contained ample evidence of wrongdoing. 'All the more chaotic abusers, which would include most of the Warsaw Pact countries, will get off only because they had no proper controls and no proper record keepers,' he commented at the time in the *Independent*.

But Matheson insisted that he saw the fact that the East Germans were doped as being a 'sidebar', concluding: 'We had silver, but we were beaten by stronger men.' Interestingly, Matheson also reflected on the strong moral stance adopted by the British crew's coach, Bob Janousek.

'Janousek knew that most of us in the British crew would do whatever it took to win,' he recalled. 'We were willing to abuse our bodies to the extent of massive fatigue and pain, and a pill or two that relieved the stress and allowed more chance of success would not have seemed inappropriate to me then. Janousek was adamant and tough. It was not an option – a decision he took knowing the eventual price in results. Thank goodness he did. However, it never worried me that others took the opposite view.'

The fall of the Berlin Wall led to some awkward questions being asked about coaches from the Eastern bloc who had presumably been involved, to varying degrees, in a state-backed doping regime, and who subsequently sought employment in Western Europe.

Jürgen Gröbler has coached Britain's elite athletes for twenty years, guiding our squeaky clean icons Sir Steve Redgrave and Sir Matthew Pinsent to their triumphs, among many others. Both men have strenuously defended his integrity. Gröbler subsequently commented: 'I have to live with what went on in East Germany. I was born in the wrong place. It was not possible to walk away.'

For a while, even more controversially, Ekkart Arbeit, a man reportedly much closer to the centre of the East German doping regime, worked briefly with Britain's Olympic heptathlon champion Denise Lewis as she prepared for what would be an unsuccessful defence of her title at the 2004 Athens Games. Arbeit had by this time spoken of 'regretting' his involvement in a doping culture, and had condemned the practice.

For a few dollars more…

Moral judgement of a different kind was called into play in athletics in 1999 following an incident that took place during the Weltklasse meeting in Zurich. Kenya's Bernard Barmasai naively admitted to reporters after winning the 3000m steeplechase that he had persuaded his compatriot, Christopher Kosgei, to ease off and let him win.

Barmasai insisted that Kosgei had happily complied with his request as it meant he, Barmasai, would thus be eligible for a share of the $1 million jackpot being offered to any athlete finishing the season unbeaten in the IAAF's Golden League series. 'He would have won today but he is a friend and we have to live together,' Barmasai said. 'The jackpot is for me and my friends.'

So, it seemed everybody was a winner. Not so. The international authorities found Barmasai guilty of bringing the sport into disrepute and disqualified him from his $250,000 share of the jackpot, three other athletes also having finished their seasons with victory in Zurich. Clearly, Barmasai was operating under that same 'collective' Kenyan philosophy that determines on occasion which man will be assisted by his teammates to a victory seen as being deserved.

Barmasai got nothing. And yet others, over the years, have profited hugely from similarly calculating approaches. Sergei Bubka, for example, whose mastery of the pole vault – in which he still holds the world record after retiring in 2001 – was such that he could simply edge up through the heights, gaining a succession of world record bonuses over a period of years. What Bubka did was entirely legitimate – he simply used the particular nature of his event in a canny fashion. In more recent years, Russia's Yelena Isinbayeva has utilised her pre-eminence in the pole vault to similar effect. The event lends itself to such calibration. Were it possible to judge how fast one ran the 100m, no doubt record bonuses would have been doled out on a similarly regular basis. And yet, witnessing such calculations in sport goes against the grain as far as many observers are concerned. The system itself works against a full expression of athletic ability.

The problem of sex

We have already remarked on the case of Samukeliso Sithole – the Zimbabwean female athlete who turned out to be a man named Ngwenya Mduduzi. But while it is not hard to agree that Ngwenya was an offender, it is more difficult to form a response to the more serious examples of transgender sporting figures that preceded his case. At the 1936 Berlin Olympics, Dora Ratjen of the host nation finished fourth in the women's high jump. No problem there. Except that Dora wasn't really Dora. She was Hermann.

Ratjen was banned from competition in 1938 after being classified as a hermaphrodite – that is, a person with both male and female organs. But in 1957 Ratjen revealed that his real name was Hermann, and that he had been ordered by the Hitler Youth movement to pose as a woman in order to improve Germany's Olympic medal tally. Given that the process involved him tightly binding his genitals, perhaps it was no surprise that he didn't manage a place on the podium.

In 1980 there was an armed robbery at a Cleveland shopping mall during which a passer-by was shot dead by a stray bullet as they crossed a car park. That person turned out to be Stella Walsh, born Stanislawa Walasiewicz, who had won 100m gold at the 1932 Games – where the Canadian official report noted her 'long, man-like strides' – and 100m silver in Berlin four years later, representing the country of her birth, Poland. She had been on her way to a discount store to buy ribbons for a reception due to be given to the Polish basketball team.

Police autopsies revealed that Walsh had male genitals and both male and female chromosomes – a condition known as mosaicism. 'She' was, legally, a 'he'. Ratjen and Walsh cheated other women out of rightful medals. And yet it can be argued they were both as much victim as offender in these cases. Moral confusion.

Oscar Pistorius – rightful Olympian?

Categorising athletes can be problematic, and there has been a similar ambivalence in the case of Oscar Pistorius, the Paralympian par excellence who made history by becoming the first double amputee to earn the right to compete with able-bodied athletes at a global championship. Shockingly, less than six months after his triumphs at the London 2012 Olympics and Paralympics, Pistorius created a more profound and disturbing conflict of opinion when he was charged with the murder of his girlfriend, the international model Reeva Steenkamp. But we limit our discussion here to the complexities of his competitive career.

Running on carbon-fibre prosthetic legs, the South African reached the semi-finals of the 2011 World Athletics Championships in Daegu and won a silver medal in the relay. The following year he competed at the London 2012 Olympics before earning two golds at the Paralympics which followed. But Pistorius's achievements have taken place amid an ongoing debate into, firstly, the legitimacy of his technological assistance and, secondly, the relative legitimacy of others.

As part of their promotional presence ahead of the London 2012 Olympics, for which Pistorius was eventually selected, Lloyds TSB featured a poster of Pistorius in full flight, with the accompanying words: 'He doesn't need feet. They'd only slow him down.' In the circumstances, this was an unfortunate choice of words.

What are the circumstances? In athletic terms, Pistorius's achievements have been magnificent. No one is disputing this. But there have been strong suggestions, from both fellow athletes and some scientists, that Pistorius may have been enjoying an unwitting advantage through the excellence of the technology supporting him.

Even before he began racing against able-bodied opponents in invitation races following his successes at the 2004 Paralympics, Pistorius had become a controversial figure. Because of the scarcity of double amputee athletes, he had to be put in a category where many of his opponents were single amputees. And there were complaints.

For instance Marlon Shirley, the American single amputee whom Pistorius defeated over 400m at the Athens Paralympics, maintained afterwards that his rival had an unfair 'locomotive advantage' with two, rather than one, of the contraptions fashioned by his team of Icelandic engineers.

Able-bodied runners, too, were beginning to feel threatened by the perceived advantages of his Cheetah blades. Some said they were too long, making Pistorius taller than he would naturally be had he not been born without a fibula in either leg. Others complained that the blades, which offered the dashing Pistorius an obvious nickname of Blade Runner, provided him with excess spring.

On 14 January 2008 the IAAF, having commissioned a scientific study conducted by Dr Peter Brüggemann at the German Sport University in Cologne, ruled that Pistorius's prostheses were ineligible for use in competitions under IAAF rules, which meant all recognised racing including the Olympics.

Brüggemann had concluded that Pistorius had 'considerable advantages' over athletes without prosthetic limbs. His report indicated that the South

African used 25 per cent less energy than able-bodied runners running at the same speed, and that his blades required 30 per cent less mechanical work for lifting the body.

But the Court of Arbitration for Sport had a different take on the subject when it heard Pistorius's appeal on 16 May. Brüggemann's findings were ruled out, partly on the basis that he had conducted his research without considering the difficulties Pistorius had in the start and acceleration phases of racing, and also in negotiating running around a bend.

It was too late for Pistorius to qualify for the Beijing Olympics – he contented himself with three golds at the Beijing Paralympics. But the way was clear for him to contest future global championships if he could run the qualifying times. Within three years, he had done so.

On the eve of the IAAF's ruling in January 2008, Britain's Tanni Grey-Thompson, who had retired a year earlier with a total of sixteen Paralympic medals, eleven of them gold, commented: 'I have been expecting him to be banned. When he was running less quickly it was all quite jolly, but as soon as he started running fast times, that's it. I think this has provoked a debate about what it is to be disabled, and what it is to be able-bodied.

'I think there's an argument both ways. People will say that he can pick the length and style of his prosthetics, so maybe that gives him an unfair advantage. I think it's probably more of a disadvantage to be running with two lower limbs missing.

'But others will say if he can be racing against able-bodied runners on two false legs, good luck to him. Oscar is a stunning talent. He is as far ahead of his Paralympic rivals as Michael Johnson was over his Olympic 400m competitors ten years ago. He has been given a glimpse of inclusion but now it looks like being taken away from him. The authorities probably shouldn't have let him compete against able-bodied athletes in the first place. They've given him a chance to get out of the ghetto but they are going to throw him back in again.'

Richard Callicott, a director of the British Paralympic Association, added: 'People are falling into two camps on this question. One argument is, let him get on with it. Let him carry on proving that having no legs is no handicap compared with natural talent. But others think his prosthetics give him an advantage. Once he gets up to speed his strides are immense, and he gets faster as the races get longer.

'Having Pistorius in the Olympic Games would also put able-bodied athletes in an impossible position if they felt he was racing with an unfair advantage. If they complained, people would say they were being spoilt, that they were whingeing and moaning. I don't think they could win, whatever they did.'

Scientific opinion on the matter has been almost bizarrely at odds. In 2011 Dr Ross Tucker, a senior lecturer at the University of Cape Town's Exercise Science and Sports Medicine Department, cast doubt on the findings which CAS used to give Pistorius a free run and raised questions about the possibility of technological advances in prosthetic blades improving performance in the manner of Formula 1 engineering.

Tucker's position, however, was dismissed almost entirely by the scientist who co-presented the Pistorius case at the CAS hearing, Professor Hugh Herr of the Massachusetts Institute of Technology and himself a double amputee following a mountaineering incident. Herr maintained that Pistorius had run on identical blades for fifteen years, and that the CAS ruling related specifically to those blades. He added that calculations of unfair advantage were completely skewed, although he acknowledged that there was still much research to be done on the subject.

The ethical argument in this case rested on the following assumption: that Pistorius should be allowed to compete with able-bodied athletes until such time as he can be proved to be operating with an unfair, even if entirely unwitting, advantage.

But the opposite principle applies in world sport when it comes to introducing new methods of testing for pharmacological products and processes which offer competitors unfair advantage – as indeed it applies to the introduction of any new drug on to the market.

As the former head of the IOC's medical commission, Prince Alexandre de Merode, once said when explaining why new tests for human growth hormone and EPO could not be brought in in time for the 2000 Sydney Olympics: 'To be fair, you can't take a medal away from someone who is tested with a method that is still not 100 per cent accurate.' Can you, then, potentially take a medal away from someone in favour of an athlete whose broad equality has not been 100 per cent established?

Paralympic sport has to wrestle with its own particular set of moral problems, mostly to do with classification. A few months after her retirement in 2007, Grey-Thompson was realistic about the continuing disputes that occurred within disabled sport over the classification of competitors. 'There were two athletes in particular, neither of them British, whom I had some concerns about,' she said. 'Both of them had requested to be moved from a category where competitors have back and stomach muscles to my category, where they were not supposed to have.

'Classifications are made in a snapshot of time, but competitors can work and train and develop until they can exceed the supposed limits of the class. There are some people who think that just because athletes are disabled, they wouldn't do such a thing, that we are all just lovely and nice to each other and what we do is just a bit of fun. That's not how it is.'

London 2012 Paralympics – Pistorius, prosthetics and politics

Pistorius was always likely to be a high-profile figure at the London 2012 Games, and so it proved as he duly became the first amputee runner to compete at the Olympics – where he reached the 400m semi-final and ran in the relay final – before going on to earn gold in the 400m individual and 4x100m relay events at the Paralympics. However, it was the South African's outraged comments immediately after being beaten to the Paralympic 200m gold by Alan Fonteles Cardoso Oliveira that caused at least as great an impact as his expected achievements.

Given his own struggles to establish his validity as an Olympian, there was a rich irony in the defending champion's reaction after his unexpected defeat in the T44 200m final by the Brazilian who passed him in the final 25 metres. But it was also a reaction that begged a very large question which still hangs over the business of amputee athletes running with the assistance of prosthetic 'blades'. Pistorius insisted that his opponent, also a double amputee, had run on blades that were too long, making him much taller and offering him an unfair advantage in terms of speed.

'We are not running a fair race here, absolutely ridiculous,' Pistorius told Channel 4's Sonja McLaughlan immediately after his race. 'I'm not taking away from Alan's performance but I can't compete with Alan's stride length. The IPC (International Paralympic Committee) have their regulations and their regulations mean that some athletes can make themselves unbelievably high... his knee-heights are four inches higher than they should be. We have spoken to the International Paralympic Committee about the length of these blades but it has fallen on deaf ears. Guys are coming from nowhere to run ridiculous times. I don't know how you pull that back. I run at ten metres per second and I don't know how someone comes back from eight metres behind in the home straight. It's not right.'

In reply, however, IPC spokesman Craig Spence commented: 'All blades are measured and Oliveira's passed the test. There has been no infringement of the rules.'

'Oscar has to choose – either he was beaten fair and square by a better athlete or blade design CAN radically affect your performance level,' tweeted Sir Matthew Pinsent, whose own involvement with blades was thankfully confined to the means by which he propelled himself and others to four Olympic rowing golds. Bizarrely, almost two hours after the race had been run, both the IPC and Pistorius appeared to have shifted their positions, as Spence said that a special meeting would be convened on the following day to discuss Pistorius's 'concerns' without the 'emotions' of the race being involved. Pistorius, meanwhile, appeared to backtrack on his earlier comments about Oliveira as he congratulated the Brazilian on 'a great performance', adding that he had shaken the victor's hand on the warm-down track after the final.

After bringing home the South African 4x100m relay team to gold in a T42–46 world record of 41.78 seconds, Pistorius stood for almost half an hour in front of journalists and repeated apologies he had already aired over the timing of his comments in the wake of his 200m defeat. But he insisted the sport still had to find a more consistent method of measurement regarding prosthetic limbs if it was to thrive.

Pistorius made it clear, however, that he would not have chosen to change to taller blades himself before the Paralympics from the blades on which he has been operating since 2004, which had been cleared for Olympic competition by the Court of Arbitration for Sport. When asked if he would have switched if he could, he responded: 'Not at all,' adding, 'I've got a teammate in Arnu Fourie, and if I beat him on the day I want to know I've beaten him by hard work and talent. I don't think every blade should be the same height, but I think it should be in relation to your body. For the sport to evolve and be taken seriously it has to happen. Obviously I regret the timing of my comments after the 200m wasn't great and it's led to a real backlash in the last two days. It's easy to be gracious when you win; it's not as easy to be humble when you lose, and I've had to learn that. I think it was just frustration in the heat of the moment, and I have apologised to Alan. But I think it is a problem and the national Paralympic committee has brought it up with the IPC. I was the first to bring up the topic, but a lot of other athletes have spoken about it in the last two days and I think it just shows that it is a huge concern and it has been in the sport for a long time. It's an important topic.'

Among those who had spoken about the issue earlier in the evening was Jerome Singleton, who had inflicted Pistorius's first defeat in seven years at the previous year's world championships over 100m. The American, a single-leg amputee, supported the comments Pistorius had made about the need for more precise rules on blade length, and added that some athletes were changing blades between the 200m and 100m races. 'It does happen,' Pistorius said. 'Jerome's right. There is a problem, and it's got to be addressed.'

Singleton also widened the debate on blade classification as he insisted that his T44 class – for single-leg amputees below the knee – should run separately from the T43 class, for double below-knee amputees such as Pistorius, a situation he likened to 'apples and oranges', adding: 'I think that the time has come that the T44s and the T43s have to split their classes. Unless we can split the classes I think we need to review or evaluate that formula. A number of athletes have made their feelings known to the IPC that we should make sure we have a formula where there is a leeway of between one or two centimetres, because no one wants to go out there and race someone totally different. We need to have an exact height for an athlete to run in, so you know you are racing the same athlete in all competitions.'

Singleton, who has degrees in applied physics and industrial engineering and who has worked as a researcher at NASA, added: 'As time changes, science changes too, so we just have to be sure it is fair to all competitors.'

Just not cricket?

Let's take a final example here of a moral debate within sport – this time from cricket. When, on 31 July 2011, Ian Bell strode to the Trent Bridge pavilion to take tea on the third day of the Second Test against India, he was in fine fettle, having already made his fifteenth century for England and pushed on to add another 37 runs.

But Bell had made what he later admitted was a 'stupid' and 'naive' decision. He had not checked to make sure that the session was over before vacating the crease. Bell's partner at the wicket, Eoin Morgan, had driven the last ball of the over to long leg, where India's Praveen Kumar made fleeting contact with the ball before falling over the boundary. Evidently believing the ball had crossed for a four – which it hadn't – he got back on his feet and, without urgency, returned it.

Bell and Morgan, meanwhile, had run three before Bell grounded his bat and both set off for tea and biscuits. By now the ball had reached the Indian wicketkeeper Abhinav Mukund, via the Indian captain Mahendra Singh Dhoni, and Mukund promptly removed the bails on Bell's untenanted wicket before appealing to the third umpire, Billy Bowden, who confirmed the dismissal.

As the two batsmen loitered palely at the boundary, Dhoni turned down two invitations to withdraw the appeal, and the Indian team, along with the umpires, were booed from the field. Boos greeted their return, too, but they were soon replaced by cheers of relief as it became clear that Bell was returning to the crease. Dhoni and his teammates had agreed to withdraw their appeal shortly before reappearing, and Bell went on to make 159 before being caught.

Neither Nasser Hussain nor Michael Vaughan, both former England captains, had much sympathy for Bell. Hussain said he would have appealed in the same situation, and Vaughan agreed, adding that Bell had been 'very dozy'. Sweetness and light had returned to Trent Bridge, certainly. But at the expense of the rules. Was that right? Many observers did not believe so. Writing in the *Independent*, James Laughton memorably described it as 'a burst of sentimental cricket illiteracy', adding: 'Laws are not there to be pushed aside when it suits the prejudices of any particular audience.'

However you analyse the sequence of events, the fact remains that this incident highlighted an ambivalence which has no obvious resolution. Should the 'spirit of the game' have primacy over the laws of the game? It remains a matter of opinion whether it was justly dealt with or not.

The power of 'we'

1. HOW DO WE REACT TO FOUL PLAY?

'Thanks Suarez'
– Uruguayan fan's poster after World Cup handball

The moral conundrums rehearsed in the previous chapter call into question what sport is supposed to be about. But who supposes? The fact is that all the vexed morality, all the debate, all the controversy is rendered meaningless without one vital element: us. Without us – the spectators, the followers – to decide on what feels right and wrong, what is just and what is just too much, the questionable activities become merely things that have happened, or things that are happening, random as asteroids.

How, then, do we as followers react to foul play? Perhaps there will be those who look down upon all wrongdoing in sporting arenas with no more than a sense of regret at human nature, and human folly. People cheat in life; people cheat in sport. We wish it wasn't so, but there it is.

For most of us, however, such a lofty overview is tempered by the awkward circumstance that we find it almost impossible to be entirely impartial when engaging with sporting contests of any kind.

For example, the increased coverage of European matches on TV now makes it relatively easy to watch matches where there may be no particular knowledge or affinity operating for many viewers. So we may find ourselves watching a match – Zaragoza versus Athletic Bilbao perhaps, or Hearts vs Motherwell – where the two sides are, to all intents and purposes, of equal merit to us. Do we then settle back to draw whatever technical and aesthetic merits we can from the match? Do we maintain a lofty indifference to the result? We don't. We take a dislike to a defender's challenge, or we respond to a flourish in midfield, or maybe one of the teams is playing in a kit we especially like. The reasons will always vary, but what tends not to vary is the fact that we will start wanting one team or the other to win.

Whatever the sport, the same thing happens. Even if we watch, say, an early heat in the Olympic 100m, involving runners who are neither Usain

Bolt nor Tyson Gay, runners with whose names we are not familiar, can we honestly say in the course of the ten seconds or so it takes for this early contest to be completed that we have not attached any kind of preference to the sprinters? Is there not always a little part of us that would prefer one competitor or another to reach the line first, whether it be the man straining to keep his lead or the man straining to take it over?

When it comes to sporting contests, trying not to want one protagonist or another to win is like deliberately trying not to think of a pink elephant. Sport is all about partiality, all about identification. For the period of time when our chosen competitor or team operates, they are, effectively, us. And we allow them commensurate latitude.

Which is where we have to be honest with ourselves. Some years ago the *Observer* columnist Katherine Whitehorn coined a phrase: 'I am firm. You are obstinate. He is a pig-headed fool.' If you follow a team, whatever the sport, can you truly say you don't view things in a similarly partial manner? 'We are resourceful. You are opportunistic. They are blatant cheats.'

Point of view is critical to the way in which we, as sporting followers, regard any instance of foul play. And depending upon that point of view, any instance of foul play can engender three broad categories of response.

Points of view

At one end of the scale, foul play can be vilified. There is a middle ground, where foul play can be justified, or its effects partially nullified. And, on occasion, taking that justification a stage further, foul play can be glorified.

Foul play tends to polarise opinion among those who witness it. If the team or individual we follow is badly done by, we will naturally feel most aggrieved on their behalf. We vilify the wrongdoers. And by the same token, those who have gained the advantage through whatever wrongdoing it may have been will be most likely to take an opposite view and, in some cases, to rejoice in the circumstances, glorifying them. Of course, if it's our individual or team who profits, then the roles are reversed. This is the basic see-saw of support.

The middle ground – what you might describe as the fulcrum of the see-saw – is more complex. Justification – with a view to explaining and perhaps even nullifying, or neutralising, the wrongdoing – is, naturally enough, something attempted by those perceived to have been guilty of foul play. But how can 'wrong' turn into 'right'? Or at least, 'not so very wrong, and maybe, in a funny kind of way, almost right'?

Such justification often involves encouraging us, as sporting followers, to change the focus of our gaze.

The justification of the bigger picture

Let's take as an infamous act of cheating Diego Maradona's 1986 handball again. For this action, nothwithstanding his miraculous second goal, Maradona was and continues to be vilified by England followers who feel that his action deprived their team of their chance to progress. For Argentinian followers, however, the handball is excused, celebrated even, as a means to a glorious and rightful end.

But that glorification was made easier by the way Maradona justified his action in the aftermath, with his infamous reference to the fact that it was a little bit the hand of Maradona, a little bit the Hand of God.

The match took place just four years after the hostilities between England and Argentina over the ownership of the Falkland Islands, or the Malvinas, as they are known in Argentina. 'Although we had said before the game that football had nothing to do with the Malvinas war, we knew they had killed a lot of the Argentine boys, killed them like little birds. So this was revenge,' Maradona later commented.

Sport borrows so much of its language from warfare – ferocious battles, courageous fightbacks, defensive lines – and the observation was well made that it can serve as ritual battle between nations, assuaging patriotism without exacting a cost in human life. And yet when the two elements are as closely linked as they were in this instance, we are on dangerous ground.

Maradona's position, as we have seen, was broadly this: 'OK, if you want to be all literal about it, it was a handball, but let's broaden the context. Let's remember the war over the Malvinas, and the young Argentinian conscripts who died there at the hands of battle-hardened British troops. From that point of view it was, in the larger scheme of events, justified. So it's a bunched fist, two fingers, to the gunboat Brits.'

Thirty years before Maradona took off for that covert flourish, the water polo players of the Soviet Union and Hungary engaged in a bitterly fought battle at the Melbourne Olympics, just days after Soviet tanks had moved in to crush a Hungarian uprising and reassert Communist rule in the country.

By the end of a ferocious contest there was blood in the water of the pool and the Soviet players were escorted away by police.

Feelings of enmity are only natural in the wake of traumatic events such as the Hungarian Uprising, or the Falklands Conflict. There were many older English people who took a particular pleasure in the fact that England beat West Germany in the 1966 World Cup final, albeit that the match occurred more than two decades after the end of the Second World War. There were more than a few German supporters, too, who questioned the motivation of the Russian linesman who advised the referee that Geoff Hurst's shot in extra time had crossed the line and should be given as a goal. Tofik Bakhramov was actually from Azerbaijan, but he had fought in the Second World War against Germany. Just a fact. But who knows how it might have played out?

The Thierry Henry handball that effectively denied Ireland a place in the 2010 World Cup provoked the Irish so fiercely that their justice minister, Dermot Ahern, demanded that FIFA organise a replay. Predictably, the idea was turned down. Henry himself had declared in the aftermath that a further game would be 'the fairest solution'. But it was all too late.

When he returned to his club, Irish followers had installed an eight-foot poster of him with the words 'I'm sorry' emblazoned over the top, and an apology to the Irish people underneath. A generation of Ireland football followers will never forgive him for what he did to their team's World Cup ambition. And so the next sporting encounter between France and Ireland will gain an extra resonance. If it is to remain sport, however, that resonance must be subsumed within the rules of the game.

Justification for foul play can be found in any sport. Take rugby union. When Neil Back executed the sleight of hand that effectively won Leicester the Heineken Cup in 2002 there was an understandable uproar, and the Munster followers were understandably outraged. The player himself produced a curious quote in the aftermath which, in a way, resembled the justifications Maradona had come out with after his own sleight of hand, attempting to put his misdeed in a greater and more forgiving context.

'That was a very crucial scrum,' Back said, 'and I did what I had to do to ensure a win for Leicester. I am not a cheat and I would be very upset if anyone accused me of being one.' How do we react to this as fans? To most followers of the game this stance appears deluded and disingenuous. And yet would we be more minded to accept such a statement if it came from a player who had just won one of the biggest prizes in sport for our team? A prize which, we may feel, we richly deserved, and which we might have won anyway without this assistance. Who knows, even if the scrum had gone the way of Munster, perhaps they would have wasted their last precious possession?

Such are the animadversions that occur within the mind of committed sporting followers as they wrestle to square their consciences in the aftermath of wrongdoing. And although Back's intervention was never forgotten it did not cause the Leicester club or indeed its followers to turn away from him, just as there was no outcry or reaction from Argentinian supporters over Maradona's action. Clearly the essential dynamic is the same in football or rugby – there are circumstances when foul play can be accepted on behalf of one's team.

In rugby union, the phrase 'getting your retaliation in first' operates on the same principle, making it clear that the violence being done unto others is merely forestalling violence that would otherwise be done unto you. It's not so much a case of being aggressive as being, in the bigger picture, actively defensive. The phrase is darkly humorous and has become common coinage. But in the end it is a justification which invites a set of sporting followers to excuse foul play.

What many of these justifications have in common is the kind of rhetorical device which Maradona employed when he invited those who had witnessed his intervention to put it into a wider context which, he felt, justified it, maybe even nullified it. It is a process akin to switching the focus on a microscope from x500 to x100, getting the bigger picture. With his reference to 'a very crucial scrum', Back attempted a similar thing. We, as followers, were given by Back to understand that, had it been an ordinary scrum, he would never have dreamed of doing such a thing. But in the big picture of the game he felt obliged to do it.

On a more prosaic level, when contentious decisions go the way of a football team – to pick a hypothetical example, let's say Manchester United are awarded a questionable penalty at Old Trafford – television commentators will be swift to offer an opinion along the lines of luck evening itself out in the course of a season. Which may detract from the fact that, on the day, an injustice has been done. Admittedly it is easier to accept this justification if one is a Manchester United supporter.

A similar 'bigger picture' process of justification occurs when athletes are found to have taken illegal substances to further their sporting ambitions – once they have accepted that their original default positions of 'I never took it' or 'I never knowingly took it' are no longer accepted. The claim – as voiced by such as the British shot-putter Neal Brunning and Ben Johnson's coach, Charlie Francis – is that such measures were necessary to ensure a fighting chance against opponents who, in the most part, were doing the same thing anyway. So in the wider context, doping was justified.

To return to the question: do we, as sporting followers, 'buy' these justifications? It depends. The tendency will always be to accept such reasoning from or on behalf of those we follow.

Glorification of Luis Suarez

Let's take another example that, depending on one's sporting viewpoint, was vilified, justified – and glorified. As we have seen, at the 2010 World Cup, Luis Suarez of Uruguay earned widespread censure and criticism for handling on the line in the last minute to deny Ghana what would most likely have been a winning goal. Suarez was sent off, the penalty was missed, and Uruguay went on to reach the semi-final by winning the penalty shoot-out at the end of extra time.

Oscar Tabárez, the Uruguayan coach, attempted to justify Suarez's actions on the basis that they were 'instinctive'. Whether they believed that or not, the vast majority of Uruguayan followers seemed content with the result, with many going a stage further by openly glorying in the actions of a player whose efforts were clearly fully appreciated by his teammates, who chaired him from the pitch after the match had finished. Suarez also appeared jubilant. (To neutral supporters, however, and without doubt to followers of the Ghana team, this spectacle was a hideous parody of sporting tradition.)

There was further justification after the match from the former Uruguayan international Gus Poyet. 'I was a little bit disappointed with some people talking about cheating,' said the former Chelsea midfielder. 'I think that is rubbish. That is taking one for the team. That is making something happen for the rest of their life. That is helping one country of 3.5 million people to get to the semi-final for the first time in so many years.' Classic 'bigger picture' talk.

Photographs of Uruguayan fans supporting Suarez's action were subsequently published, and they included a snap of a young male and a young female fan, both smiling broadly, the former brandishing a poster with the words 'THANKS SUAREZ' on it, and the latter holding up one depicting a giant hand of Uruguayan blue. Here was graphic evidence of foul play being justified – the means had justified the end, which was that the team in the pale blue shirts progressed in the competition through foul play. And that was something to celebrate, to glorify.

Glorification of foul play was set in motion on this occasion by a player reacting to the random circumstance of the ball coming within reach of his hand at a critical juncture. In football, however, such partisan celebration more often follows instances of violent behaviour on the pitch.

Glorification of hurt

There is no question that most teams include some members who are more willing to transgress than others; and there is no question that, for some, part of the satisfaction of following a team is the relish, the glorification even, of such transgression.

As far as football is concerned, the perfect scenario is like that in all the best westerns, where the hero is drawn reluctantly by a series of escalating outrages to exact righteous retribution. By the time he slugs the brutish newcomer on the jaw, or fills him full of lead with the townswomen watching from behind their curtains, the violence is commensurate with the wrong-doing that has provoked it. And so the nasty newcomer slinks out of town with his tail between his legs, or sinks into the dirt of the main drag. Justice.

An enduring example of this is related in Stanley Matthews's autobiography *The Way It Was*, where the legendary England winger recalls a punishing afternoon at Stamford Bridge when he was a venerated – but vulnerable – fortysomething while still playing for Stoke City. A series of brutal assaults on the doyen of dribble by Chelsea's young defender Ron Harris earned firstly a warning from Matthews's 'minder', Eddie Clamp, and then – after one more outrageously violent tackle on the national treasure – cataclysmic retribution. It was monumental foul play on behalf of the Stoke player, sure, but it was foul play that the main proportion of visiting fans will have treasured down the years. At that moment, Clamp was Charles Bronson, returning to the New York Metro with face hardened, gun at the ready, and revenge in mind.

The relish we feel as football followers when our 'hard man' sorts out a member of the opposing team is palpable. During the Leeds United glory years of the 1970s one of their most feared operatives, Norman Hunter, earned the nickname of Norman 'Bites Yer Legs' Hunter. His exploits were celebrated, mythologised even, by Leeds fans.

Now Hunter was an accomplished player who would have won even more than the twenty-eight England caps he earned had he not been rivalled for his place by the captain, Bobby Moore. But many of his challenges – some of which are now turning up in clips on YouTube – were simply foul play. One collision with Everton's Howard Kendall – celebrated by whoever posted it as a 'brilliant tackle' – was a piece of action you might wince to see in American football.

Jason Leonard's hair-raising tales from the rugby field, we have already seen, gave evidence of a relish that many spectators will have shared. Contact sports such as football and rugby access some of the more primal instincts of the viewing public, and the admiration for those who visit violence upon the enemy is an ancient, tribal one. The protagonist makes the enemy afraid; therefore he keeps us safe. We glorify the act of violence performed on our behalf.

2. HOW DO WE INFLUENCE FOUL PLAY?

'If we want justice we must change!'
– Bruno Grandi, president of the International Gymnastics Federation

Thus far we have been looking at the various ways in which we, as followers, react to sporting misdeeds and misdemeanours. But the power of 'we' is more than reaction. The power of 'we' is influence, and it shapes the sports we watch.

As spectators, we can have a malign effect by cowing or intimidating opponents on behalf of those we follow. As spectators, and more generally as followers, the pressure of our expectations and demands can exert pressure on sporting protagonists to cheat.

In benign fashion, as sporting followers, we effectively temper elements of our games that are clearly felt to be 'not right', which eventually results in rule changes. Beyond this we also adjust the 'spirit of the game', effectively determining the rules within rules which operate in all sports – that is, the etiquette of sport.

Foul crowds

The most basic influence of the spectator is upon those they have come to watch, and in this respect spectators can often be responsible for 'foul play' themselves. While it is not unusual to hear from elite sportsmen and women that they are 'oblivious to the crowd' once they are 'in the zone', that is not always true. Sports psychologists might like it to be so, but it isn't. Thus when Gail Emms played badminton matches in China with her regular mixed doubles partner Nathan Robertson, with whom she won the Olympic silver for Britain in 2004, she said the pair always prepared themselves for crowd noise that would, whether they wanted it to or not, break through the bubble of their concentration and impinge upon their consciousness.

As spectators, we can directly influence the results of the spectacles we witness. Does that constitute us being guilty of foul play ourselves? Arguably, yes. At the 2010 Commonwealth Games in Delhi, the exploits of India's wrestlers and archers were followed with particular intensity, and by and large the effect on the medal count was positive. But there were rumbles of discontent from some of the visiting competitors, particularly in the archery, where several of those taking part complained about the partisan noise putting them off.

Most painfully for the England women's team, one of the competitors most obviously affected was twenty-three-year-old Amy Oliver, whose six-out-of-ten score on her last effort in the final – amid a cacophony of local anticipation – was a significant contributory factor in the host nation moving past her team, which included five-times Olympian Alison Williamson and Naomi Folkard, to claim gold by one point.

'In Delhi I think many of the crowd at the archery had probably never seen the sport before and some people were making a noise when archers were shooting, which is a bit like shouting when tennis players are serving,' Williamson told insidethegames.biz. 'The spectators were very enthusiastic, and the message was soon relayed to them to please respect the archers. By the time I was in the individual competition it was a lot better. I think we all learned a lot from Delhi – particularly the younger members of the team. But you can't guarantee silence at an event.'

The point at which vocal support is legitimate, and the point at which it becomes unfair, is not a clearly defined one. While what occurred in Delhi seemed no more than a mixture of exuberance and failure of understanding, at the other end of the scale the power of the crowd can become something akin to a tidal wave of hostility.

It is one of football's clichés that one's home ground turns into a 'fortress'. It is a faintly misleading image, as fortresses are built for defence and the idea behind its use is more aggressive – the 'fortress' envisaged is a wall of inimical noise, perhaps abuse, directed towards visiting players by an aggressive home crowd, with the home team responding in like fashion. But without the 'we', without the sound and fury of partisan supporters, the whole idea of a fortress falls flat.

There are many descriptions of what it is like to experience such treatment from supporters. As an example, let's take the recollections of the former Manchester City and England forward Mike Summerbee, who recalls in his excellent autobiography co-written with Jim Holden (*The Autobiography: The Story of a True City Legend*) the atmosphere in which he and his teammates found themselves in their first big European Cup away trip in 1968, the season after they had won the First Division title. After drawing their home leg at Maine Road 0–0 with the then unheralded Turkish club Fenerbahçe, City's relatively inexperienced players discovered a world of stress in the away leg.

Summerbee relates how, at 9 a.m. on the day of the match, he went to his hotel desk to ask what the waves of noise were that he had woken up to, which he likened to the sounds of a plane. He was told it was the noise of the Fenerbahçe fans who were already in the stadium preparing for the match in the evening, by which time Summerbee observed: 'I had never known such an intimidating atmosphere.' Unnerved, and preyed upon by home players who knew their visitors could not risk retaliation for fear of causing a riot, City lost 2–1. Over the years a similar pattern of behaviour from football spectators – whether it be tooting their horns all night outside the opposition's hotel, or creating a seething hotbed of aggression within the home stadium – has brought about similar results in terms of demoralisation.

Don't go letting us down...

But the power of the follower goes beyond the impact they can have upon a particular sporting contest. It can be argued that we, sport's followers, contribute to and in some cases encourage foul play among those we support through the weight of our expectation. While money remains perhaps the prime motive for sportsmen and women to cheat, the lure of glory – that is, satisfying public demand – comes a close second. Public expectation is a strong contributory factor in the stimulation of foul play.

As the latest cheating sportsman or woman is flushed out – literally, in some cases – and given the eternal tabloid label 'drugs cheat', softening over the years to 'former drugs cheat', we, the viewing public, take up our stance over the issue. (Is the sportsman one of ours? Then it's regrettable. He's not one of ours? Then it's despicable.) But do any of us have the feeling that we might be in some way to blame?

The phrase 'bread and circuses' ('*panem et circenses*') originates from one of the Roman poet Juvenal's *Satires*, from around 100 AD, as a disparaging summary of the debased concerns of a Roman people which had long since 'abdicated its duties'. Politicians came to bolster their support by providing citizens with free supplies of wheat and regular diverting and often bloody entertainments, including circus games and gladiatorial spectacles.

Those slaves who gathered in the dark tunnels under the Colosseum before emerging to an arena glaring with light, noise and likely death were victims, even in victories which only put off their final fall. How different were they from some of our modern day sporting gladiators who feel the need to distort their bodies and risk shortening their lives by enhancing their performances with drugs?

There is pressure on top sportsmen and women to win, particularly when they represent their country. Here is a factor which, at times, towers over the lure of money in the mind of sporting protagonists. Sport becomes a visceral, tribal affair. Or it becomes a political thing – equally potent. But the generating force is us, the sporting following, willing and even demanding our representatives to win on our behalf, or else demanding that performances reach ever increasing levels.

Victory may be the essential demand as far as the sporting follower is concerned, but there is also an ancient imperative to be entertained by mighty deeds. There is a basic thrill to be had in witnessing feats never achieved before, and in sports measurable by time or distance it is easy to recognise if this is the case. As we watch the latest 100m runner flash across the line in a time never registered before, or see the latest swimmer thrash through their final stroke to stop the clock in unknown territory, how much do we care at that moment what the price for the performance has been? How much do we wonder whether the centre of attraction has earned their pre-eminence by the illegal and quite possibly damaging means of doping?

When one gigantic American football player batters another to earth, or when the time we never thought would be eclipsed is, does the possibility of doping become like a blind spot in our vision, willed out of existence?

An athlete taking illegal, performance-enhancing substances – it could be argued – is simply looking after number one, seeking glory and accompanying cash by illicit means, perhaps justifying their actions with the default position that everyone is at it anyway, so it is only a case of operating on a level playing field. But no matter how many drugs they put into their system, they gain nothing unless their performance is valued. Only that monetises it. And the valuation comes from us, the sporting followers.

When something has to change

There is another more benign aspect to this process, where abuses of the rules of a game are perceived by the general public to erode the spirit of that game so flagrantly that pressure builds, and is sooner or later transmitted to the sport's governing body, which changes the rules in an effort to prevent further instances.

Luis Suarez was not the first footballer to handle on the line to prevent a goal, of course. As with the Maradona goal against England, such actions – using a hand in a game which is, as its name implies, all about feet – have an especially alien feel about them to the football follower. The key difference between these two incidents was that while the Argentinian got away with it, the Uruguayan didn't.

But even as he reached out his hand to Adiyiah's header, whether it was instinctive or not, Suarez was taking himself out of the game – and the next game. FIFA had put in place a rule by which any such instance of deliberate handball would mean the player involved being automatically dismissed and facing a subsequent ban.

Had that rule been in place during the 1966 World Cup, England might not have won the trophy, as they would have played the final against West Germany without the man at the heart of their defence, Jack Charlton. The Leeds defender gave away a penalty in the semi-final against Portugal by handling the ball off the line. England were 2–0 up at the time, and Eusebio successfully converted from the spot, so it could be argued that no great harm was ultimately done to the Portuguese cause in the manner that it was to Ghana forty-four years later. However, there was no sending-off for Charlton, and he was allowed to play in the final, where his efforts at the centre of England's defence were crucial in helping to defeat West Germany 4–2.

But to return to the point: the rule has changed. Not because someone at FIFA decided it ought to, but because such a change was demanded by growing opinion within the game, opinion which derived, ultimately, from the way football followers felt about the game. At some point, as such offences became more frequent, opinion within the game began to demand extra sanctions for such cynicism. Sure, handling the ball on the line was against the rules. And the sanction was a penalty kick. But because it is such an egregious offence against the game, because it so offends what we might venture to call the 'spirit of the game', the rules have been changed in order to make it a more punishing option for the offender and his team.

The glaring anomalies of the gymnastics judging at the 2004 Athens Olympics prompted protests from spectators at the time and widespread criticism in the media. Rule alterations swiftly followed. 'If we want justice we must change!' exclaimed Bruno Grandi, president of the International Gymnastics Federation. Numerous changes were made to the international code of points, including the replacement of 10.00 points as a maximum score with an 'open score', an increase of value for the quality of execution, and technological improvements in the way the judging took place – although many believe the balance is still not right.

Similarly, the perceived injustice of many of the boxing judges' decisions at the 1988 Seoul Olympics provoked a popular demand for changes in the rules. Alterations were duly made which meant that, henceforth, scoring shots in amateur bouts would be recorded and displayed contemporaneously, so that everyone could see how a bout was progressing.

A less profound but nevertheless important change in the rules occurred as a result of a football match at the 1982 World Cup between West Germany and Austria during the Group B qualification. What occurred was technically within the rules but was deemed beyond what was acceptable by many who watched it. Because all the other qualification matches had already been played, the two neighbours were able to go into their meeting knowing exactly what they needed to do to ensure progression. A 1–0 win for the Germans would suit both teams perfectly.

Horst Hrubesch put West Germany ahead after ten minutes, after which the match effectively ended as a competition. Despite boos and whistles from the crowd – one German fan was seen setting fire to his national flag – the phoney contest continued until the final whistle, at which point both teams had earned their places in the next round.

During the game one German TV commentator simply ceased commentating and allowed the 'action' to progress in silence. Meanwhile one Austrian TV commentator suggested to viewers that they might like to turn off, or turn over. Algeria, the team that missed out on qualification in the same group, protested to FIFA, but to no avail. However, at the Mexico World Cup four years later, FIFA ensured that the last round of matches in the group stage took place simultaneously.

It might be asked whether there was an onus on the players to resist the temptation put before them. Perhaps they were acting as directed by their management. Perhaps they felt that it was more important to ensure that, whatever the weather, they progressed to the next round without any further uncertainties or alarms. Perhaps at that moment the twenty-two players on the pitch felt they were, effectively, one team, and that if they all worked together for the same end they would all be successful, while their 'opponents', Algeria, would be the ones to suffer.

In an ideal world there should have been no hint of collusion, as such doubts about the fundamental integrity of sporting contest can swiftly erode the vital sense of faith in the game. Without that faith, it is nothing. Such, hearteningly, was the belief of many football followers, including some from Austria and Germany. Here was compelling evidence that, within any set of rules, there are unwritten rules that are profoundly important. Clearly, supporters and commentators alike found what happened made a mockery of the game of football, and FIFA's swift reaction endorsed that view.

The same broad reaction to public opinion occurred in November 2012, three months after the scandal at the London 2012 Games involving badminton players trying to lose group matches in order to gain a more advantageous draw in the knock-out stages. The Badminton World Federation altered the rules 'to ensure such a regrettable spectacle is never witnessed in badminton again' – all teams placing second in the group stages at the Rio 2016 Games would be subject to another random draw for the knock-out stages, thus removing the risk of any unsporting calculation in early matches.

A similar process had occurred half a century earlier when Douglas Jardine's touring England side appalled their Australian hosts – and cricket's broad following – with the introduction of their inimical 'fast leg theory' bowling, which left a physical mark on several of the home batsmen and a metaphorical mark on the sport itself. The effects of the English tactic proved extraordinarily damaging to relations between the two countries for at least a decade. It also caused a change to be made to the rules in 1935, whereby umpires were given the power to intervene if they felt a bowler was deliberately aiming at a batsman with intent to injure. Here was another clear example of 'follower power', where something nominally within the rules came to be viewed as being beyond the pale as far as the general consensus was concerned, prompting change from the authorities. This dynamic operated again, shortly before the changes to the badminton rules, with the International Paralympic Committee's acknowledgement of the unease caused by competitions pitting male single against double-leg amputee athletes and their plan to separate the categories at the Rio 2016 Games.

We – the fans, the followers – ultimately rule on what is and is not acceptable behaviour within sport. A self-correcting principle operates as we react to incidents or activities which, in our hearts, feel wrong. And that emotion is writ large as sporting legislation.

Rules within rules – sporting etiquette

There is another, fundamental way in which we, as sports followers, exert influence on the sports we watch, in that we shape the very codes within which sports operate. And when those codes are abused by those indulging in foul play, we respond in ways which seek to correct and balance their behaviour.

There are rules in sport, of course. There have to be. But within each sport there are rules within rules, whereby certain kinds of wrongdoing are regarded as being worse than others, and others are deemed to be almost acceptable. In other words, in the view of the committed follower of any given sport, there is an etiquette which has to be observed. When sporting protagonists expected to abide by it do not, their failings flap in the faces of those who follow and support them.

For instance. Brian Moore, the former England and Lions hooker who, with props Jeff Probyn and Jason Leonard, formed one of the most formidable front rows ever to play the game of rugby union, did not get to that position without a working knowledge of the dark arts practised in the scrum. And yet when Moore, who has been a regular commentator for BBC television in recent years, witnessed an incident in a 2011 Six Nations match where a forward fouled one of his opposite numbers, he was outraged. 'That's a red card!' Moore announced, instinctively. What was the offence? A high tackle? A massive punch or a brutal trampling? No. It was a simple trip-up, and a very ungainly, slow-motion trip-up to boot.

Footballers move at least as swiftly as rugby players, due to many of the latter being considerably heavier on average. And yet the incident which so exercised Moore, had it occurred during a football match, would have occasioned no more than a rumble of grumbles on behalf of the man tripped, particularly as it occurred during a passage of play broadly in the middle of the park.

The International Rugby Board's Rule 10.4, on Dangerous Play and Misconduct, classifies Tripping along with other offences such as Punching or Striking, and Stamping or Trampling. Historically the offence has been viewed similarly in rugby league, where on the rare instances that a trip took place it used to incur a mandatory sending-off, although that decision is now down to the discretion of the referee.

Rugby, both codes, encourages players to get on with the lumps and bumps of a game in which all manner of harsh physical contact is regarded as normal. So it seems that the heinous quality of the trip, within rugby union and rugby league circles, is about more than safety considerations. It is viewed as being both abhorrent and aberrant – not just cheating, but *really* cheating.

Another example. After relating a history of mayhem from his playing days with some relish, Moore's old comrade Leonard revealed that he still feels bitter about a mere tap on the ball imparted by Australia's David Campese, who knocked down what Leonard felt was a possible try-scoring pass to Rory Underwood in a 1991 World Cup final that England went on to lose. Underhand, in all senses.

The classic position of the rugby player and follower is that they prefer a sport (as the ancient and apparently untraceable axiom has it, the 'hooligan's game played by gentlemen') which is more 'honest' than football, which, as any rugby player and follower will tell you, is essentially a sport of posturing and diving played by those who wouldn't last five seconds on a rugby pitch playing a proper man's game. The classic position of the football player and follower is that they prefer a sport ('gentleman's game played by hooligans') which does not regularly allow levels of physical attrition on an industrial scale, with occasional instances of shocking brutality.

What is evident is that sports have their own culture, within which different forms of cheating, or gamesmanship, are ascribed internal values – graded, effectively. Part of the reason rugby followers so hate the trip is that it is seen as a base and cowardly action which undermines the flow and the trust of the game. It has been seen historically as an alien offence, unlike a good old honest thump. It offends against the etiquette of the sport. The same discrimination was voiced in the autobiography of Martin Johnson, the forward who captained England to their Rugby World Cup victory in 2003, when he explains how he was moved to knee and then 'walk over' Saracens' Australian fly half Duncan McRae while playing for Leicester after McRae had obstructed one of Johnson's team mates and prevented him receiving a pass. 'I hate this sort of offence,' said Johnson, whose intervention – for which he was suspended, and which he admitted he regretted – left McRae with broken ribs. Johnson made it clear that had McRae simply been 'winded and bruised', justice would have been served.

The etiquette of a sport is not set in stone, however. We have heard from Leonard first-hand recollections of violence on the rugby field, and how, for example, an exchange of good honest thumps with his French rival Pascal Ondarts in 1991 led to a state of affairs where neither man had 'any problems after that'. Such traditional interactivity in rugby has not been a case of pushing the boundaries of the game's laws, so much as operating in a separate domain within them bounded by unwritten rules. It is something players and spectators have instinctively understood over the years, and as such has become an accepted element of the game. Spectators have therefore been complicit in the tacit acknowledgement that the occasional good honest thump, where merited within the unwritten code, is not really cheating.

However, a recent online debate following the sending-off of a Scottish club player for punching an opponent highlighted that this is an etiquette seemingly in evolution. There were several comments bemoaning the severity of the punishment in what has always been known as 'a man's game'. But that view was numerically outweighed by those suggesting that such overt violence should be consigned to the past – that it would be sufficient to incur a prison sentence if such action occurred beyond the field of play, and that it was becoming an increasingly anachronistic feature of an increasingly professionalised and commercial game.

That debate aside, were football to witness even occasionally the level of physical aggression that is at the heart of rugby, there would be an outcry. Although the rugby authorities have made serious efforts to curb the most damaging practices within their game – for example, spear tackling – there is still a routine physicality about the game that would seem appalling in football. This physicality constantly seethes at the borders of the rules, and frequently crosses those borders.

And yet, were a rugby player to exaggerate an injury – something, to be fair, that you hardly ever see – in the manner frequently witnessed in football, can you imagine how that would play? The reaction would make a spear tackle look benign. Etiquette can appear as a historical oddity, unimportant at first glance. But upon further inspection it is revealed as something which operates in all sports, as vital as a tendon to a muscle. And when the etiquette that holds a sport in place is infringed, the result, as Mr Micawber would put it: misery.

When the Bloodgate scandal was revealed, it came at a particularly bad time for rugby union in Britain, where cases of eye-gouging and drug-related issues resulting in the suspension of five Bath players had also emerged. But the very idea of a rugby union player biting on a blood capsule purchased from a joke shop in order to precipitate a bogus tactical change provoked the followers of the game to a new level of outrage. It was out of order. It was the creeping culture of an alien game… which brings us back to football.

Everton's Irish midfielder Seamus Coleman reflected in 2011 on the differences he had observed between football and the game he had played as a youth, Gaelic football, which he described as the harder of the two games. 'If you get pushed you get straight back up,' he added. 'You don't roll around looking at the referee for a free kick and you wouldn't get one if you did in Gaelic. It's a fight – nothing too serious.' As we have seen earlier, however, there are those who do roll around in football.

So what is the supporter to do in all this, if he sees one of his own performing such a routine? It's tricky. As we have already heard from Robin van Persie, going to ground can sometimes be a grey area. Are you cheating? Or are you merely calling attention to cheating, amplifying it, as it were, crying out, like Simon and Garfunkel's Boxer, in your anger and your pain? And from the spectator's point of view, is it the case that 'our' players amplify, while 'their' players falsify?

While each individual supporter may have to wrestle with his or her conscience in this regard, there is, historically, an intrinsic disapproval on the part of the British spectator for footballing histrionics. The classic British stance is memorably exemplified by a sequence of events that took place back in the 1970s during a match involving Burgess Town.

Bill Collins, a local undertaker who was one of the Sussex County League side's small band of regular followers, was known for his vocal support, as was his friend Sandy Powell, a Town director, and their comments could always be clearly heard among crowds that averaged less than one hundred.

In 1972 the visitors to Town's Leylands Park ground were Rye. Powell and Collins were soon on their case for feigning injury. As yet another Rye player rolled in apparent agony, it became more than the funeral director could stand. Collins ducked under the rope, ran on to the pitch and crouched next to the stricken visitor before reaching into his wallet and shouting to all and sundry: 'Here you are, mate – have one of my cards!'

Are we more accepting of simulation nowadays? Certainly we are more aware of it, as television replays offer us repeated opportunity to inspect every nuance of play. Ashley Young, the Manchester United forward, attracted particular interest in this regard in April 2012 when he won penalties on successive weekends for his team against QPR and Aston Villa after appearing to make the most of two defensive challenges.

Commentators looking at the second penalty decision implied that Young had actually moved his leg towards the tackling Villa defender, Ciaran Clark, before falling forwards in an exaggerated fashion. Young's manager, Alex Ferguson, defended the actions in characteristically robust fashion, but his words made it clear just how convoluted opinions are on the topic – an uncertainty reflected in the reaction of football supporters. 'It's a penalty kick,' Ferguson said of the Villa incident. 'No doubt. The only fault is that Ashley went down too easy, but it's a penalty. If he [Clark] doesn't stretch his foot out and take him, it's a goal.'

Ferguson then referred to a match he had seen between Bayern Munich and Real Madrid in the Champions League, which he described as being 'absolutely ridiculous' because of 'players diving and rolling about'. And yet the United manager went on to admit that he was concerned about Young earning a reputation as a diver because it might inhibit referees from awarding future penalties involving him. Clearly this is an area where etiquette may be evolving, as the traditional British attitude to a practice perceived to be more typically employed elsewhere in the European game is forced to adapt to its increasing occurrence. When you hear someone as plain-speaking as Ferguson struggling to define the correct etiquette in this situation, you know it is complex.

Do we care, as followers? The anecdotal answer to that, as we have seen, is yes. For followers of the British game there is still a general distaste for 'simulation' that cannot be dissimulated. Other instincts on matters of etiquette also run deep. As was evident in the case of the 1999 FA Cup fifth-round tie between Arsenal and Sheffield United.

A United player, seeing one of his teammates was injured, hoofed the ball into touch so the trainer could come on. In such circumstances the etiquette of the game dictates that the resulting throw-in is returned to the team that conceded it. In this case, that didn't happen. The Arsenal throw went to

Arsenal's Nigerian international, Kanu, who then compounded the outrage already forming among United's players and supporters by running down the wing and crossing for Marc Overmars to score the winning goal.

There followed, as Anthony Buckeridge's Jennings would have put it, the biggest hoo-hah since the Battle of Britain. Upon which Arsenal's manager, Arsène Wenger, offered Sheffield United's manager Steve Bruce a replay, purely on the basis of this travesty of convention, of etiquette. It was, in its way, exemplary. And the offer was taken up ten days later, although it did United no good in the end as the result was the same. On the face of it, this turn of events was relatively unimportant. Arsenal won 2–1. The game got replayed. Arsenal won 2–1 again. But in what it demonstrated about the etiquette operating within the explicit rules of a game – and what we, the fans, demand when it comes to that etiquette – it was profoundly important.

Conclusion

Why cheat? Why not cheat?

The young baseball fan who made his plaintive demand of Shoeless Joe Jackson in the wake of the 1919 World Series fixing scandal – 'Say it ain't so, Joe!' – might well have gone on to ask, 'Why?' History does not record. But what history has recorded – and continues to record – is a multiplicity of elements within the world of sport that constitute what most sensible people would regard as foul play.

Indeed, when one reflects upon the depth and range of dodgy dealing through to outright cheating that has occurred within the sporting realm since the days of the ancient Greek Olympics, the more apt question might be: 'Why not?'

As we have seen, there are many shades of foul play, some so faint that it almost seems the play is not foul at all. The latter description is often operative within the category of mind games, where much of the activity is nothing but positive and free from any hint of rebuke. Who's harmed by a competitor visualising themselves in control, focusing their mental energy on a maximal performance and setting their controls for the heart of a victory? No one. It is hard, for instance, to criticise the mastery maintained by Arthur Ashe in the 1975 Wimbledon final when he mentally destroyed his opponent, the bumptious young champion Jimmy Connors. The tactics and discipline maintained by the elder man simply underlined the potency of mental factors in elite sport. Ashe was indulging in smart play, not foul play.

But it only takes a small shift for such strategies to become more inimical, and less acceptable.

Scales of infringement

If this infraction of sporting behaviour lies at one end of the scale in terms of mind-games malpractice, tactics such as 'sledging' lie at the other end – deliberate, premeditated and often orchestrated assaults upon an opponent's psyche.

Muhammad Ali's calculating, albeit amusingly delivered, abuse of upcoming opponents clearly struck home, provoking alarm and demoralisation in Sonny Liston, and prompting Joe Frazier to allow his feelings of anger to undermine the discipline of his performance in the ring.

Similar scales of severity are evident in the other key areas of foul play – basic physical manipulation, doping and financial malpractice – all of which may be accepted, or even celebrated, by followers of sport. Depending upon their point of view, that is.

With applied manipulation there is a rich field of operation to be observed – from bogus blood capsules, dodgy boat designs, and altered bats and balls, to bowls which do not conform to the required bias, mysteriously opening stadium doors, 'magic' épées, doctored birth certificates, subterfuge and espionage involving everything from high-street photocopiers to divers with cameras, and yes, even baked and pickled conkers. While this may make for an entertaining inventory, it also involves a darker aspect of foul play in that the hardware is employed in a preconceived and crooked context. You could argue, with some success, that these instances constitute more serious offences in the overall scheme of things. Such practices effectively destroy the sport they feed on, rendering it invalid and risking the ultimate ignominy of public indifference or antipathy.

The vital bond between sport and spectator

Imagine if they held an Olympics, or a World Cup, or a Test match, and nobody came. Not likely, admittedly. But once the bond of trust between spectators and sporting protagonists is broken, once it becomes impossible to trust what one witnesses as a spectator, the mainspring has gone and the whole exercise becomes effectively meaningless. The only way forwards for sport at that juncture would be to advance down the path trodden by professional wrestling, where sport becomes mere entertainment, with spectators complicit in the show.

In the end we – the sporting followers, the spectators – are the ones who must give sport credence and meaning. Yet we are all human, and fallible, and – inevitably – partial. Thus any instance of foul play, whether slight or severe, is not instantly censured across the board. It is judged according to our point of view. No doubt there are some who manage to retain absolute clarity with regard to the transgression of rules or the spirit of rules within any game. But for most the tendency is to be more forgiving of the transgressions of 'our' player or team, even to the point of openly celebrating their efforts, and correspondingly more censorious of those of the opposition.

So every sporting follower has their own sliding scale that ranges from vilification, through to justification, and on to glorification, with events registering at certain points depending on circumstances.

We, the sporting followers, also have a fundamental role in shaping and maintaining 'rules within rules' – that is, the etiquettes of various sports which can point the way to their essential values. Violation of these core values generates instinctive dismay and disapprobation in the heart of the sporting spectator.

Such emotions ultimately lead to shifts in sporting etiquette – and indeed changes to sporting rules. The governing bodies of our sports, ultimately reliant on our continuing interest and goodwill (and money), make it their business wherever possible to react to public opinion by correcting obvious examples of foul play or bad practice. As FIFA president Sepp Blatter, that most business-minded of men, remarked recently, changes within the world game to implement goal-line technology were critically prompted by the glaringly obvious mistake made by officials at the 2010 World Cup in ruling that Frank Lampard's shot for England against Germany had not crossed the line.

Much was made at the time of how sport, like life, can demonstrate the dictum: 'What goes around comes around.' German football followers have always believed they were done a disservice in the 1966 World Cup final when Geoff Hurst gave England a 3–2 lead in extra time with a shot which bounced down off the underside of the bar and, in their view, failed to cross the line completely.

Can there be such a thing as sporting kismet? Do cosmic forces such as hubris and nemesis actually come into play? Politics and conflict lurk under the surface of many sporting encounters. But if sport is to remain sport, rather than an excuse for further belligerence, it needs to be insulated from such history. Otherwise where do such calculations stop? A French player hacks down an England forward in full flight. 'That's for Waterloo, my friend…'

In sport, as in life, there has to be forgiveness. Years after the 2004 Athens Olympics, at which most observers believed Bulgaria's Jordan Jovtchev had been deprived of the gold medal in the gymnastics rings competition – which the judges gave to home athlete Dimosthenis Tampakos – he reflected on the position of his Greek rival: 'What is his guilt for what happened to me in Athens? The two of us are sweating in the gym pretty much all our lives; like all the rest of the gymnasts in the world. He is trying to do his best, I am trying to do mine...'

Earning the right to forgive

Sporting victims of foul play, or what appears to be foul play, earn the right to offer such forgiveness if they can find it in themselves. Reflecting upon the honours and medals she might have won had the East German women against whom she competed throughout her athletics career not been boosted by their country's doping regime, British sprinter Kathy Cook concluded that there was 'too much water under the bridge' for the results to be reversed. She admitted to a mixture of 'sadness and anger' about the whole business, but the most intense anger was reserved for a Canadian athlete who, she reasoned, had doped without coming under the same pressure to do so as the East German women, saying that she could 'have more sympathy' for them.

Reflecting further, she added: 'One of the saddest things is that those East German athletes were never able to show how good they really were without the help of drugs. Their whole careers were flawed. I don't know how you could win a race knowing that you had cheated and gain any satisfaction from it. Once the excitement was over, the lap of honour and the medal ceremony, I don't think I could live with knowing that I had cheated. It's the way you are made, I suppose.'

Cook, a 'victim' of the East German doping regime, clearly makes the case that the East Germans themselves were the greatest victims of their own, state-sponsored foul play. This stance gets to the heart of what competing in sport is about and how foul play – especially damaging, premeditated, systematic foul play – can disfigure and devalue its intended rewards. In the end, you have to ask, as protagonist, as spectator – is cheating worth it? What do we lose when we gain unfairly? As Cassio laments in *Othello*: 'O, I have lost my reputation! I have lost the immortal part of myself...'

The concomitant emotion here is an urge towards redemption. The urge to do right, to repair, is profound in the human psyche – and sport offers all of those emotions full play. Had the sporting authorities not relented in the case of the 1904 Olympic marathon stunt played by Fred Lorz, the American would have been doomed for ever as no more than the man who hitched a lift in the Olympic marathon before briefly pretending, 'as a joke', to be the winner.

But a year after his Olympic shame, his life ban having been rescinded, Lorz won the Boston marathon, running himself into a state of collapse in the process. Would he have pushed himself so hard, you wonder, had his miscalculated manipulation of the previous year not driven him to prove himself an honest and able sportsman? To restore his standing among those who followed the sport? Fair play followed foul for Lorz as he strove to attune himself to the spirit of the game, and we applaud him for it. Lorz got the chance of redemption in the eyes of the sporting public that was never offered to the young sportsmen and women who came to maturity in the German Democratic Republic in the 1970s and 1980s.

Foul play, as a concept, exists only as a variant of fair play. Therefore it requires an audience, a judgement – otherwise it is a meaningless term, just as whatever happens in sport, or indeed life, is meaningless. Judgement gives it meaning. And so, as sporting followers, we watch and experience and judge, we deem some actions fitting, others less so. We alter the rules, or cause the rules to be altered. And we observe the spirit in which games are played within those rules, altering those rules within rules in a more subtle but equally effective manner. Otherwise the whole thing is not worth a candle.

As Bobby Jones, the great US golfer who won a unique grand slam of professional and amateur titles in Britain and the United States in 1930, once reflected: 'The rewards of golf, and of life, too, I expect, are worth very little if you don't play the game by the etiquette as well as by the rules.' Foul play will always exist – but we will always know it for what it is, and we will always judge it through our instinctive sense of the alternate pole: fair play.

Acknowledgements

This book has drawn upon numerous sources and experiences, but I am particularly indebted to the kind help offered by Matthew Engel, James Willstrop, Steve Cram, Steve Backley, Mauri Plant, David Powell, Bryn Vaile, Sally Jones, David Rhys Jones, Tony Allcock, Malcolm Arnold, Tim Brabants, Darren Campbell, Hugh Matheson, Ervin Zador, Michele Verroken, Tanni Grey-Thompson, Ben Ainslie, Paul Goodison, Colin Hart, Alan Hubbard, Mark Butler, Chris Turner, Bob Ramsak, Greg Wood, Olaf Brockmann, Mary Wittenberg and Vera Atkinson.

Thanks to the *Independent* for access afforded to stories past, and to all at insidethegames.biz, notably Duncan Mackay, Sarah Bowron and David Owen. Also to Charlotte Atyeo and Nick Humphrey at Bloomsbury for their help and encouragement.

Thanks to all my family for their support – Sarah, that Greek research was great; Stella, those Olympic cuttings were invaluable.

I am also indebted to the following publications:

Bowls Skills by Tony Allcock and David Rhys Jones (Hamlyn, 1988)

The 1908 Olympics: The First London Games by Keith Baker (SportsBooks Ltd, 2008)

Race Against Me: My Story by Dwain Chambers (Libros International, 2009)

Tommy Gemmell: Lion Heart by Tommy Gemmell with Graham McColl (Virgin Books, 2005)

Martin Johnson: The Autobiography by Martin Johnson (Headline, 2003)

The Peleton by Timm Kölln (Rouleur, 2010)

Taking Le Tiss by Matthew Le Tissier (Harper Sport, 2010)

The Way It Was by Stanley Matthews (Stanley Paul, 2000)

The 1948 Olympics: How London Rescued the Games by Bob Phillips (SportsBooks Ltd, 2008)

The Theory and Practice of Gamesmanship (or the Art of Winning Games without Actually Cheating) by Stephen Potter (Rupert Hart-Davis, 1947)

Mike Summerbee, The Story of a True City Legend by Mike Summerbee with Jim Holden (Optimum, 2010)

The Complete Book of the Olympics by David Wallechinsky and Jaime Loucky (Aurum Press, 2012)

The Complete Book of the Winter Olympics by David Wallechinsky and Jaime Loucky (Aurum Press, 2010)

Index